Preface Books

A series of scholarly and critical studies of major writers intended for those needing modern and authoritative guidance through the characteristic difficulties of their work to reach an intelligent understanding and enjoyment of it.

General Editor: MAURICE HUSSEY

The 'Nickleby portrait', Daniel Maclise, 1839

A Preface to Dickens

Allan Grant

Longman, London and New York

LONGMAN GROUP LIMITED
Longman House,
Burnt Mill, Harlow, Essex, CM20 2JE, England

Published in the United States of America by Longman Inc., New York

© Longman Group Ltd., 1984

All rights reserved. No part of this publication
may be reproduced, stored in a retrieval system
or transmitted in any form or by any means, electronic,
mechanical, photocopying, recording or otherwise,
without the prior written permission of the Publishers.

Library of Congress Cataloging in Publication Data
Grant, Allan.
  A preface to Dickens.

  (Preface books)
  Bibliography: p.
  Includes index.
  Summary: A critical introduction to the life,
thought, and art of the great Victorian novelist.
  1. Dickens, Charles, 1812–1870. 2. Novelists,
English — 19th century — Biography. [1. Dickens,
Charles, 1812–1870.   2. Authors, English] I. Title.
PR4588.G68   1984   823′.8 [B]   [92]   82–10064

ISBN 0–582–35271–1
ISBN 0–582–35272–X (pbk.)

Set in 10/11pt Baskerville, Linotron 202

Printed in Singapore by
The Print House (Pte) Ltd

The late **ALLAN GRANT** was Senior Lecturer in the Department of Humanities at Chelsea College, University of London. His speciality was English literature of the nineteenth and twentieth centuries. He is the author of the volume on Coleridge in the 'Preface' series, now unfortunately out of print.

Contents

List of illustrations

Foreword

The size of Dickens's output forbids comprehensive treatment in a volume of this scope but Allan Grant has selected those areas that he believes to be most valuable towards an understanding of his developing art. In recent years academic opinion and industry have made many assumptions about the growth of the novelist's psychology and realism and given them the currency that Mr Grant would prefer to question or to reject. This is his firm statement of belief which can hardly be bettered as a motive for embarking upon a volume to substantiate it. 'His novels are the product of an intelligent, humanely sensitive, imaginative vision of life, determined neither by his childhood nor by the times in which he lived.'

Part One of the study reveals Dickens the reformer and humanitarian but culminates more unusually in a stimulating section on the literature of Victorian London life which was the testing ground or seedbed of his artistry. Therein he encountered the institutionalized images of offices, shops and prisons with all their inmates and also the entertainments and domesticities which are the special realm of Dickensian light relief. The two worlds of Mr Wemmick in *Great Expectations* are shown as a comic example of this dual life and it is in that novel that Mr Grant finds the centre of his critical estimate of the author as a whole. There the treatment of childhood, so realistic as to convince readers that a child might have written it, is properly understood as a continuation of the search for innocence and experience inaugurated previously by Romantic poets such as Blake and Wordsworth and now the central thread in the world of Victorian fiction. Here the novel is also the poem.

Also in Part Two I would single out the close readings of sections of Dickens's prose. The style that is so unmistakable is nevertheless rarely examined as helpfully as here.

To our deepest regret Allan Grant died before being able to correct the proofs of this book. Readers of his earlier *Preface to Coleridge* will find the same cogency of argument and concern for the student seeking a critical path through the complex works of literature. Dickens was indeed an author for whom he had the fullest admiration and he completed his articulation of that respect, fortunately for the reader, a short time before his final illness.

MAURICE HUSSEY General Editor

Introduction

The traditional view of the novels of Dickens is that they contain humour and pathos, exciting plots and a parade of characters who are larger than life in their improbabilities and eccentricities. It follows that the tendency implicit in such a view is to prefer the earlier to the later work. It is exemplified in John Forster's *Life of Dickens* written shortly after the novelist's death which places *David Copperfield* at the pinnacle of his achievement.

Recent serious criticism, on the other hand, has tended to value the later novels above the earlier and to see a developing seriousness of concern and a growing mastery of technique and organisation from novel to novel. Within this larger change of view, there is a great variety of approaches and differences of judgment about the kinds of serious pleasure and meaning to be derived from the novels. Some studies emphasise the relationship between Dickens and the history of the nineteenth century, others that between the work and the life in attempts to interpret the work as psychologically dependent on the man's experience.

To those historicist critics of literature who assume that all human activities are ground out by an inevitable, if sometimes superficially disorderly, movement of historical forces in one decisive direction I can only respond that the writer of genius transcends his own time and that great literature, therefore, is always contemporary. If, on the other hand, it is asserted that the writer is some kind of neurotic and that his works are always referrable to early life experiences which are the reality underlying the imaginative work that is only the 'sublimation' or illusory appearance, then I must think that modern varieties of psychological theories of the imagination are simply inadequate to account for phenomena as complex as works of art. For it is clear to me, if anything is clear about Dickens, that his novels are the product of an intelligent, humanely sensitive, imaginative vision of life, determined neither by his childhood nor by the times in which he lived. Indisputable as it is that he used his own experiences, friends, glimpses of chance acquaintances as materials for his novels, what I hope to show in the following pages is that these materials are transformed into art. It is an art of an idiosyncratic, uneven and paradoxical kind, but it is art and not 'native wood-notes wild'. It is also not automatic writing.

The paradoxes are plentiful. He was the most popular writer of his own day and yet he did not always give his public what he thought it wanted. Yet there is never a hint of condescension in what he writes. If confirmation were required to show that he was a conscious artist, it lies in the fact that he never repeated himself. Each novel is a fresh beginning, a departure from what had already been achieved. The changes entail changes of technique, an increase in the complex notion of what a fictional character is, and a deepening exploration of moral judgments made firmly through the action. Judgments are not only made, but become part of the process and are qualified to the extent that they can sometimes be reversed. Sir Leicester Dedlock in *Bleak House* is a good example of the process.

The paradox can be stated differently if one thinks of Dickens's work in relation to his own time. For all his continuous popularity, there was no more radical and often bitter critic of his own time. His spirit opposed the major tendencies of both evangelical puritanism and utilitarian calculation which between them characterised Victorian society. Henry James saw this feature as one of the significant differences between his own position as a novelist in America and Dickens's and Thackeray's in England. Equally important in any consideration of Dickens in his time is one's sense that our view of the society of Victorian England in the middle years of the nineteenth century was created for us by Dickens. He makes it visible and gives it the form by which we recognise it. As adjectives, 'Dickensian' and 'Victorian' are almost synonymous.

And yet not quite, as about 'Dickensian' plays is an atmosphere of pathos, of humour and, above all, of fantasy that enlarges it and removes it from historical or social accountability.

That he should have remained, across the intervening century and its accelerating changes in the ways in which the world we live in is perceived and described, a most popular story-teller and inventor of characters which we still know better than many of our close friends, is witness to the transcendence of his art and a powerful strand of continuity in the human condition to which he originally addressed himself.

To talk satisfactorily about the art is not easy. Despite Forster's emphatic assertion that Dickens was a serious artist rather than a popular entertainer, Dickens talked and, in his letters, wrote more frequently about the craft and profession of letters than about art in any consciously deliberate fashion. He does not appear to have articulated any considered theory of art, his own or in more general terms. Through the character of Podsnap in *Our Mutual Friend*, and in Tigg Montague's dinner for Jonas Chuzzlewit in *Martin Chuzzlewit* where Shakespeare is the subject of discussion, Dickens wittily satirises attitudes he despised. Yet there is not much in the pages of Dickens that could not comfortably be offered to Podsnap's Young Person. If, like Matthew Arnold, he attacked Victorian philistinism, then it is still the case that he shared many of the attitudes to art and life of the rising middle classes of that period.

To Forster he revealed an anxiety that his writing should be 'realistic'. Yet to say only that is to say nothing. Dickens is not a realist in either the special technical sense or the more general and more difficult sense of that over-used word. More helpful is the comment he makes in a letter of reply to an aspiring contributor to *Household Words* on her 'manner of relating the tale. The people do not sufficiently work out their own purposes in dialogue and dramatic action. You are too much their exponent; what you do for them, they ought to do for themselves.' (To Miss King, 9 February 1855).

The purposes of Dickens's novels work themselves out in the characters and what they do and say. The method is dramatic and his exemplar is Shakespeare to whom his novels are indebted at many levels, not only at that of those uproarious parodies of Shakespearean performances that his characters put up with on occasion. His preoccupation with the relationships between parents and children is Shakespearean in its mode, and the mechanical business of plot construction occasionally provides muted echoes of a memory or a borrowing. It has always seemed to me, for example, that *The Chimes* owes something to the plot of *The Winter's Tale* despite all the differences of setting and authorial idiom in its abrupt reversion from the darkness of the dream to the brightness and promise of the day.

To Shakespeare and the eighteenth-century English novelists of the picaresque I want also to add an emphasis on the importance of the work of the English Romantic Poets to his vision of life which, as it develops from its beginnings in comic facetiousness and exuberance, becomes poetic in its concentration and intensification.

To say as much is not to dismiss his early writings. It is the mark of the great artist that his apprentice pieces have in them already an authority and distinctness that inform them even when such pieces are themselves close imitations of the work of earlier artists. In chapter thirty-two of *The Pickwick Papers* that Tony Weller should express views on art at all is comically unlikely: that he should emerge at that moment as a fiercely energetic proponent of a Wordsworthian naturalism in the matter of diction is a wild, yet convincing absurdity.

Although I agree with W. H. Auden's dictum that the relations between a writer's life and his work are oblique and best ignored, the account of his life which follows portrays the life as an example of a Victorian success story and as an introduction to the complexities of Victorian life and thought. Just as his own experience provided the occasion for a freely invented, imaginative art, so Dickens acted out his life and made his art at the very centre of his age. It is a contention of what follows that he speaks equally powerfully to our own; his accounts of modern urban life and of what it is like to grow up in towns are perfectly familiar to us.

I have followed the general format of the series in that Part One contains the biographical material, Part Two pursues critically a central concern — that of childhood — and a central, frequently discussed novel, *Great Expectations*. In it examples of Dickens's prose are also presented and discussed. Part Three contains background and related information together with references to further critical guides in the inexhaustible pleasure of tracing for oneself the extent and significance of Dickens's achievement as a novelist.

Part One
The Writer and his Setting

Charles Dickens's Family Tree :

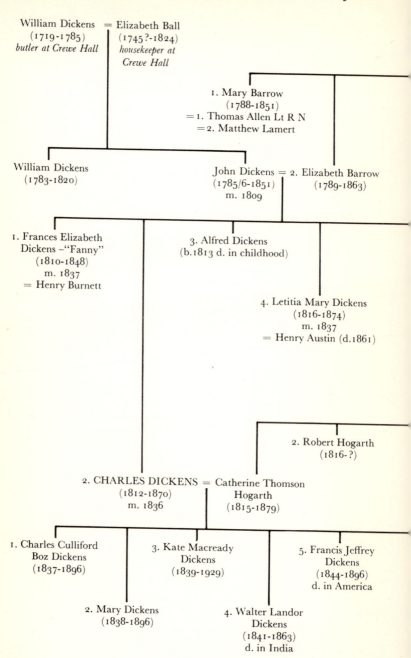

William Dickens
(1719-1785)
butler at Crewe Hall
= Elizabeth Ball
(1745?-1824)
*housekeeper at
Crewe Hall*

1. Mary Barrow
(1788-1851)
= 1. Thomas Allen Lt R N
= 2. Matthew Lamert

William Dickens
(1783-1820)

John Dickens = 2. Elizabeth Barrow
(1785/6-1851)   (1789-1863)
m. 1809

1. Frances Elizabeth
Dickens –"Fanny"
(1810-1848)
m. 1837
= Henry Burnett

3. Alfred Dickens
(b.1813 d. in childhood)

4. Letitia Mary Dickens
(1816-1874)
m. 1837
= Henry Austin (d.1861)

2. Robert Hogarth
(1816-?)

2. CHARLES DICKENS = Catherine Thomson
(1812-1870)   Hogarth
m. 1836   (1815-1879)

1. Charles Culliford
Boz Dickens
(1837-1896)

3. Kate Macready
Dickens
(1839-1929)

5. Francis Jeffrey
Dickens
(1844-1896)
d. in America

2. Mary Dickens
(1838-1896)

4. Walter Landor
Dickens
(1841-1863)
d. in India

The Dickenses, The Barrows, and the Hogarths

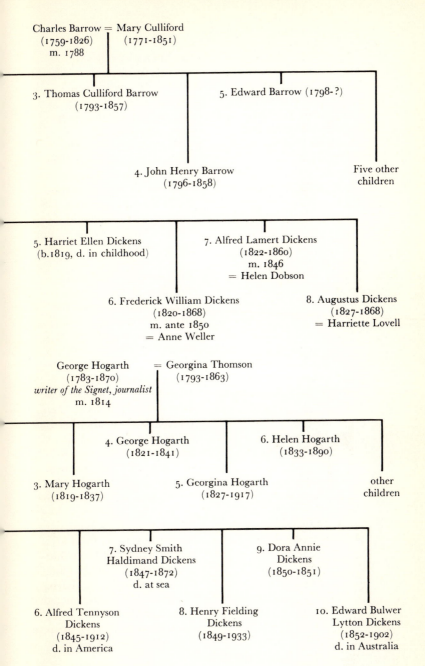

Charles Barrow = Mary Culliford
(1759-1826)   (1771-1851)
m. 1788

3. Thomas Culliford Barrow
(1793-1857)

5. Edward Barrow (1798-?)

4. John Henry Barrow
(1796-1858)

Five other
children

5. Harriet Ellen Dickens
(b.1819, d. in childhood)

7. Alfred Lamert Dickens
(1822-1860)
m. 1846
= Helen Dobson

6. Frederick William Dickens
(1820-1868)
m. ante 1850
= Anne Weller

8. Augustus Dickens
(1827-1868)
= Harriette Lovell

George Hogarth   = Georgina Thomson
(1783-1870)   (1793-1863)
writer of the Signet, journalist
m. 1814

4. George Hogarth
(1821-1841)

6. Helen Hogarth
(1833-1890)

3. Mary Hogarth
(1819-1837)

5. Georgina Hogarth
(1827-1917)

other
children

7. Sydney Smith
Haldimand Dickens
(1847-1872)
d. at sea

9. Dora Annie
Dickens
(1850-1851)

6. Alfred Tennyson
Dickens
(1845-1912)
d. in America

8. Henry Fielding
Dickens
(1849-1933)

10. Edward Bulwer
Lytton Dickens
(1852-1902)
d. in Australia

Chronological table

1816		Charlotte Brontë born. Jane Austen's *Emma*. S. T. Coleridge's *Kubla Khan* (written 1797). Walter Scott's *Old Mortality*.
1817	John Dickens is moved to Chatham, where Charles goes to school.	Jane Austen dies. G. F. Watts born. John Leech born. S. T. Coleridge's *Biographia Literaria*. *Blackwood's Magazine* founded. Habeas Corpus suspended following a secret Parliamentary report that insurrection is imminent after rioting against prices up and down England.
1818		Walter Scott's *Heart of Midlothian* and *Rob Roy*. Mary Shelley's *Frankenstein*.
1819		John Ruskin born. Charles Kingsley born. George Eliot (Mary Ann Evans) born. The Peterloo massacre occurs when militia charge on a Manchester crowd demonstrating in favour of Parliamentary reform and the repeal of the Corn Laws.
1820		George III dies and is succeeded by the Prince Regent as George IV. Florence Nightingale born. Walter Scott's *Ivanhoe*. Shelley's *Prometheus Unbound*. Charles Lamb's *Essays of Elia*.
1821		John Keats dies. Feodor Dostoevsky born. Shelley's *Adonais*. Thomas de Quincey's *Confessions of an English Opium Eater*.

1822	John Dickens is transferred to London and the family lodge in Camden Town.	Shelley dies. Matthew Arnold born. Royal Academy of Music founded.
1823	Mrs Dickens tries to open a Young Ladies School at 4 Gower Street. John Dickens is arrested for debt and imprisoned in the Marshalsea where he is joined by his wife and younger children. Charles lodges alone and is sent to work at Warren's Blacking Factory. Following his father's release, Charles is sent to school after his sister Fanny goes to the Royal Academy of Music.	*Forget-me-not*, the earliest illustrated annual published. First Mechanics' Institute founded by George Birkbeck.
1824		W. S. Landor's *Imaginary Conversations*. National Gallery, London, founded. *Westminster Review* appears.
1825	John Dickens retires from Admiralty service with a small pension.	W. Hazlitt's *The Spirit of the Age*. George Stephenson builds 'The Rocket' and starts the first passenger-carrying railway line.
1826	John Dickens becomes a reporter for the *British Press*.	
1827	Charles Dickens joins a firm of solicitors as a clerk.	William Blake dies. Ludwig van Beethoven dies. Baedeker's first travel guide published.
1828		George Meredith born. Leo Tolstoy born. Franz Schubert dies.
1829		Balzac begins *La Comédie Humaine*. Roman Catholic Relief Bill passed by both Houses of Parliament.

6

Robert Peel, Home
Secretary, establishes the
Metropolitan Police in
London.

1830	Dickens first meets Maria Beadnell.	George IV dies. The Duke of Clarence succeeds to the throne as William IV. Tennyson's *Poems, Chiefly Lyrical*. William Cobbett's *Rural Rides*.
1831	Dickens becomes a reporter on Henry Barrow's *Mirror of Parliament*.	Victor Hugo's *Notre-Dame de Paris*. R. H. Surtees starts *New Sporting Magazine* with the first episode of *Jorrock's Jaunts and Jollities*. A Bill to reform Parliament is vetoed in the House of Lords.
1832	Dickens becomes a journalist on the *True Sun*, and falls in love with Maria Beadnell.	George Crabbe dies. Jeremy Bentham dies. The Reform Bill becomes law.
1833	Dickens breaks with the Beadnell family. His first published piece, 'A Dinner at Poplar Walk', appears in December, in the *Monthly Magazine*.	Thomas Carlyle's *Sartor Resartus*. British Factory Act passed to prevent children under nine from working in factories and those between nine and thirteen from working more than a nine-hour day.
1834	Dickens becomes a staff reporter on the *Morning Chronicle*, in which several 'street sketches' appear. Dickens meets Catherine Hogarth. John Dickens is again arrested for debt.	S. T. Coleridge dies. Rev. T. R. Malthus dies. Charles Lamb dies. W. H. Ainsworth's *Rookwood*. Bulwer Lytton's *Last Days of Pompeii*. Slavery abolished throughout the British Empire. At Tolpuddle, in Dorset, labourers are sentenced to transportation for taking illegal oaths in forming a Trade Union.

Having succeeded Lord Grey, Lord Melbourne is dismissed as Prime Minister in favour of Peel. In October, both Houses of Parliament almost destroyed by fire. Joseph Hansom patents his Hansom Cab.

1835 Dickens contributes 'Sketches of London' to the *Evening Chronicle*, and becomes engaged to Catherine Hogarth.

'Mark Twain' (Samuel Clemens) born. Hans Andersen's *Fairy Tales*. F. Marryat's *Mr Midshipman Easy*. Opening of Madame Tussaud's waxworks in London.

1836 *Sketches by Boz* published and *Pickwick* begun. Dickens and Catherine Hogarth married in Chelsea. Dickens's first play *The Strange Gentleman*, adapted from *The Great Winglebury Duel*, runs for sixty nights at the St James's Theatre. He agrees to edit Richard Bentley's *Miscellany*, makes a friend of John Forster, and has another play, *The Village Coquettes*, produced at the same theatre.

R. W. Emerson's *Nature* published.

1837 *Pickwick* completed and issued in book form, and *Oliver Twist* begun in *Bentley's Miscellany*. *Is She His Wife?* produced at the St James's. Charles Culliford Boz Dickens born and the family move to Doughty Street where Catherine's sister, Mary, dies suddenly.

Thomas Carlyle's *The French Revolution*. William IV dies and Victoria becomes Queen aged seventeen. Isaac Pitman invents his shorthand system. T. N. Talfourd introduces a new Copyright Bill in House of Commons.

1838	*Nicholas Nickleby* begins in monthly instalments. *Memoirs of Grimaldi* published. His first daughter Mary (Mamie) born.	Thackeray's *The Yellowplush Correspondence* appears in *Fraser's Magazine*. Anti-Corn Law League founded in Manchester by Richard Cobden. The Working Men's Association publish The People's Charter. Regular transatlantic steam ship service started.
1839	Family move to Devonshire Terrace and Dickens sends his parents off to live in Devon. Kate Macready Dickens born. *Nickleby* completed and published in book form.	Charles Darwin's *Voyage of the Beagle*. Riots break out after the Chartist Petition is rejected by Parliament.
1840	*Master Humphrey's Clock* begins to appear weekly and from the fourth number carries *The Old Curiosity Shop*	Thomas Hardy born. Ainsworth's *The Tower of London*. Queen Victoria marries Prince Albert of Saxe-Coburg. Roland Hill's penny post introduced. New Houses of Parliament built. Column to Lord Nelson erected in Trafalgar Square.
1841	*Barnaby Rudge* appears in *Master Humphrey's Clock*. Walter Landor Dickens born. Dickens is made a Freeman of Edinburgh and tours Scotland.	Carlyle's *On Heroes and Hero Worship*. *Punch* first published. Bradshaw's first *Railway Guide* appears. Thomas Cook arranges his first passenger tour.
1842	January–June, Dickens and his wife tour America. *American Notes* published. Begins *Martin Chuzzlewit*.	Tennyson's *Poems*. Lord Macaulay's *Lays of Ancient Rome*. *Illustrated London News* first published. House of Commons rejects the second Chartist Petition, and renewed rioting results.

1843	*Chuzzlewit* appears in monthly parts. *A Christmas Carol* published in time for Christmas.	Henry James born. Carlyle's *Past and Present*. Bulwer Lytton's *The Last of the Barons*. John Ruskin's *Modern Painters* begins to appear. Wordsworth succeeds Robert Southey as Poet Laureate. Brunel's Thames Tunnel opened. First printed Christmas cards.
1844	In Italy, from where Dickens returns to London to read to friends his new Christmas book, *The Chimes*.	Robert Bridges born. Frederick Nietzsche born. B. Disraeli's *Coningsby*. Factory Act to restrict female workers to a twelve-hour day and children aged eight to thirteen to six-and-a-half hours. 'Ragged School' Union founded. Rochdale Pioneers found Co-operative Society.
1845	Back in England Dickens produces *Every Man in his Humour* with friends. *Cricket on the Hearth* written for Christmas. Alfred D'Orsay Tennyson Dickens born. Begins *Pictures from Italy*.	Disraeli's *Sybil, or the Two Nations*. E. A. Poe's *Tales of Mystery and Imagination*. Friedrich Engel's *The Condition of the Working Classes in England* published in Germany. Austen Layard begins excavating Nineveh. British Museum built.
1846	Dickens launches the *Daily News* but resigns as editor after only seventeen days. *Pictures from Italy* appears as letters in the newspaper. In June the family travel to Lausanne, where Dickens starts *Dombey and Son*, issued in twenty monthly parts from October. November in Paris. *The Battle of Life: a love story* appears for Christmas.	*Poems* by the Brontë Sisters. Thackeray's *The Book of Snobs*. Edward Lear's *Book of Nonsense*. Defeated after repeal of the Corn Laws, Peel is succeeded as Prime Minister by Lord John Russell. The Fleet Prison is pulled down.

1847	Back in London, Dickens arranges a benefit tour of *Every Man in his Humour*.	Anne Brontë's *Agnes Grey*. Charlotte Brontë's *Jane Eyre*. Emily Brontë's *Wuthering Heights*. Thackeray's *Vanity Fair* serialised. Disraeli's *Tancred*. The Californian 'Gold Rush' begins.
1848	Fanny dies. Dickens arranges performances of *The Merry Wives of Windsor* to raise funds to preserve Shakespeare's birth-place. The company perform before the Queen. His final Christmas book *The Haunted Man* published.	Emily Brontë dies. Elizabeth Gaskell's *Mary Barton*. Anne Brontë *The Tenant of Wildfell Hall*. J. A. Froude's *The Nemesis of Faith*. Macaulay's *History of England* and Thackeray's *Pendennis* begin to appear. Marx and Engels issue the *Communist Manifesto*. Holman Hunt, D. G. Rossetti, and Millais, painters, found the Pre-Raphaelite Brotherhood. A year of revolutions in France, Germany, Austria-Hungary, Poland and Italy.
1849	Henry Fielding Dickens born. Dickens begins *David Copperfield* and the first number appears in May.	Charlotte Brontë's *Shirley*. Charles Kingsley's *Alton Locke*. Matthew Arnold's 'The Strayed Reveller'. David Livingstone begins his exploration of Central and South Africa.
1850	*Household Words* appears with Dickens as editor. Discusses with Bulwer Lytton the idea of founding the Guild of Literature and Art. Dora Annie Dickens born, but dies within a year.	Tennyson publishes *In Memoriam* and becomes Poet Laureate on the death of Wordsworth. Wordsworth's *Prelude*. Public Libraries Act passed.
1851	A year of theatrical fund-raising activities by Dickens and his circle of literary and artistic friends.	Ruskin's *Stones of Venice*. H. W. Longfellow's *The Golden Legend*. Herman Melville's *Moby Dick*.

The family move to Tavistock Square. John Dickens dies.

Crystal Palace built in Hyde Park for Prince Albert's Great Exhibition. Lord Palmerston dismissed as Foreign Secretary. Thackeray's *History of Henry Esmond*.

1852   Serial publication of *Bleak House* begins. Dickens and his wife tour with friends in Lytton's *Not so Bad as we Seem*. The first bound volume of *A Child's History of England* published. Edward Bulwer Lytton Dickens born.

Duke of Wellington dies. Victoria and Albert Museum opened in Kensington.

1853   Visits to Boulogne and Italy. First public readings from the Christmas Books given at the Birmingham Mechanics' Institute.

Charlotte Brontë's *Villette*. Elizabeth Gaskell's *Cranford*. Thackeray's *The Newcomes*. W. E. Gladstone introduces a Free Trade Budget in Parliament.

1854   *Hard Times* appears weekly in *Household Words*, and is published in book form.

Charles Kingsley's *Westward Ho!* Coventry Patmore's *Angel in the House*. Britain and France allied with Turkey against Russia land armies in the Crimea.

1855   Supports the Administrative Reform Association. *Little Dorrit* issued in monthly parts from December. The family in Paris at the end of the year where Dickens meets leading writers, publishers, actors and artists.

Charlotte Brontë dies. Tennyson's *Maud*. Browning's *Men and Women*. Longfellow's *Hiawatha*. Whitman's *Leaves of Grass*. Anthony Trollope's *The Warden*. Lord Palmerston becomes Prime Minister. Allied forces occupy Sebastopol after a long siege and Russia capitulates. Livingstone discovers the Victoria Falls on Zambesi River.

1856	Buys Gad's Hill Place. Family return from France to London.	Oscar Wilde born. George Bernard Shaw born. Gustave Flaubert's *Madame Bovary*. Crimean War ended by the Peace of Paris. Thomas Cook leads the first travel tour to Europe.
1857	Collins's melodrama, *The Frozen Deep*, acted at Tavistock House, and the company tours to Manchester where the female parts are taken by professional actresses, Ellen Ternan and her sister. *The Lazy Tour of Two Idle Apprentices*, a collaboration with Collins, appears in *Household Words*.	Charlotte Brontë's *The Professor*. Thackeray's *The Virginians*. Trollope's *Barchester Towers*. George Eliot's *Scenes from Clerical Life* appears in *Blackwood's Magazine*. Charles Baudelaire's *Les Fleurs du Mal*. Transportation for crime ended in Britain. Indian Mutiny.
1858	Articles from *Household Words* published as *Reprinted Pieces*. Gives readings in aid of the Hospital for Sick Children. In May, Dickens and his wife separate; he makes a personal statement in *Household Words* and breaks with his publishers, Bradbury & Evans. He later undertakes a tour of 87 readings for his own profit.	Trollope's *Dr. Thorne*. William Morris's *The Defence of Guenevere*. Robert Owen dies. Palmerston resigns and Earl of Derby forms a Conservative Government. I. K. Brunel's iron ship S.S. *Great Eastern* launched. W. P. Frith paints *Derby Day*.
1859	Begins a new weekly, *All The Year Round*, with himself as 'Conductor', and buys out and incorporates *Household Words*. *A Tale of Two Cities* appears weekly from April, and is published as a volume in December.	Leigh Hunt dies. Thomas de Quincey dies. Lord Macaulay dies. Charles Darwin's *On the Origin of Species by Natural Selection*. J. S. Mill's *On Liberty*. George Eliot's *Adam Bede*. Tennyson's *Idylls of the King*. George Meredith's *The Ordeal of Richard Feverel*.

Edward FitzGerald's *The Rubaiyat of Omar Khayyám*. Disraeli's Reform Bill defeated; Derby's administration falls and Palmerston again becomes Prime Minister.

1860   Removes to Gad's Hill. *Great Expectations* begins in weekly instalments in *All The Year Round*.

Wilkie Collins's *The Woman in White*. George Eliot's *The Mill on the Floss*. Thackeray becomes first editor of *The Cornhill Magazine*. Garibaldi proclaims Victor Emmanuel King of Italy. Abraham Lincoln is elected President of the United States.

1861   *The Uncommercial Traveller*, pieces from *All The Year Round*, published. A second series of readings.

Prince Albert dies. Elizabeth Barrett Browning dies. George Eliot's *Silas Marner*. Charles Reade's *The Cloister and the Hearth*. Horse-drawn tram-cars introduced into London. Civil War in America. Emancipation of serfs in Russia. Bismarck becomes Prime Minister of Prussia.

1862   A year of readings. In Paris with Mamie and Georgina Hogarth.

George Meredith's *Modern Love*. Ruskin's *Unto This Last*. J. S. Mill's *Utilitarianism*. Victor Hugo's *Les Misérables*. Ivan Turgenev's *Fathers and Sons*. Gilbert Scott designs the Albert Memorial, erected in Kensington Gardens.

1863   More readings, in Paris and London. Elizabeth Dickens dies.

Thackeray dies. Kingsley's *The Water Babies*. Abolition of slavery in USA. Work begins on London's underground railway.

1864	*Our Mutual Friend* appears in monthly instalments for Chapman and Hall.	Landor dies. John Leech dies. Trollope's *The Small House at Allington*. J. H. Newman's *Apologia pro Vita Sua*. Leo Tolstoy's *War and Peace*. International Red Cross founded in Switzerland.
1865	*Our Mutual Friend* published in book form. Involved in the Staplehurst railway accident in June. Second collection of *The Uncommercial Traveller* published.	Elizabeth Gaskell dies. Joseph Paxton dies. Lord Palmerston dies. Rudyard Kipling born. John Ruskin's *Sesame and Lilies*. A. C. Swinburne's *Atalanta in Calydon*. Lewis Carroll's *Alice in Wonderland*. *Fortnightly Review* and *Pall Mall Gazette* founded. Lord John Russell made Prime Minister with W. E. Gladstone as Leader of House of Commons. U.S. Civil War ended. President Lincoln assassinated.
1866	Thirty provincial readings.	H. G. Wells born. George Eliot's *Felix Holt*. Kingsley's *Hereward the Wake*. A. C. Swinburne's *Poems and ballads*. Dostoevsky's *Crime and Punishment*. Henrik Ibsen's *Brand*. Government resigns after defeat of Gladstone's Reform Bill. Derby becomes Prime Minister. War between Prussia and Austria, and Austria and Italy.
1867	Fifty provincial readings. Sails on American reading tour in November, to Boston and New York, during which his health deteriorates.	Arnold Bennett born. John Galsworthy born. Trollope's *The Last Chronicle of Barset*. Emile Zola's *Thérèse Raquin*. Karl Marx's *Das Kapital* Vol. 1.

Fenian Rising in Ireland and
bomb attacks in Manchester.
Disraeli's Reform Act
extends adult male franchise
to tenants and lodgers.
Further Factory Acts to
regulate hours and conditions
of work for children,
young persons, and women.

1868   Sails for England in April,
and tours with further
readings.

Collins's *The Moonstone*.
Browning's *The Ring and the
Book*. Morris's *The Earthly
Paradise*. Louisa M. Alcott's
Little Women. Dostoevsky's
The Idiot. Disraeli becomes
Prime Minister but is defeated
at the December General
Election, and Gladstone
forms a Liberal Ministry.

1869   First public reading of the
murder of Nancy from
Oliver Twist, but his doctors
order him to discontinue
the tour. Begins writing
The Mystery of Edwin Drood.

Earl of Derby dies. R. D.
Blackmore's *Lorna Doone*.
Matthew Arnold's *Culture
and Anarchy*. Mark Twain's
The Innocents Abroad. Jules
Verne's *Twenty Thousand
Leagues under the Sea*.
Imprisonment for debt
abolished. Suez Canal opened.

1870   Twelve farewell readings in
London. Six parts of *Edwin
Drood* appear between April
and September. Dies at
Gad's Hill on 9 June, aged
58, and is buried in Poets'
Corner, Westminster
Abbey.

Alexandre Dumas dies.
Disraeli's *Lothair*. D. G.
Rossetti's *Poems*. Herbert
Spencer's *Principles of
Psychology*. Education Act
establishes Board Schools.
Civil Service reformed and
opened to entry by
competitive examination.
War between France and
Prussia leads to revolt in
Paris, the collapse of the
Second Empire and the
establishment of the Third
Republic.

1   His life and times

And one man in his time plays many parts.
                    (*As You Like It*, Act II, Scene vii)

The story of Dickens's life is bold and epic in outline, rich and fascinating in its inexhaustible detail. To explore any one strand of his life is to be drawn into the grand spectacle of Victorian life and thought where one stands before an immense and bustling conversation piece on a scale quite beyond that of the largest canvas of the many genre painters of the time.

From the days of his earliest successes, Charles Dickens lived several lives and pursued several careers simultaneously. Everything he did was done with a ferocious energy. Although my primary concern with him is as an artist and novelist, he was also a man of the theatre, a tireless supporter of good causes and social reforms, a radical campaigning journalist, the head of a large, demanding family and their dependants who often fell short of his expectations of them, an ardent friend to a large circle of his contemporaries and, in a way that needs stressing, a professional man. An artist can be a great writer and care little for his profession. Not so Dickens who was, throughout his writing life, always sensitive on the subject of the status of the writer in Victorian society. And yet, paradoxically, one does not gain from his correspondence or from his biography any sense that he lived only in order to write. His appetite for life, for fun and for experience was as full of zest as his writings. Nor is it the case that his life and art were separate existences for him. It is a large part of his modernity and, I suggest, of his inheritance from the English romantic poets, from Wordsworth in particular, that his own experiences, especially those of his first twenty-five years, were the materials out of which he created his fictional worlds. Yet, in life, he was extremely reticent about his origins. No hint of these was revealed to his reading public until after his death with the appearance of John Forster's biography. For Forster, he began an autobiography in 1847 of which only a fragment remains as he broke it off at a painful moment in his youthful past and never resumed it. Two years later he drafted much of the material into the early chapters of *David Copperfield* which began to appear in 1849. I shall leave to a discussion of the novel itself (see p. 109) the question of the connections between these two related writings. The main outlines of the early life can be established independently of them.

Charles John Huffam Dickens was born at Landport, Portsea, on

7 February 1812. His father, John Dickens, was at that time a clerk in the Navy Pay Office at Portsmouth Dockyard, a post he probably attained through the influence of Lord Crewe, whose steward his father, William Dickens, had been for many years at Crewe Hall, and where his mother was housekeeper. In 1809 he had married Elizabeth Barrow, whose father, Charles Barrow, was an important Admiralty functionary, the Chief Conductor of Moneys in Town. In the following year Barrow confessed to the embezzlement of navy funds and absconded to the continent. John Dickens may have relied on Barrow for financial support occasionally for, although he worked well and was a good family man, he was also convivial and enjoyed offering generous hospitality, so that for most of his life he was quite unable to manage on his income. He was explicitly the origin of Mr Micawber.

After a brief spell in London, he was sent to the large naval dockyard at Chatham early in 1817. Here he could afford a three-storey house and two servants for his growing family. Charles was the second of eight children. At Chatham his mother, who apparently had some powers as a comic mimic, taught him to read and he listened to terrifying bed-time stories told by his young nurse, Mary Weller. His older sister Fanny played the piano and Charles sang comic songs to the delight of his father, who would exhibit his son's talent to friends. Here Charles was at school under William Giles, the son of the local Baptist minister, who recognised the boy's quick intelligence and encouraged it. Dickens was not a very healthy child, and he was often at home reading while the other children played outside. Forster reports that David Copperfield's account of his childhood reading in chapter four is in every word faithful to the autobiographical account. The list includes the novels of Fielding, Smollett, Goldsmith and Defoe and, most importantly, *The Arabian Nights*. At the age of ten Dickens wrote a tragedy called *Misnar, The Sultan of India*, and he was often taken to the theatre by James Lamert, an aunt's step-son, who lived with the family both at Chatham and later, in London, where John Dickens was recalled in 1822. Charles was apparently left in Chatham to finish his school term, and followed the family to London by coach, bearing a copy of Goldsmith's miscellany *The Bee*; a parting gift from his teacher. Here, in temporary lodgings, the family were immediately worse off as John Dickens had only his salary of £350, having lost the allowances that outpost positions carried, and Charles felt himself utterly neglected according to his own later account, which is fully reported in Forster's *Life*. His sister entered the Royal Academy of Music as a pupil-boarder while he did housework, wandered about the neighbourhood of Camden Town and was sent as occasion demanded to the pawnbroker or to the bookseller with the precious collection of cheap novels from his Chatham days. His mother then rented a house in Gower Street where she hoped to establish a school. But, despite the brass plate and the leaflets that Charles distributed, no pupil ever came. John Dickens was continuously on the point of being arrested for debt and so accepted an offer of work for Charles from James Lamert, at Lamert's brother-in-law's blacking factory at Hungerford Stairs.

The close parallels between these experiences and their central importance in *David Copperfield* is part of every reader's knowledge of the novel. Whether or not his later recollections of it were accurate in detail, this was an episode that marked Dickens for life, and one which he hugged close to himself secretly and continuously. As he wrote later:

> No words can express the secret agony of my soul as I sunk into this companionship; compared these everyday associates with those of my happier childhood; and felt my early hopes of growing up to be a learned and distinguished man crushed in my breast. The deep remembrance of the sense I had of being utterly neglected and hopeless; of the shame I felt in my position; of the misery it was to my young heart to believe that, day by day, what I had learned, and thought, and delighted in, and raised my fancy and my emulation up by, was passing away from me, never to be brought back any more; cannot be written. My whole nature was so penetrated with the grief and humiliation of such considerations, that even now, famous and caressed and happy, I often forget in my dreams that I have a dear wife and children; even that I am a man; and wander desolately back to that time of my life.

It is the powerful, dream-like memory of it all that masters him and shakes his grip on reality. It is a dream of Romantic horror that is often re-shaped as fiction in his later life. The hopelessness of his situation was compounded when, at about the same time, his father was arrested for debt and imprisoned in the Marshalsea, the prison which is at the centre of the vision of life in *Little Dorrit*. Here, paradoxically, the family were better off than they had been, as John Dickens was still drawing his pay and there was no house to keep up. Charles was put into lodgings, first in Camden Town and then, after complaining to his father of being totally cut off from the family, nearby in the Borough. He and Fanny went each weekend to stay in the Marshalsea but spent the rest of the week quite alone. Charles fended for himself on the six or seven shillings a week which he earned at the blacking factory. At some stage during his time there, the factory moved premises to Chandos Street where Charles and his young fellow workers laboured at papering over, neatly tying round with a string and labelling the pots of blacking. They worked in the window for the sake of the light:

> And we were so brisk at it that the people used to stop and look in. Sometimes there would be quite a little crowd there.

The core of Dickens's remembrance of these months is his sense of having been neglected to the point of abandonment. What comes through the writing is an indifference to the plight of his existence, not only on the part of his immediate family, but also on the part of the larger human family from whom he felt himself to be cut off by that large window, through which others stared at him and — I take this to be the importance of what he is expressing — failed to recognise him as 'a child of singular ability: quick, eager, delicate, and soon hurt, bodily or mentally. No one made any sign. My father and mother were quite satisfied. They could hardly have been more so, if I had been twenty years of age, distinguished at a grammar school, and going to Cambridge.' This denial of his own sense of himself is marvellously transformed in *David Copperfield* into the Murdstones' denial of David's right to exist after his mother's death. But it is tempting to see in the image of the child, unacknowledged, gazing through the window, a deeper significance in the development of Dickens's comic art. His comic characters are comic often in that the author records them, their appearance, their gestures and their language, as though they were inexplicable objects and not persons. He withholds that assumption of the other's humanity which is essential to all our relationships. This, I take it, is what is meant by calling Dickens a caricaturist and thinking of his fictional characters, insofar as they have character, which not all of them do, as caricatures. But they seem to me quite different from caricature, as I hope to be able to show in discussing the novels.

John Dickens was released from prison in May 1824. He received a legacy of £450 from his mother: it went to pay his creditors and there was nothing left for the family, but what followed was Charles's release from the drudgery and shame he reports himself as having suffered. His father quarrelled with Lamert and took him away from the factory. 'With a relief so strange that it was like oppression, I went home.' Whatever one makes of Dicken's reconstruction of his sufferings of that time, the very ambiguity of his feelings on his escape is a sign of the truth of those feelings and of the experience that provoked them.

Like Keats, Dickens is very accurate in his evocations of powerful dream states and dream-like confusions and, like Wordsworth in the *Prelude*, able to persuade us that such ambiguous experiences and feelings are profoundly significant. The episode does seem to be one of the Dickens's earliest experiences which he felt in his secret, innermost being marked his whole future:

Hungerford Stairs, Thomas Shepherd

21

My mother set herself to accommodate the quarrel, and did so next day. She brought home a request for me to return next morning, and a high character of me, which I am very sure I deserved. My father said I should go back no more, and should go to school. I do not write resentfully or angrily: for I know how all these things have worked together to make me what I am: but I never afterwards forgot, I never shall forget, I never can forget, that my mother was warm for my being sent back.

From that hour until this at which I write, no word of that part of my childhood which I have now gladly brought to a close, has passed my lips to any human being. I have no idea how long it lasted; whether for a year, or much more, or less. From that hour, until this, my father and my mother have been stricken dumb upon it. I have never heard the least allusion to it, however far off and remote, from either of them. I have never, until I now impart it to this paper, in any burst of confidence with anyone, my own wife not excepted, raised the curtain I then dropped, thank God.

Until old Hungerford Market was pulled down, until old Hungerford Stairs were destroyed, and the very nature of the ground changed, I never had the courage to go back to the place where my servitude began. I never saw it. I could not endure to go near it. For many years, when I came near to Robert Warrens' in the Strand, I crossed over to the opposite side of the way, to avoid a certain smell of the cement they put upon the blacking-corks, which reminded me of what I was once. It was a very long time before I liked to go up Chandos Street. My old way home by the Borough made me cry, after my eldest child could speak.

For the next two years he attended Wellington House Academy in Mornington Place. The school is described as 'Our School' in an article in *Household Words* for October 1851, and was later demolished to make way for the same railway line that destroyed Stagg's Gardens, the home of the Toodle family in *Dombey and Son*. Its Master, Mr Jones, was apparently an ignorant tyrant who provided the outline for Mr Creakle of Salem House, where David Copperfield was sent to school.

In May 1827 he began work as a solicitor's clerk in Gray's Inn, but after about a year began to think of journalism as a career. His father had been retired from the Navy Pay Office following his discharge from prison as an insolvent debtor, and, after learning shorthand, had become a parliamentary reporter for the *British Press*. Charles struggled with shorthand and joined a distant relative as a shorthand reporter in the Consistory Court of Doctors Commons, near St Paul's; a muddled and archaic legal survival from the Middle Ages. His experiences here would seem to have given him his life-long contempt for the law. As soon as he was eighteen he applied for a reader's ticket to the British Museum where, during the next three or four years, he read widely and generally, mainly in literature and history but with, as far as one can now tell, little sense of an intellectual programme of study.

Journalism and early fiction

In 1828 his maternal uncle, John Henry Barrow, had started a new record of verbatim reports of parliamentary debates, the *Mirror of Parliament*. This Dickens joined early in 1832. At the same time he was reporting for a new evening daily newspaper, the *True Sun*. In Parliament he 'made a great splash' as a reporter and came to the attention of the Chief Secretary, Edward Stanley, later Lord Derby. He was remembered in later years as the greatest shorthand writer ever. What partly spurred him on was the fact that he had fallen in love with the young daughter of a Lombard Street banker, Maria Beadnell. When it became clear what the young man's intentions were, Maria was sent to Paris out of the way. On her return he found her changed towards him. She returned his letters and called him a boy; so, at about the time of his twenty-first birthday, he came to the conclusion that his position was hopeless and broke off the affair. Undoubtedly Maria Beadnell re-emerges in *David Copperfield* as Dora, his child-wife, but they did meet again in later life, when it was Dickens's turn, after writing passionately in reply to her letter, to flee from the fat middle-aged lady she had become. He put something of her into Flora Finching in *Little Dorrit*. As he wrote to Forster: 'No one can imagine in the most distant degree what pain the recollection gave me in Copperfield. And, just as I can never open that book as I open any other book, I cannot see the face (even at four-and-forty), or hear the voice, without going wandering away over the ashes of all that youth and hope in the wildest manner.' Apart from the character of Flora, the one thing he caught from Maria Beadnell was a bad cold. Yet, as he explains in reliving the memory of Dora, this was yet another of the experiences that marked him permanently and made him what he became, especially in his relations with women. This passionate and hopeless love affair 'made so deep an impression on me that I refer to it a habit of suppression which now belongs to me, which I know is no part of my original nature, but which makes me chary of showing my affections, even to my children, except when they are very young'. Nevertheless, within three years he was an acknowledged writer, bound for an extraordinary fame and popularity, and a married man.

His experiences of parliamentary debate at this time left him utterly sceptical of the ability of the institution to reform or govern the country. In 1833, again with the help of his uncle Barrow's connections, Dickens became a reporter for the *Morning Chronicle* which was then under the editorship of a Scotsman, John Black. Black was a radical campaigner on behalf of reform and his influence was considerable. Under his guidance the *Morning Chronicle* came to rival *The Times* and promoted the cause of the Liberal Party. Meanwhile, Dickens had begun to write a series of sketches of London life, the first of which, entitled 'A Dinner at Poplar Walk', had appeared in the *Monthly Magazine* for December 1832. When he bought the copy with his anonymous piece 'in all the glory of print' he had to hide himself in Westminster Hall, 'my eyes so dimmed with pride and joy that they could not bear the street, and were not fit to be seen'. Even though the editor could not pay his writers, Dickens contributed four more sketches in quick succession, and more again from August 1833 under the pen name of Boz. In September he was sent to Edinburgh to cover a reception for Earl Grey and, in the same month, his sketches began to appear in his own newspaper. They had already attracted critical notice, and some of them had been pirated and either reprinted or adapted for the theatre.

It was in the offices of the *Chronicle* that Dickens met Harrison Ainsworth, the historical novelist whose *Rookwood* had been a bestseller. It was he who introduced Dickens to his publisher John Macrone, and Macrone suggested publishing a volume of *Sketches by Boz* with illustrations by George Cruikshank who was already a well-established artist and illustrator. Macrone would pay £150. The offer was timely as John Dickens was yet again in serious financial difficulties. He had been sacked by Barrow and, although earning as a reporter for the *Morning Herald*, he was utterly incapable of living within his means. In November 1835, Charles took matters into his own hands, put his parents and family into cheaper lodgings and rented cheap chambers for himself and his brother Frederick in Furnival's Inn. He also moved to the *Chronicle's* new sister paper, the *Evening Chronicle*, whose editor was George Hogarth, a music critic. Here Dickens contributed beyond his regular assignments twenty more sketches for which he was paid. Others appeared elsewhere under the pseudonym of Tibbs — a name he took from Goldsmith's essays. Through Ainsworth he also at this time met Daniel Maclise the painter, Edward Bulwer (later Bulwer-Lytton, see page 169), Benjamin Disraeli, and Cruikshank.

Sketches by Boz appeared on his twenty-fourth birthday and immediately attracted favourable critical reviews. A second edition followed in August 1836 and two more in the course of the following year. Dickens's extraordinary career was launched. In February 1836 he was visited by the head of a new publishing firm, William Hall, whom Dickens recognised immediately as the counter assistant who had sold him his copy of the *Monthly Magazine* containing 'A Dinner at Poplar Walk'. Dickens had already produced for Chapman and Hall's Library of Fiction a sketch entitled 'The Tuggses at Ramsgate' to be illustrated by Robert Seymour. Seymour had had the idea of producing a series of sporting prints with extended captions depicting, in the manner of R. H. Surtees's *Jorrocks's Jaunts and Jollities* with coloured plates by Henry Alken, the adventures and mishaps of a so-called 'Nimrod Club'. Dickens seized the notion, turning it round so that he would provide a series of scenes of English life and people which could then be illustrated. Hall agreed and suggested a series in monthly parts, each an instalment of about twelve thousand words, totalling twenty issues at a shilling each. Pierce Egan's *Tom and Jerry* had appeared in this form between 1821 and 1823 with illustrations by the Cruikshank brothers. The full title of this not uninteresting forerunner of the *Sketches* and *Pickwick* is *Life in London, or the Day and Night Scenes of Jerry Hawthorn, Esq. and Corinthian Tom*. The genre existed, but it took the genius of Dickens to transform it in *The Posthumous Papers of the Pickwick Club* into one of the greatest English comic novels.

The first issue of *Pickwick* appeared on 31 March 1836 with Seymour's green cover and illustrations, but the venture hung fire at around four hundred copies until, in the fifth number, Dickens introduced Sam Weller, Mr Pickwick's cockney servant. In April Seymour shot himself, possibly over a disagreement with Dickens, before the third number was prepared. Among the applicants Dickens interviewed to replace Seymour was William Makepeace Thackeray, newly returned from a Paris art school. He was unsuitable and the final choice fell on Hablôt K. Browne, still not twenty-one, but already well-known and who would become famous as 'Phiz' during his long years of collaboration with Boz. Suddenly, *Pickwick's* sales grew enormously and reached a circulation of forty thousand before it was completed.

Meanwhile Macrone wanted to pay Dickens £200 for a novel, and Richard Bentley, a publisher whom he had recently met, made an offer in August of £400 for each of two novels; an offer quickly raised to £500. Dickens seemed to be in a mood to accept any offer, and committed himself eagerly to more contracts than he could possibly hope to fulfil. After an engagement that lasted a year he married Catherine, eldest daughter of George Hogarth, by special licence quietly at St Luke's Church, Chelsea in April 1836. Catherine was pretty and plump, still only twenty and, although lively and gossipy, inclined to moods of depression. Their relationship was quite different from the entanglement with Maria Beadnell. From the first, Dickens firmly took the upper hand. He was working almost continuously either for the newspaper or at the *Sketches* and wrote to her:

I really have no alternative but to remain at home tonight, and 'get on' in good earnest. You know I have frequently told you that my composition is peculiar; I never can write with effect — especially in the serious way — until I have got my steam up, or in other words until I have become so excited with my subject that I cannot leave off; and hoping to arrive at this state tonight, I have, after a good deal of combatting with my wish to see you, arrived at the determination I have just announced — I hope to do a good deal.

I will not do you the injustice to propose that knowing my reason and my *motive* for exertion, *you* of all people will blame me one instant for my self-denial. You may be disappointed; — I would rather you would — at not seeing me; but you cannot feel vexed at my doing my best with the stake I have to play for — you and a home for both of us.

The stakes were higher than domestic content. Dickens's determination forced him through nearly two million words in the course of the next four years, during which time he gained an international reputation.

Bentley wanted an editor for a new monthly miscellany and was persuaded to offer the post to Dickens. In November Dickens accepted at a salary of £20 a month and another twenty guineas for his own contributions. With his earnings from the accelerating sales of *Pickwick* reaching £300 a year, Dickens would have at the age of twenty-five nearly £800 a year. He resigned from the *Morning Chronicle* and set about gathering contributors for the new venture. The first issue appeared early in January 1837, a few days after the birth of his first son, also called Charles. Macrone became very angry at the news, asked Ainsworth for advice and continued to advertise a forthcoming novel, *Gabriel Vardon*, despite Dickens's insistence that Macrone had released him from the contract. Dickens only escaped the consequences of Macrone's refusal to yield by abandoning to him outright the entire copyright of two series of *Sketches by Boz*. It was at Ainsworth's at Christmas that he first met John Forster, his life-long companion, literary adviser and biographer.

Oliver Twist was launched in the February issue of *Bentley's Miscellany* and was a success from the start. Dickens's youthfulness at this time came as a surprise to the many figures he was beginning to meet. But he was already a family man and looking for a house to match his needs and expectations. This he found at 48, Doughty Street, which is now the headquarters of the Dickens Fellowship and a Dickens museum. Then it was a private street with a porter's lodge and gates at each end. Late in March, Chapman and Hall gave Dickens a dinner and a large cheque to celebrate the first anniversary of *Pickwick*. Very shortly afterwards he was elected to the

48, Doughty Street, London

Athenaeum Club by that distinguished body. Nevertheless, he still had to face difficulties and immediate trials of very different kinds.

In setting up house in Doughty Street Dickens took with him as part of his immediate family not only his younger brother Fred but also Catherine's next sister, the sixteen-year-old Mary. Early in May they had all been to the theatre to see Dickens's own farce *Is She His Wife?* from which they had just returned home in very good spirits. Scarcely had Mary closed the door of her room than Dickens heard her cry out strangely. He rushed in to find her choking for breath, held her in his arms, sent Fred for a doctor and held her until 'she sank under the attack and died — died in such a calm and gentle sleep, that . . . I continued to support her lifeless form long after her soul had fled to Heaven'. It was a shock from which he never recovered. Just as he wore her ring until he himself died, so he never freed himself from the grief of this sudden and numbing loss. Child mortality was a common enough fact of life in early nineteenth-century England. Early death was a close and distressing accompaniment to the whole business of growing up. The story of the Brontë family and their childhood friends is harrowing to read, and the death of Little Nell at the end of *The Old Curiosity Shop* is the most famous or, in many modern critical judgements, the most notorious of Dickens's repeated rehearsals of the motif that arose out of Mary Hogarth's death. As Edgar Johnson says: 'It is impossible to exaggerate the significance of this early loss and early sorrow.' Her place in his household and her role in his life were taken by another younger sister, Georgina, who maintained a ferocious loyalty to him throughout his later domestic troubles.

He could not write and, abandoning the instalments of *Pickwick* and *Oliver Twist* for June, escaped with Catherine to a farm on Hampstead Heath and, a little later, to the continent. Hablôt Browne persuaded them to take a trip to Brussels and Antwerp. This was Dickens's first of many experiences of European life for which he conceived an insatiable passion. Throughout his life he was to spend months on end travelling and living abroad, whether in America, Italy, Switzerland or France. Everywhere he went he enjoyed the friendship and admiration of his peers.

It was John Forster who sorted out his other trial, thereby cementing an enduring friendship and role as Dickens's adviser. Dickens was committed to three publishers, Bentley, Chapman and Hall, and Macrone, and Macrone intended, on Ainsworth's advice, to hold him to his contract. Moreover, when Macrone saw the spectacular success of *Pickwick*, he expressed an intention to re-issue the *Sketches* in very similar monthly parts with the now familiar green cover. Forster tried to buy Macrone out but, at the price of £2,000 which Macrone demanded, he advised Dickens to leave well alone.

Portrait sketch of John Forster, Daniel Maclise

At Dickens's enraged insistence, however, Chapman and Hall agreed to buy the copyright for more than that amount against the security of Dickens's further share in *Pickwick*, and another novel. At that moment Macrone died, and for his widow Dickens edited a volume, *The Pic-Nic Papers* which raised £300 for her. At the bottom of Dickens's contractual problems was, of course, his rapidly rising popularity and his awareness that he was enriching his publishers rather than himself. Relations with Bentley deteriorated rapidly when Bentley could well have afforded to be generous. Dickens edited for him a life of the clown Grimaldi for £300 and a half share in the profits. Although Dickens thought nothing of it, the book sold very well. But in the negotiations conducted through Forster, particularly for the second novel, relations became very strained and Dickens finally resigned the editorship of the *Miscellany* on completion of *Oliver Twist* in February 1839. It was taken up by Ainsworth.

Since April 1838 *Nicholas Nickleby* had been appearing in monthly parts and sold fifty thousand copies for Chapman and Hall on its first day. *Pickwick* was also selling very well in a complete, three volume edition. All Dickens's novels appeared first in serial form. Book publication was arranged to coincide with the final double number of the serial. Single volume cheap editions of his works only began to appear much later. He made his next step as a writer in an attempt to combine his functions as novelist and editor. In the course of 1839 he proposed first to Forster and then to his publishers a weekly miscellany for which the final title of *Master Humphrey's Clock* was chosen. He had found the name in Richmond, Yorkshire, where he paid a visit early in 1838 to look up examples of the infamous Yorkshire boarding schools in preparation for *Nicholas Nickleby*. The novel ran until October 1839 and the first number of *Master Humphrey's Clock* came out in April, 1840. His original note proposing the scheme is dated July 1839:

> The best general idea of the plan of the work might be given perhaps by reference to the *Tatler, The Spectator*, and Goldsmith's *Bee*; but it would be far more popular both in the subjects of which it treats and its mode of treating them.

The idea of the old story teller, Master Humphrey, and his quaint clock full of old manuscripts, followed shortly afterwards. The scheme shows that Dickens's ambition was not limited to the success as a novelist which he had already achieved. During the two years of the meteoric growth of his fame he had become a public figure of considerable vigour and glamour. These other lives are important to the later novels and bear heavily on our understanding of him in his own time. However, in order not to have to compress them all into a single narrative, I have divided what I take to be the main strands into separate elements, pursuing here his career as novelist. Later in this chapter I shall turn attention to outlines of his role as journalist and editor, to his life-long passion for the theatre and to his place in public life.

The novels of the 1840s

Although *Pickwick* and imitations of him were known in France and Germany, and although an American publisher who had pirated *Oliver Twist* tried to make Dickens a token payment which was firmly refused, it was *The Old Curiosity Shop*, or perhaps rather the character of Little Nell, which secured for him both an international reputation and that sense of triumphant progress he created whenever, in later years, he travelled abroad. The novel began as a tale in weekly episodes in his new periodical and only grew in the writing into a full length novel. In the Preface to the first cheap edition of 1848 he said that even by the time *The Old Curiosity Shop* began to appear in his magazine he 'had already been made uneasy by the desultory character of that work . . .. The announcement of a story was a great

The Dickens children, Daniel Maclise

satisfaction to me.' It was also what his readers had come to expect of him, and the narrator figure, Old Humphrey, bows out of the story after a few chapters. The magazine sold up to one hundred thousand copies during the run of the novel.

Despite the difficulties Dickens had to face in writing short episodes to a weekly deadline, *The Old Curiosity Shop* was followed immediately by *Barnaby Rudge*, a historical reconstruction of the Gordon Riots of the 1780s in London against parliamentary legislation designed to achieve the emancipation of Roman Catholics in Britain. Angus Wilson says of it that it was the novel in which Dickens's greatness first announced itself. It was a much deferred

product. First contemplated as early as 1836, Macrone had advertised its forthcoming publication in 1838, and Dickens was well ahead with it by the time it appeared. It ran from February to November 1841.

He was now established with a growing family in a large house in Devonshire Terrace, Regent's Park, and much in demand as a public speaker and dinner guest. Exasperated by his father's continued incompetence in money matters, he had ruthlessly bundled both parents off into the country when he discovered that John Dickens had been borrowing in his name unknown sums from his publishers, and was still likely to be arrested yet again for debt. Dickens had refused the offer of a seat in Parliament and had been invited to Edinburgh to be made a freeman of the city. The completion of *Barnaby Rudge* allowed him to pause, to abandon the weekly grind and to think about travel.

Other writers, such as Anthony Trollope's mother who herself a novelist, and Harriet Martineau had already reported unfavourably on America towards which Dickens's thoughts had turned more than once. Through his work and his political affiliations Dickens had identified himself with liberalism as a political force and with the lives of the population of ordinary people whose fictional counterparts filled the pages of his novels with their miseries and their happinesses. It was inevitable that he should identify their aspirations in Britain with what, in anticipation, he took to be their fulfilment in the new, vigorous, if somewhat rough-edged republic. Tony Weller in chapter thirty five of *Pickwick Papers*, offered through Sam the advice to Pickwick to disappear to 'Merriker until Mrs Bardell should die when he could come back and write a book about the "Merrikins as'll pay all his expenses and more, if he blows 'em up enough'. Publishers and distinguished writers had also urged him to come.

Dickens and his wife sailed on the *Britannia*, the first Cunard transatlantic liner, in January 1842, letting the Devonshire Terrace house for six months, leaving the children in the care of his close friend W. C. Macready, the distinguished actor, and carrying a travelling portrait of all four children painted by Daniel Maclise for the purpose.

Chapman and Hall paid for the expedition on the strength of a travel book to be written on his return. The storms of the crossing were nothing to compare with his stormy journey across the civilised western states of America. From the beginning his reception was tumultuous. 'I wish you could have seen the crowds cheering the Inimitable in the streets.' The very scale of the crowds everywhere and their intrusive insistence exhausted and occasionally frightened

Opposite: The Britannia, *Clarkson Stanfield*

the young travellers. The hospitality was everywhere extravagant and those scenes, more than anything else, convinced Dickens, if he needed convincing, that he and his works were at least as well known in America as at home. Nothing more would be needed to persuade him that here lay an immense flourishing market for him and his fellow writers from which no one received a penny by way of royalties. His six years or so of dealing with publishers had sharpened and refined his extremely keen awareness of his own worth, and so in his public speeches to the Americans he launched a major campaign on behalf of an international copyright act. For this boldness, even as he continued to be universally fêted, he was almost universally reviled in the American newspapers for what they called a flagrant abuse of hospitality.

American Notes is not a good book. In one way or another America was bound to disappoint his excessive hopes ('This is not the republic I came to see; this is not the republic of my imagination'), but he did see much to admire, quite apart from Niagara Falls where he stood and thought of Mary Hogarth. He also made a large number of new friends among writers and intellectuals, many of whom he would meet again, either in London or on his later American visits. Longfellow, the poet, he met again almost immediately in London. He was excited and glad when the family were reunited at Devonshire Terrace. 'I feel my power now more than ever I did, I have a greater confidence in myself than ever I had,' he wrote. He passed the summer seeing friends in London, and at Broadstairs where he often established his family and their dependants for the long summer holidays. Nevertheless, he was still continuously occupied. A jaunt with Forster, Maclise and Clarkson Stanfield took him to Cornwall. He enquired of Lady Holland about the possibility of capturing a newspaper, perhaps the *Courier*, for the Liberal Party and the cause of reform. He also had to face his publishers who were pressing him for his next novel. He shut himself up:

> In agonies of plotting and contriving a new book; in which stage of the tremendous process, I am accustomed to walk up and down the house, smiting my forehead dejectedly; and to be so horribly cross and surly that the boldest fly at my approach. At such times even the postman knocks at the door with a mild feebleness, and my publishers always come two together, lest I should fall upon a single invader and do murder on his intrusive body.
> . . . In starting a work which is to last for twenty months, there are so many little things to attend to, which require my personal superintendence, that I am obliged to be constantly on the watch; and I may add, seriously, that unless I were to shut myself up, obstinately and sullenly in my own room for a great many days

without writing a word, I don't think I should ever make a beginning.

Even in the exaggerated ironic comedy he directs against himself in this letter of apology, we feel some hint of the way in which Dickens had to fight to prepare himself to undertake a new story, and of the energies that had to be summoned up. It was, on occasion, almost like an act of self-hypnosis. He did not, however, write automatically and, although occasionally he is known to have written in company, he was more usually stern with himself, locking himself away to 'get up steam'. He sometimes had great difficulty in getting the words down at all, but usually managed his deadlines if at cost of severe symptoms of headaches, chills and other complaints indicative of the strain he suffered in order to write. Yet, at the same time, the letter reveals something of the extraordinary energies that play almost continuously about his writings.

He finally set about the new novel, *Martin Chuzzlewit*, and Forster notes that the first instalment, which was to be published in the following month, was not quite complete by 8 December 1839. Dickens had great difficulty with *Chuzzlewit*, partly with the writing but, more acutely, with the advance planning of the complexities of the story for which he had conceived an initial design: an attack on hypocrisy. The problems with this novel decided him that hereafter he must plan further ahead. The early instalments did not sell well, although my feeling is that, within what is a great comic achievement, chapter ten, 'Town and Todgers', which appeared in the fourth part, has a peculiarly powerful comic force. Following a celebratory dinner with the lodgers in Mrs Todger's boarding house, Pecksniff's secret lecherousness, released by drinking a great amount, remains incapable yet obstinately irrepressible when he is finally got to bed. It is a wonderfully controlled, dramatically realised chapter, played out to the accompaniment of the gnomic derisive commentary of the demonic serving boy, Young Bailey. Nevertheless, Dickens decided to attempt to raise sales by sending young Martin to America; without a great deal of effect. The novel only sold well later in book form where the full deployment of Pecksniff and, that wonderful creator of language and creation of Dickens's language, Sarah Gamp the nurse and midwife, can be appreciated in the context of the novel as a whole. I shall return to aspects of this novel in the chapter on Dickens and London (p. 70).

After the problems of *Chuzzlewit* Dickens decided firmly that, at whatever cost, he needed a year off to travel in Europe. 'What would poor Scott have given to have gone abroad, of his own free will, a young man, instead of creeping there, a driveller, in his miserable decay?' The example of the old Sir Walter Scott for whom he had a great admiration, bankrupted and writing only for his creditors, haunted Dickens frequently and hovered about his dealings with publishers, intensifying his resolve always to drive a bargain advantageous to himself. But even while he was still grappling with '*Chuzzlewit* agonies', he conceived the idea of writing a short book to sell specially at Christmas. Christmas annuals, usually anthological in character, had become an established convention, and Dickens looked to being able to exploit this large market in order to recoup something of the disappointments of *Chuzzlewit* and to pay for his planned journey abroad. He wrote *A Christmas Carol* in six weeks, weeping and laughing, and weeping again 'thinking whereof he walked about the black streets of London fifteen and twenty miles many a night when all sober folks had gone to bed', so that it was ready by November 1843. Chapman and Hall were to publish it on commission.

Afterwards Dickens, as he said, 'broke out like a madman' into Christmas capers and conjuring tricks which he had been practising secretly. Six thousand copies of the *Carol* sold on the first day. Thackerary wrote, 'Who can listen to objections regarding such a book as this? It seems to me a national benefit, and to every man or woman who reads it a personal benefit.' It was immediately pirated and, in a fury, Dickens took the publishers to court. He won the case but the pirates pleaded bankruptcy, paid their own costs and left Dickens to face the mass of legal problems and a bill for £700 for his own expenses at a moment when he was in considerable financial difficulty and awaiting the profit from the extraordinarily successful Christmas book. In February, the accounts showed a profit to him of £230 only, at which Dickens panicked. He was bitter at Chapman and Hall and immediately told them that he would leave them, setting about making arrangements for future publication with their printers, Bradbury and Evans.

After the dinner at Greenwich to celebrate the completion of *Chuzzlewit* in July 1844, Dickens and his family were on their way to spend eleven months in Italy in an enormous old coach he had bought ('it is about the size of your library', he told Forster), and a specially engaged courier. Arriving wthout adventure at Albaro near Genoa, he found himself faced with a 'lonely, rusty, stagnant old staggerer of a domain', the Villa di Bella Vista which he had rented for three months through a friend, where 'the mosquitoes would tempt you to commit suicide'. He set about transforming the place with characteristic energy and, after some hesitation during which he reported that he was missing the inspiration that the streets of London always gave him, settled down to his next Christmas story, *The Chimes*. He made his way back to England just in order to read the finished story to his friends before Christmas. At his house in Lincoln's Inn Fields, Forster assembled ten close friends for the

Sketch of the reading of The Chimes to friends

reading which had an immediate and powerful impact. A second reading had to be arranged at which Macready sobbed undisguisedly as Dickens read. Twenty thousand copies sold immediately of this satirical attack on political economy, which provides evidence of both Dickens's concern with the society of his time and its doctrines and his admiration for the work of Thomas Carlyle whose close friend he had now been for several years.

On his return journey he stopped in Paris where Macready was presenting a Shakespeare season. Here Macready introduced him to Théophile Gautier, Alexandre Dumas and Victor Hugo, Régnier of the Théâtre Français and the painter Delacroix, among many others. In Genoa the family had moved house to the Villa Peschiere and from there they toured south to Rome, which Dickens thought, apart from the Colosseum, was not *his* Rome; to Naples where they struggled up Vesuvius and down again in the dark through ice and sulphurous smoke and cinders. *The Chimes* meanwhile had brought him in nearly £1,500. His combined earnings from Chapman and Hall amounted to almost £4,000 and so, by the time he was ready to return to London in June, he was no longer pressed for money and could afford to have the Devonshire Terrace house sumptuously redecorated in good time. The family travelled by way of the St Bernard Pass and through Switzerland.

On his return he drew up and sent to Forster a prospectus for a weekly magazine to be called *The Cricket*, which he was persuaded to abandon only with difficulty. The idea was nevertheless reshaped into his Christmas book for 1845, *The Cricket on the Hearth*. He also plunged into private theatricals with benefit performances of Ben Jonson's *Everyman in his Humour*, and began to make enquiries regarding the expense of running a newspaper, about which he had been thinking in Italy. By October he had an agreement, backers who would provide capital for a newspaper to be conducted on behalf of progress and reform, a staff of reporters which included his father and his father-in-law, and a set of offices next to his printers. From then, things moved swiftly until the first number of the *Daily News* appeared on the streets, badly printed and badly made up, on 21 January 1846. From the beginning the whole affair was disastrous: editor, proprietors and printers all clashed, and Dickens resigned as editor after only seventeen days, handing the newspaper over to a reluctant Forster who, in turn, handed it on in October. Although he continued to write for the *News*, contributing Italian letters which were later published as *Pictures from Italy* with illustrations by Samuel Palmer, by March he was having 'vague thoughts' of a new book '. . . and I go wandering about at night into the strangest places, according to my normal propensity at such a time — seeking rest, and finding none'. The *Daily News* had been a mistake and he now wanted to resume his old ways. In May he decided he would write his next novel abroad and, despite being busy with the subject of the so-called Ragged Schools, about which he had written in the *News*, he left with his family for Switzerland at the end of May. They settled themselves in a pretty villa overlooking the lake near Lausanne and, on 28 June, he was able to write to Forster with the words:

BEGAN DOMBEY!

The first instalment would appear in October, so Dickens had time in hand to make friends, both Swiss and among the English visitors, receive a stream of house guests and explore the area and the mountains in long walks. As to the writing, however, he found difficulty in getting on fast even when invention seemed the easiest thing in the world. He also hesitated over that year's Christmas book which he did, however, manage to finish in time and which was called *The Battle of Life: a Love Story*. For the first time Dickens, after a pause of nearly two years, was able to plan and write well in advance, if only with the now familiar 'agonies', headaches and bouts of restlessness.

In late November the family moved to Paris for three months, from where Dickens made flying trips to London. The novel was selling well and one old lady who belonged to a circle where the instalments were read aloud thought, as Forster reports, that three or four men must have put together *Dombey*. *The Battle of Life* meanwhile earned Dickens well over a thousand pounds. *The Times* judged it 'the very worst ... of ... the deluge of trash' that flooded the Christmas book market. Thackeray called it 'a wretched affair,' but of the death of little Paul Dombey he said, 'There's no writing against such power as this — one has no chance! Read that chapter describing young Paul's death: it is unsurpassed — it is stupendous!'

The next year, 1847 was the year of the English novel. For the first time Dickens's unquestioned supremacy as a writer was challenged by the appearance of Thackeray's *Vanity Fair*, by *Jane Eyre*, *Wuthering Heights* and by other novels which were published in that extraordinary year. Apart from some journalism and an inferior Christmas story, *The Haunted Man*, Dickens wrote nothing between completing *Dombey* and starting on *David Copperfield*. It was Forster who suggested that his next novel might be written in the first person. Dickens began it in February 1849, and publication followed in the May of that year. He had contemplated writing an autobiography, abandoned it to Forster as a fragment, but used elements of it in the novel. 'I really think I have done it ingeniously, and with a very complicated interweaving of truth and fiction.' Dickens always thought of this novel as his special child, but in falling under the spell of its charm, commentators have often seemed to ignore just how completely successful it is as a work of fiction. Sales hung

An illustration from Pictures from Italy, Samuel Palmer

fire at about twenty-five thousand copies per number and Dickens began to revive the idea of a weekly periodical as an additional source of income. The final result was *Household Words* 'the gentle mouthpiece of reform'; not reform of a 'mere utilitarian spirit, no iron binding of the mind to grim realities', rather it was to 'cherish that light of Fancy which is inherent in the human breast' with 'the sympathies and graces of imagination'. As sub-editor he took on W. H. Wills who had been his secretary at the *Daily News* and who proved to be extremely efficient and business-like. John Dickens handled a monthly supplement entitled *The Household Narrative of Current Events*. Dickens kept a sharp eye on his contributors, directing and persuading but also encouraging younger writers such as Elizabeth Gaskell. He failed to recruit George Eliot. Establishing himself as 'Conductor', he sustained a continuous attack on current social abuses, crusaded on behalf of education, sanitary reform, prison reform, decent houses for the poor and safety in factories. At the same time Dickens threw his energies and the resources of the magazine into the promotion of the cause of the arts. Edward Bulwer Lytton, with whom he was now on very friendly terms, wanted to use land on his estate at Knebworth where he had had constructed a grand Gothic mansion to build homes for deserving artists and writers, making the functions over to a Guild of Literature and Art. Dickens proposed to mount a tour with friends who had already taken part in his amateur theatricals in order to raise the necessary funds for the charity. Bulwer proposed to write a play for the scheme and Dickens secured the patronage of the Duke of Devonshire as well as the library of Devonshire House in Piccadilly for the opening production. The promotion of the Guild was well-timed to coincide with Prince Albert's Great Exhibition of 1851 which opened on 3 May. Two performances, the first in the presence of Queen Victoria, took place at Devonshire House later in the month and were enthusiastically received. Everywhere they played it went 'like wildfire', and in the course of the following year the group made over £3,000 for the Guild. The Great Exhibition, on the other hand, upset Dickens considerably, despite the prominent display in the Grand Hall of statues of Oliver Twist and Little Nell. After only one visit, his eyes refused to focus and the sheer amount and scale of exhibits bewildered him and made him feel 'used-up'.

The major works of the 1850s

In the middle of 1851 Dickens had to give up the Devonshire Terrace house. He bought Tavistock House, facing Tavistock Square in Bloomsbury, and turned to his next novel, *Bleak House*. If *David Copperfield* is a watershed in Dickens's career, then *Bleak House* is the first of the great series of late novels in the course of which he described an England corrupted by its obsolete institutions. In these novels, social misery is no longer laid at the door of evil individuals, but is felt to be part of the fabric of a rotten society. *Bleak House* uncovers the invisible threads that connect the most notorious decaying slums of the capital with the grand melancholy estates of the aristocracy. By this time Dickens had had a vast practical experience of attempts at social reform and private philanthropy, quite apart from what he had written as novelist and journalist. *Hard Times* followed within six months in *Household Words* in an attempt to rouse a flagging circulation, but again, Dickens had enormous difficulty in confining himself to the compression demanded by weekly instalments. The writing exhausted him and, for all the praise that has been expended on this short novel (John Ruskin thought it 'in several respects the greatest he had written'), it does seem to me, despite the intelligence of its conception, to bear the marks of a strained imagination. This is not merely a matter of the mechanical and formal constraints so much as the tight rein put on the author's invention by the attempt to stay close to what is an identifiable idea: the incompatibility of, on the one hand, human life and imagination, and the tyranny of abstract, statistical theories of education and human worth on the other.

Despite the pressures and constraints of writing in weekly instalments, he took the family to Boulogne for the summer where he finished the novel in sight of the military preparations for the Crimean Campaign. He dedicated the finished work to Carlyle. 'I know it contained nothing in which you do not think with me, for no man knows your books better than I.'

Portrait sketch of Thomas Carlyle, Daniel Maclise

With the novel completed, he found himself utterly used up, 'in a state of restlessness, impossible to be described — impossible to be imagined — wearing and tearing to be experienced'. The Crimean War, which began in March 1854, had put a complete stop to any further attempts to reform Parliament and government, and by the winter the news of the catastrophic incompetence of the conduct of the campaign had become a national scandal. Of the army of fifty-four thousand sent to Russia only fourteen thousand were still alive and, of those, only five thousand fit for service. The government of Lord Aberdeen fell as a result of these appalling reports. Cholera accounted for the majority of the deaths and the same disease had swept through England during the year. Dickens's daughter Mary caught it in Boulogne, but recovered without any danger to the others in the house. *Household Words* took up the cause of reform; inveighing against the administration of Lord Palmerston, 'Twirling Weathercock' as Dickens called him, and supporting the Administrative Reform Association which was set up on the initiative of Austen Layard, the explorer of Nineveh and a member of Parliament. At the same time, Dickens organised another round of private theatricals. This time it was to be *The Lighthouse*, a melodrama written by Wilkie Collins. Its success in private encouraged the group of friends to give public performances for charity benefits on several occasions.

It was his preoccupation with public affairs, however, that directed him towards his next novel which he started in May 1854. Originally entitled *Nobody's Fault*, it became, in the writing, *Little Dorrit*, a sustained attack on the issue of the condition of England, the topic to which Carlyle addressed himself continuously during this period in a series of tracts and pamphlets. Monthly publication began in December, 1855. By then Dickens and his family were living in Paris in an apartment on the Champs Elysées where he was continuously entertained during the following eleven months by the leaders of intellectual and artistic life. What struck Dickens most forcibly about the Parisian scene were the high style of living and the importance to public life of the most famous artists, writers and publishers. There was, he felt, no such regard or respect paid to their counterparts in England. Furthermore, intellectual Paris took him seriously as an artist. Henri Taine wrote an article in the *Revue des Deux Mondes* placing him among the immortals of art. From Paris, and later from Boulogne where the family again spent a late summer, he made at least one business trip to London each month. He often had engagements to fulfil, public charity readings or speeches to give. It was while he was abroad that he bought Gad's Hill Place, a country house near Rochester, which was to be his final home in England. His father had shown him the house on a walk when he was still a small boy and had even said that he might live

there if he grew up to become rich and famous. The other association with Gad's Hill is one which gave Dickens intense satisfaction.
It was the scene of the memorable robbery enacted by Sir John
Falstaff in Shakespeare's *Henry IV* Part 1. Dickens had Falstaff's
words copied and framed for his visitors to read:

> But, my lads, to-morrow morning, by four o'clock,
> early at Gadshill! There are pilgrims going to
> Canterbury with rich offerings and traders riding to
> London with fat purses: I have vizards for you all
> you have horses for yourselves.

Dickens also noted that the growing railway system would connect
him with the coastal towns of Kent and with London and so add
to the convenience and value of his purchase.

He was, however, still in the middle of writing *Little Dorrit* and,
once again, absorbed in producing another play of Wilkie Collins's,
The Frozen Deep, which he had re-written to a considerable extent.
He also played the main part of the hero who sacrifices himself to
save the life of his rival in love. Dickens's playing of the role had an
extraordinary effect on audience and actors alike. A private performance was arranged for the Queen, Prince Albert and the King of the
Belgians: also present was Dickens's long-staying house guest of that
summer, Hans Christian Andersen, the Danish writer of fairy tales.

It was the sudden death of his friend, Douglas Jerrold, the playwright and humorist, that decided Dickens to give more readings
of *The Christmas Carol* and performances of *The Frozen Deep* in public
in order to raise money for Jerrold's family. Public performances
meant professional actresses rather than his daughters and the wives
of the company, and for the female roles he engaged two sisters and
their mother, Mrs Ternan, a well-known actress. After performances
in Manchester, the Jerrold fund had passed £2,000. Following these
exertions, and after a dash north with Collins for a short walking
tour, Dickens was still restless and in great distress and wrote so to
Forster. In the letter he confessed that he could no longer avoid the
feeling that he and his wife were 'not made for each other'. Over
the years she had been able to contribute increasingly little to his
domestic life, though she had borne him eight children, and almost
nothing to his public career. She had probably had little opportunity
to do so whether or not she had the inclination. Even her part as
mother had been taken over by Georgina who had devoted her own
life to the children and their father. What was also clear to Catherine
by this time, although nothing was revealed publicly until 1934, was
that Dickens had become infatuated with the younger Ternan sister,
Ellen, during the final rehearsals in the Dickens's house for the
public performances of *The Frozen Deep*. It was not the first time that
she had grieved over her husband's relations with other women. In

Portrait of Wilkie Collins, Charles Collins

Genoa in 1848 he had given mesmeric treatment to the wife of a
local bank official, often in the middle of the night, ostensibly for
depressive headaches and hallucinations. Over many years, as far
as one can tell from the surviving correspondence, Dickens carried
on apparently light-hearted affairs with a number of women. Even
though his daughter Kate later wrote that her father never understood women, what is clear is that he was often attracted to them
and, being the man he was, as often attracted them. Furthermore,
Dickens had in recent years followed the lead of the younger sybar-

itic Collins into a pursuit of pleasures more hedonistic than he had allowed himself hitherto. It was the intervention of Catherine's family, the Hogarths, that brought matters finally to a head and led to the break-up of the family. In June 1858 Dickens, in an astonishing and unattractive display, begged his readers' confidence in an article in *Household Words* headed 'Personal'. He wanted to put it also in *The Times* and *Punch*, an invitation which both journals refused. As the printers of Punch were also his publishers, he began to plan to free himself of them. At the same time he cut himself off from any friend who, for whatever reason, remained loyal to Catherine. She was swiftly settled in a separate house with Charlie, while Georgina now took full charge of the household and the children. Charles and Catherine Dickens had been married twenty-two years; he was forty-six, she three years younger.

Before all was, as he wrote to Forster, 'despairingly over' in June 1858, he had already begun the series of public readings from his works which now became an important feature of his life and travels and his main source of income. He felt that he needed something to do to take him out of his unhappiness and he also needed to earn more money in order to pay for Gad's Hill Place and the improvements he was continually proposing for the house. After an initial series in London, he took his readings on a tour of the principal cities of England and Scotland with such success that he was earning at the rate of £500 per week. Beginning with the *Carol* and *The Chimes*, he created sixteen readings in all from among short stories and scenes from the novels.

Back in London he completed his arrangements to break free of his publishers and return to Chapman and Hall. Refusing any compromise, Dickens forced Bradbury and Evans to sell to him at auction their portion of the stock of *Household Words* and advertised the last number of that magazine for 28 May, and the first of his new weekly magazine, *All the Year Round*, for April 1859. From the beginning the new venture carried *A Tale of Two Cities*, one of his most popular stories even though, as a novel, it is in many ways much inferior to his best writing. In the midst of everything else that occupied him or otherwise obstructed him in his private life, he had managed to get down to the writing in March after an appeal for background reading to Carlyle, author of what was at that time the best-known history of the French Revolution. Carlyle sent his friend two cartloads of books from the London Library. In addition to the weekly magazine instalments, the novel was published simultaneously in monthly parts in the green covers. It was the last novel on which Phiz worked as illustrator. In June Dickens moved himself finally to Gad's Hill to finish writing the novel. The weather was hot and the 'small portions drive me frantic; but I think the tale must have taken a strong hold'. It did, and the new venture was even more profitable to him than *Household Words* had been. Forster turned 'white with admiring approval' and Carlyle found the story 'wonderful'.

After a summer at Gad's Hill and an autumn reading tour, he tried and failed to persuade George Eliot to write a serial for him. Collins's *The Woman in White* was a sensation, but the following serial failed to attract readers and so, in the next year he began, at a moment's notice it would seem, *Great Expectations* for the magazine (see p. 128). He sold off Tavistock House and, at Gad's Hill, burned all his past correspondence, expressing the wish that all the letters he had ever written were also on the bonfire. He gave away his eldest daughter Kate in marriage to Collins's brother, a Pre-Raphaelite painter and writer whose work Dickens admired sufficiently to print occasional pieces by him. Allston Collins was seldom in good health and was twelve years older than his bride and Dickens had advised her against marrying him. He was absent from his oldest son's wedding in November, but was delighted a year later by the 'unmitigated nonsense' of becoming a grandfather.

The final years

Between 1861 and 1863 he made more tours with readings, published seventeen occasional papers from *All the Year Round* as *The Uncommercial Traveller* and faced the problems that his sons' growing up had caused him. Only one of them distinguished himself in a way that pleased his father; two of them died abroad still very young, and Charlie, after several attempts at different positions, joined him in the office of the magazine. Dickens's earning capacity was now extraordinary. He received £1,000 for a short story, the same for the advance sheets of a novel and, when he next proposed to Chapman and Hall a novel, *Our Mutual Friend*, they agreed to give him £6,000 in return for a half-share in the profits.

In these years he also travelled, occasionally to Paris where he gave readings for charity at the British Embassy, and sometimes with Ellen Ternan who also stayed from time to time at Gad's Hill. They were travelling together when they were involved in the Staplehurst Railway disaster on 9 June 1865. Although not injured himself and extremely helpful to those who were, the incident left him occasionally shaking and dizzy. He seemed never totally to recover complete health after the accident, and from that time began to suffer spasms and dizzy spells, quite apart from a painful left foot which was beginning to affect his habit of taking exhausting long walks. Nevertheless he at last accepted the offer of an American reading tour and, in November, sailed for America with a strenuous programme of eighty readings in prospect, from which, as his manager reported on his return from a preliminary survey, he might

Gad's Hill Place, with Dickens's Swiss writing chalet inset. The chalet is now in the Rochester museum, Kent

make as much as £15,000 profit. He very much wanted Ellen Ternan to join him in America but, once arrived, decided that it would not be possible.

His reception was everywhere decorous in contrast with his first visit, but the performances were received with wild enthusiasm. 'It is idle to talk about it: you must beg, borrow or steal a ticket and hear him. Another such star-shower is not to be expected in one's life-time.' Five hundred undergraduates excluded from the Cambridge, Massachusetts reading, begged Longfellow to intercede on their behalf. Shuttling between Boston and New York, Dickens caught a heavy cold which refused to yield to any kind of treatment and which prevented him from eating. Still, faced with immense crowds, he persisted with the readings and with an exhausting round of entertainment and dinners. His final New York readings left him prostrated each night unable to eat or sleep, and he was very ill on the occasion of his farewell dinner. He left by boat limping, his left foot swathed in black silk. He had made about £20,000.

Before even leaving for America he had negotiated a further reading tour of England with £8,000 for a hundred occasions. For these he added to his established readings a version of the death of Nancy from *Oliver Twist*. Charlie overheard him practising the piece, and told him it was the finest thing he had ever heard, but that he should not do it. When he performed it in public, members of the audience fainted. 'There was a fixed expression of horror of me, all over the theatre, which could not have been surpassed if I had been going to be hanged.' For all the excitement and enjoyment of so moving an audience, Dickens was now feeling seriously the effects of the continual strain and effort. His left side felt dead and he could not raise his hands to his head. The tour was interrupted for a consultation with a London specialist who diagnosed that he 'had been on the brink of an attack of paralysis of his left side, and possibly of apoplexy'. The rest of the reading tour was severely curtailed and postponed for some months, and by October 1869, he was at home at Gad's Hill, entertaining guests and beginning a new novel, *The Mystery of Edwin Drood*. The last readings were resumed twice a week in London in January 1870 only at great physical cost. They exhausted him and raised his pulse rate alarmingly. His doctor and Charlie were present on every occasion, but he survived even the final farewell performance. In March 1870 he was presented to the Queen, after being offered a baronetcy. In April, much to Dickens's sorrow, Daniel Maclise died. The first instalment of *Edwin Drood* appeared in that month and '*very, very far outstripped every one of its fellows*'. In May he breakfasted with Mr Gladstone, now Prime Minister, and dined with many of his eminent comtemporaries, such as Disraeli, Lord John Russell and Arthur Stanley. Dean of Westminster. He organised friends' theatricals at the end of the month before returning to Gad's Hill and *Edwin Drood*. He now wrote in a chalet in the garden, a gift from the French actor, Charles Fechter, who had long been a close friend and admirer. Fechter had acted in Paris and London in dramatisations of Dickens's stories. On 8 June he worked all day at the novel and dined at six in the evening with Georgina who thought he was looking very ill. During dinner he suffered a stroke from which he never recovered, and died twenty-four hours later on Thursday, 9 June 1870. He was fifty-eight years old. 'It is no exaggeration to say,' wrote Longfellow from America to Forster, 'that this whole country is stricken with grief.' The sense of loss was universally shared. By his own wish his funeral was private and conducted without any ceremony; but by the wish of the public as expressed in a *Times* article, he was buried in West-minster Abbey in Poets' Corner in the south-west transept. The plain coffin lay uncovered for two days as an endless stream of mourn-ers filed past it.

Publication of the unfinished mystery novel continued into September of that year. The fact that it was unfinished and that later attempts to deduce the outcome of its central puzzle have been largely unsatisfactory confirm one's feeling that what was being mourned in the death of Charles Dickens was the sense of loss and the certain knowledge that more would have flowed from his powerful, imaginative invention. He himself, on the other hand, had expressed the view that he was incapable of rest and that it was 'Much better to die, doing.'

2. Dickens and the theatre

That Dickens's passion for the theatre, awakened in his earliest years, was not a relaxation or distraction from his writing is clearly shown in any account of his life or by reading any of his novels. For John Ruskin it was a limitation of his art and insight as a writer that 'he wrote in a circle of stage fire'. But the theatre and the drama, especially the plays of Shakespeare, are inseparable from the sources of his art and are profoundly connected with his imagination. Among all the anecdotes that are told of Dickens, two in particular reveal something of the spell that the idea of acting cast on him. Taking the lead in *The Frozen Deep* at Tavistock House in January 1857, he moved audience and actors alike to tears and, in one of his last act exits, would toss other actors aside so violently as to leave them bruised. Professional actors who saw his performances wondered why he ever did anything else. The second incident is recorded by his daughter Mary in her reminiscences of her father. As a girl she had been ill for a long time and had lain convalescing in her father's study as he worked, a privilege he rarely allowed:

> Although I was fearful of disturbing him, he assured me that he desired to have me with him. On one of these mornings I was lying on the sofa endeavouring to keep perfectly quiet, while my father wrote busily and rapidly at his desk; when he suddenly jumped from his chair and rushed to a mirror which hung near, and in which I could see the reflection of some extraordinary facial contortions which he was making. He returned rapidly to his desk, wrote furiously for a few minutes, and then went to the mirror. The facial pantomime was resumed, and then turning inwards, but evidently not seeing me, he began talking rapidly in a low voice. Ceasing this soon, however, he returned once more to his desk, where he remained silently writing until luncheon-time.

The idea of energetic impersonation, which this description suggests, seems inadequate to explain Dickens's relationship with his fictional characters. That he was an actor is undeniable, and there is a great deal of evidence to show that he was a very moving actor in his frequent theatrical performances and his late series of readings. There plays also about his voluminous correspondence more than a hint that he not only adjusted his tone each time to suit each correspondent, but also that his letters presented a variety of personae. This is a better word than 'mask' as, from the letters, one receives the strongest impression that he lived in his richly varied

Dickens (in the front of box) and Thackeray (second row) at the theatre, Thomas Sibson. See also p 171, entry for Macready

personae and that these are what the man was. It is not as though there were some further personality behind, deliberately hidden and out of reach. My impression is that, in the letters as elsewhere, what we are faced with is not so much a man who dramatised himself on every occasion as someone who lived in and through his dramatis-ation. Biographers have often responded to the complexities of the evidence by choosing among the possibilities: the generous, kindly, humorous and indefatigable companion or the driven, frenetic product of childhood misery. If Forster tends to the former view, and his closeness to his subject must make it persuasive, Edgar Johnson contradicts it strenuously. There is no middle ground between these views, the complexities and discontinuities are what we experience when we contemplate the man Dickens. He himself is finally elusive, but what matters is that, although the dramatisations and the art are intimately a part of each other, the former do not determine the latter. The novels are not a product *determined*, shaped by the man's or the child's experiences and sufferings in his life. That the form of his novels is largely dramatic is evidence enough of his freedom to create and to invent; to invent Mr Pickwick or to be Sarah Gamp. Mrs Gamp even stepped out of *Chuzzlewit* to accompany him and his company of actors to 'Manjestir' and Liverpool in a long letter to Forster describing the company's exploits on the tour of 1858. His letters contain small evidence of his reading but are full of long accounts of visits to the theatre, especially abroad in Europe. He seems to have spent most of his evenings at one performance or another, whether of opera or of drama, bringing to each occasion a sharply critical and professional attention.

As a youth in London he had frequented all kinds of theatres: there is a splendidly observed piece on 'Private Theatres' among the *Sketches* as well as another describing 'Astley's Circus'. He admired in particular Charles Matthews who performed a one-man show, filling the stage with his impersonations. At the time of his courtship of Maria Beadnell he thought of applying to Matthews for an audition. Even as a child in Chatham he had seen Matthews, the great clown Grimaldi, some Shakespeare and modern plays and entertainments. He took lessons in acting from Robert Keeley, a well-known actor of the day who later, with his wife, took leading roles in some of the dramatisations of Dickens's novels. Dickens also approached the manager of Covent Garden theatre for an audition, and was only prevented from attending by a swollen face.

He tried writing for the theatre when he was looking around for ways of earning money. He had already written burlesques and performed them in his parents' home with his sister Fanny and friends. One of these was a composer, John Hullah, for whom he wrote the libretto of an operetta, *The Village Coquette*. He also turned one of his sketches, 'The Great Winglebury Duel', into a farce, *The Strange Gentlemen*, for the St James Theatre where it ran with some success just as *Pickwick* was beginning to make a stir. The very success of his first novel put an end to his professional dramatic attempts, but he continued to mount private shows, and his Christmas family entertainments for which he often wrote or adapted whole plays, became a legend. After giving up attempts to defeat pirated dramatisations of his early works, he often collaborated on them, writing and advising. But, as he got older, it was in acting that he progessively found more release from the pressures of writing, and he seized any occasion to dragoon his friends into charity and benefit performances. What is striking is that, in these ventures, he always took the lead as manager, producer and actor. There is no evidence that he ever joined in someone else's scheme except, as in other cases, to subvert it, change it beyond recognition and make it his own. The series of 'splendid barnstormings' of 1857 led finally to the break-up of his marriage when he met Ellen Ternan. His role as actor-manager was, however, not the origin of his later tours with dramatic readings from his works. The idea for these occurred to him first at Lausanne in 1846, when he read chapters of *Dombey and Son* to his friends. The first time he read in public was in December 1853 in Birmingham where he appeared in order to raise funds for the newly established Birmingham and Midland Institute. He gave three readings of *A Christmas Carol* and *The Cricket on the Hearth* with such success that he was deluged with invitations to read elsewhere. He gave readings in 1857 to audiences of two thousand and more in order to help the Jerrold benefit, for which performances of *The Frozen Deep* were being given at the same time. It was when all these excitements were over, and when he had completed *Little Dorrit*, that his mind turned again to the idea of the profitability of public readings from his own works. Forster still opposed the idea on the grounds that it would only lower the dignity of a serious author. Dickens disagreed. Thackeray was giving lecture tours in America in an attempt to earn enough to provide for his daughters, and yet, from the descriptions that Dickens gave in his letters of his subsequent, exhausting tours up and down England and Scotland by train, and across to Ireland, it is hard to believe that he undertook such a strenuous ordeal only for money, important as money always was to him. His letters to Forster insist repeatedly on the success of each occasion, the numbers present and excluded and, above all, on the *hypnotic rapport* he was able to create between himself and the thousands in front of whom he read. What he describes is a more immediate and sensational awareness of the closeness of author and audience that Dickens sought during his entire writing career. As novelist he fostered it by means of serial publication and, as editor of periodical magazines, appealed to his readers in his own voice.

Each reading was carefully prepared, rehearsed and adapted for performance with stage directions. He read from a specially constructed lectern which he took with him everywhere. For his second tour of England he learned each piece by heart, acting it out many times and perfecting it in order to have complete control over the performance and the audience. From the evidence of the copies of his works that he prepared for his readings, it is clear that many parts of his novels and complete stories are intensely dramatically conceived. They continue to attract precisely that kind of attention, but the adaptations of recent years, whether for the stage, for the cinema or for television, I take to have been no more successful than the contemporary stage versions that so often infuriated Dickens during his life-time. Dramatic conception is not at all the same thing as dramatic representation. Yet it is evident that, as a writer, Dickens consciously borrowed from the stage and from the conventions of the popular theatre of his time. The theatre is a particular kind of reference point in his novels; the chapters in *Nicholas Nickleby* in which the hero throws in his lot with the Crummles's troupe of strolling actors, or the presence in Coketown of Sleary's Circus in *Hard Times* are perhaps only the two most obvious examples in what could be a long list. Dickens also borrows from the traditional popular theatre for both character and situation. Much of the comic atmosphere of *Pickwick* grows from such borrowings. The technique of comic disclosure leading to the discomfiture of the hidden or deceived character, as so often of Pickwick himself, derives from a long theatrical practice. Some characters in the early novels seem also to have been conceived in terms of almost purely theatrical language and gesture. Ralph Nickleby is primarily a stage villain, and his speeches are couched within the style and vocabulary of the stage villain of popular melodrama. Nicholas, when he also has to show high passion, is the young hero drawn from the same rhetorical conventions:

> 'One word!' cried Ralph, foaming at the mouth.
> 'Not one,' cried Nicholas, 'I will not hear of one — save this. Look to yourself, and heed this warning that I give you! Day is past in your case, and night is coming on.'
> 'My curse, my bitter, deadly curse, upon you, boy!'
> 'Whence will curses come at your command? Or what avails a curse or blessing from a man like you? I tell you, that misfortune and discovery are thickening about your head; that the structures you have raised, through all your ill-spent life, are crumbling into dust; that your path is beset with spies; that this very day, ten thousand pounds of your hoarded wealth have gone in one great crash!'
> 'Tis false!' cried Ralph, shrinking back.
> 'Tis true, and you shall find it so. I have no more words to waste. Stand from the door . . .'
>
> (*chapter 54*)

For all its energy, this kind of theatricality is far from representing the limit of Dickens's involvement with theatre in this novel. Many of the characters in it are actors, creating roles for themselves. Mrs Wititterly and the Kenwigs are actors of this kind. In chapter fourteen the Kenwigs give a supper to honour Uncle Lillyvick, the water-rate collector. Afterwards:

> The party composed themselves for conviviality; Mr Lillyvick being stationed in a large arm-chair by the fire-side, and the four little Kenwigses disposed on a small form in front of the company

with their flaxen tails towards them, and their faces to the fire; an arrangement which was no sooner perfected, than Mrs Kenwigs was overpowered by the feelings of a mother, and fell upon the left shoulder of Mr Kenwigs dissolved in tears.

The scene has been deliberately arranged or produced, and the well-coached actors know their parts 'to perfection'. Any hint of human warmth and spontaneity has been forcibly excluded in the paradoxical phrase 'composed themselves for conviviality'. Unlike the Crummleses, however, the Kenwigs cannot relax out of their chosen roles into themselves. Their selves are the roles they have adopted and practised in the struggle towards gentility. Here the effect is comic and the metaphor of role-playing works to great effect.

Serious moments of heightened emotion in the earlier novels do, however, tend to drive Dickens back on to the conventions of melodrama. In *Dombey and Son* chapters fifty-three and fifty-four bring us to one of the major climaxes of the novel, as Edith Dombey flees from her husband to join, as he thinks, James Carker, Dombey's assistant manager, secretly at Dijon. Both chapters are disclosures of information essential to the reader and to the plot. Chapter fifty-four is very consciously staged; the rhetoric of the exchanges between Edith and Carker is composed of questions, repetitions and disclosures. She undeceives him as to both her purposes and his role in long, heightened sentences that never quite fall into blank verse. The undeception and the defeat of Carker's expectations of the encounter are characteristically theatrical in conception. The gestures of the protagonists, flaring nostrils and quivering lips from her, muttered oaths and foam at the lips from him, are at once explicit and redundant in the manner of the convention. At one moment Carker entreats Edith to act out her play quickly, and later she in turn casts up at him the part he has played. The room is described like a stage set and the chapter ends, as though the curtain were about to drop, with the thunderous beating at the door of their pursuer Dombey, and the darkness in which, Edith having fled before, Carker makes good his escape by the light of a single lamp.

The conventions of melodrama here as on other occasions allow Dickens no room to deal with interesting women characters whose qualities and intelligence unfit them for the society they are obliged to live in. The treatment of this kind of woman, of for example, Rosa Dartle in *David Copperfield*, displays a complex set of limitations that bears down heavily on Dickens's art: his notions of what a woman should be, the conventions of their representation in the theatre of his youth and early manhood and importantly, the moral constraints of mid-Victorian society which, unlike those of the earliest years of the century, left little room for such women to find ways of occupying and expressing themselves adequately. Such limitations make up a major theme of George Eliot's *Middlemarch* (1871–72). Although some of his male villains share a similar staginess of speech and gesture, a whole range of Dickens's male characters are drawn from other and older theatrical conventions. Grimwig in *Oliver Twist* and, despite his importance to the theme of delinquent and culpable fathers, Mr Wickfield in *David Copperfield*, are drawn from the stock figure of the crotchety, elderly gentleman associated with the comedy of the humours which descends from the theatre of the Elizabethan playwright Ben Jonson. Such characters display a single trait of speech or gesture which establishes and identifies them. Wickfield's first words are about motive. 'You know my motive. I have but one.' We learn later that he is in the habit of seeking out other men's motives which he takes always to be single and hidden. His suspiciousness, however, is only sketchily outlined and the irony of his blindness to Uriah Heep's powerfully displayed motive is scarcely pursued in the unfolding of the plot. It is a measure of the maturing of Dickens's art that, after *David Copperfield*, he falls back less and less readily on such devices while sacrificing nothing of the intensely dramatic energy of his portrayal of character in action. The discussion in Part Two of *Great Expectations* will, I hope, make plain the essentially dramatic character of his achieved technique as a novelist.

Theatre in the 1830s

Laying aside the question of the worth of his early plays and adaptations, the dramatic qualities everywhere apparent in his fiction suggest the possibility that Dickens might have continued to write for the stage. As a young man he was ambitious, however, and the theatre could provide only an uncertain income to a writer in the early years of the nineteenth century.

From the reopening of the theatres following the restoration of the monarchy in 1660, only two theatres at a time were licensed by Royal Patent to perform plays. As a result, both the Drury Lane Theatre and Covent Garden had been rebuilt on a huge scale which, of itself, would defeat subtlety of writing or acting. The many other playhouses were considered 'illegitimate', despite the popularity of the theatre among generations of Londoners. Taste was dominated by spectacle and pantomime and the greatest actor of an earlier generation, Edmund Kean, reviled the audiences' demands for spectacle, and lamented the fate in such a situation of the classical and Shakespearean drama. Although a number of the Romantic poets had written plays, it was with the Elizabethan poetic drama in mind rather than contemporary stage conditions, and the live theatre had

Portrait sketch of Edward Bulwer Lytton, Daniel Maclise

declined sadly since the days of Goldsmith and Sheridan. Edward Bulwer Lytton, the author of several successful plays, complained in 1824:

> What sensible independent writer will attend to an ignorant manager — 'Sir, you must write to please the reigning taste' — consent to get up processions for bipeds, and curvettings for quadrupeds — and become the pandar to such a taste?

and his Theatre Bill which he brought before Parliament in 1832, having passed through the House of Commons, was defeated in the Lords.

Furthermore, the playwright was usually paid only a lump sum for a work by the theatre manager, no matter how long it might run. This double inhibition on the writer was only removed in 1834 by an Act of Parliament to regulate theatres which finally broke the archaic and damaging monopoly system. By that date, Dickens was already the internationally celebrated novelist to whom Sir Walter Scott, a generation earlier, had shown what could be done in the way of earning as a writer of prose fiction.

3 Dickens and public life

Dickens's career as novelist and journalist spans the years of the great movement of political and social reforms which laid the basic groundwork of modern, urban, commercial and industrial Britain. The Reform Act of 1832 was passed a year before *Sketches by Boz* appeared and that of 1867 less than two years after the publication of his last completed novel. He began as a reporter of Parliamentary debates in the unreformed House of Commons in time to hear the closing speeches in the 1832 debate before the Bill was passed at its third reading and sent to the House of Lords. It was May before the Bill became law after a great deal of political manoeuvring. Despite the jubilation in the country that accompanied the event, and despite Dickens's early identification with the spirit of reform, his four years of parliamentary reporting taught him to despise the whole apparatus of parliamentary procedure. It would be a mistake to dismiss his opinion as merely the arrogant scepticism of an ignorant upstart. William Hazlitt had also been a parliamentary reporter and summed up his experience in a later essay:

> You serve an apprenticeship to a want of originality, to a suspen-
> sion of thought and feeling. You are in a go-cart of prejudices, in
> a regularly constructed machine of pretexts and precedents . . .
> there is a House of Commons jargon that must be used by
> everyone . . . you are hemmed in, stifled, pinioned, pressed to
> death. . . . Talk of mobs! Is there any body of people that has this
> character in a more consummate degree than the House of
> Commons?

An age of reform

Dickens's four years in the two Houses were an education in themselves; they brought him into acquaintance with and close knowledge of the whole class of legislators, many of whom were still, after
1832, drawn from the aristocratic land-owning interest, The 1832
Reform Act certainly diminished but did not destroy their power.
Its main achievement was to redistribute one hundred and forty
parliamentary seats, removing the so-called rotten boroughs from
the pockets of the country magnates and giving them instead to the
rising power groups of industrial and commercial interests that were
growing up in the rapidly developing provincial centres and towns.
The accompanying extension of the franchise increased the number
of parliamentary electors by less than half, and many of the powerful

figures in the Parliaments elected between 1832 and the second Reform Act of Disraeli's government of 1867 were the same individuals. Elections were more frequently than not of the Eatanswill kind described in *Pickwick*. Covering elections was part of the young Dickens's general reporting duties. Perhaps the most important effect of the 1832 Reform Act was that of releasing the brake on the processes of change and improvement. The following year saw the enactment of bills, largely inspired by the efforts of the reforming philanthropist Anthony Ashley Cooper, later seventh Earl of Shaftesbury, to regulate working conditions in factories. An important feature of the Factory Act was the establishment of an Inspectorate to enforce its observation. In 1834 the Poor Laws were amended in such a way as to rouse Dickens's wrath in *Oliver Twist*. Even in the postscript to *Our Mutual Friend* he is prompted to return to the subject:

> But that my view of the Poor Law may not be mistaken or misrepresented, I will state it. I believe that there has been in England, since the days of the STUARTS, no law so often infamously administered, no law so often openly violated, no law habitually so ill-supervised. In the majority of the shameful cases of disease and death from destitution, that shock the public and disgrace the country, the illegality is quite equal to the inhumanity — and known language could say no more of their lawlessness.

The central inhumanity of the 1834 Poor Law amendments lay in their attempt to make conditions within the workhouses less tolerable — 'less eligible' in the official terminology — than the outside world of work in a time of general economic depression. The workhouses were intended to be as like prisons as possible, with the separation of the sexes and families into male and female wards, strict discipline and a diet worse, according to Dickens, than in prison. Outdoor relief was terminated as this was dependent on the poor rate, any considerable increase in which in turn created more paupers. The old system had operated locally through the Justices of the Peace, but the new Act established a central government Commission to direct the workings of the locally elected boards of guardians. Relief under the old laws had long been essentially a local matter which, naturally, in times of hardship and distress worked to the advantage of those who exercised local authority; the landowning employers and their agents. But their power could not survive in the rapidly changing social situation.

Utilitarianism and radicalism

The spirit that lay behind the new Poor Laws and many other reforms of the period less unpopular in character was that of Utilitarianism. The Secretary to the Poor Law Commissioners was Edwin

Chadwick, a disciple of the philosopher Jeremy Bentham (1748–1832). Bentham, primarily a philosopher of law, was the founder of a school of thinkers known as the Philosophical Radicals, whose influence on the shapes that emerged from the political and social movements of this whole early Victorian period was all-important. If many of his proposed reforms at law were gradually adopted, his more general ideas aroused the opposition not only of Dickens. William Hazlitt wrote of Bentham in *The Spirit of the Age* (1825) as 'reducing law to a system, and the mind of man to a machine'. The cast of Bentham's philosophical thought is determinist and owes much to the associationist psychology of David Hartley and the economic theories of David Ricardo. Ricardo held that the 'natural price of labour' was only as much as to enable the labourer to survive and perpetuate his race 'without either increase or diminution'. Behind Ricardo's thought lay Malthus's *Essay on the Principle of Population* (1798) with its gloomy prediction of an accelerating population growth outstripping food supply. It was central to Bentham's political and ethical theories that man is motivated to increase his pleasure and diminish his pain, that these are calculable quantities and that any act is a moral act which contributes in this, rather than in the reverse direction. 'It is the greatest happiness of the greatest number that is the measure of right and wrong', he wrote in his *Introduction to Principles of Moral and Legislation* (first printed in 1780).

For Bentham, pleasure and happiness were synonymous and the ends which all men seek. The ultimate ambition of his philosophy is to manipulate pleasure and pain by means of a code of laws and, more generally, a social system in such ways that men would be determined towards virtue. The calculus of pleasures and pains leads logically to egalitarianism, and Bentham's thought evolved into Radicalism, partly as a result of the logic of his view, and partly under the influence of James Mill, together with whom, in 1824, he founded the *Westminster Review* as the organ of philosophical radicalism. He became an opponent of monarchy and the hereditary aristocracy and an advocate of complete democracy, including votes for women. He rejected both imperialism and religion as irrational follies, but had only contempt for revolutionary and libertarian ideals. Liberty was of no importance to his system of law. Perhaps the most notable critic of Utilitarianism in its own time was Thomas Carlyle who thundered against both the doctrines and their effects in *Past and Present* (1843).

The offence of Utilitarianism and its related social and economic doctrines, for Dickens as for Carlyle, was that it reduced all relations between men to a matter of abstract calculation.

True, it must be owned, we for the present, with our Mammon-Gospel, have come to strange conclusions. We call it a Society: and go about professing openly the totalest separation, isolation.

Our life is not a mutual helpfulness; but rather, cloaked under the due laws-of-war, named fair competition and so forth, it is a mutual hostility. We have profoundly forgotten everywhere that *Cash-payment* is not the sole relation of human beings; we think, nothing doubting, that *it* absolves and liquidates all engagements of man.

(Carlyle: *Past and Present*)

Mr Gradgrind sat writing in the room with the deadly statistical clock, proving something no doubt — probably, in the main, that the Good Samaritan was a Bad Economist.

(*Hard Times*)

Philosophical radicalism, for all its influence on the course of modern British society, pointed in a direction quite contrary to those notions of reform that Dickens stood for in his novels, in his journalism and in his actions on the public stage. It is not only in *Hard Times* or *The Chimes* that he gives rein to his hostility. In these works he conducts a frontal attack on Utilitarian doctrines and practices to the detriment of his art, as I think, because he found such doctrines uncongenial to contemplate. In many of the major novels, from *Oliver Twist* to *Our Mutual Friend*, we learn to recognise characters who exemplify versions, diluted and distorted in one way or another, of what he took to be, at bottom, a mechanistic and deterministic instrument of oppression.

Evangelical religion

Often such characters display at the same time what Dickens thought of as a related oppression with similar tendencies. He heartily detested the serious, evangelising aspects of early nineteenth-century religion. These come mainly from two sources: from the rapid spread in the later eighteenth and early nineteenth centuries of the dissenting sects such as the Wesley brothers' Methodist Society, and from the new spirit of seriousness in the Church of England. Both emphasised personal salvation through faith, atomising society in a way different from that of the Utilitarians but with the same effect of breaking the bonds between man and man. Some of Dickens's most energetic and effective satire is directed against such ecclesiastical figures as Chadband in *Bleak House* and the Reverend Mr Stiggins in *Pickwick* who is finally exposed by Tony Weller. Dickens cast his satirical net widely in this sea of conflicting currents, landing in it figures as different as Miss Murdstone in *David Copperfield* and Mrs Pardiggle, a prominent example of the do-gooders in *Bleak House*. As in the case of Mr Gradgrind in *Hard Times* or of Mr Filer in *The Chimes*, what Dickens objects to in his creation of such characters for satirical end, is the impoverishment of human life by those who apply its harsh and unremitting doctrines, the effect of which is an oppressive constraint on human spontaneity and love. In his postscript to *Our Mutual Friend* he wrote that he preferred to put his trust rather in 'the common sense and senses of the common people' than in doctrines and political systems. The Preliminary Word to *Household Words* asserts that the publication will 'teach the hardest workers at this whirling wheel of toil, that their lot is not necessarily a moody, brutal fact, excluded from the sympathies and graces of imagination' and, further, that it will 'bring the greater and the lesser in degree, together, . . . and mutually dispose them to a better acquaintance and a kinder understanding'.

It is not the case, however, that Dickens thought through an alternative philosophy to Utilitarianism or to the particular shifts of politics in its confrontations with radical movements like the Chartism of the 1830s and 1840s. Although he was on his own admission influenced by what Carlyle was writing at the time on the question of the 'condition of England', even this influence is transformed when it is assimilated into what Dickens wrote. It seems often that what his position is varies from novel to novel where ideas as such are pressed into fictional shape according to the double demand of his creative imagination and the form of the particular novel as it works itself through. There is little evidence of a coherent system of belief carried over from novel to novel, just as there is little evidence of a coherence between his fictional imagination and his journalism. Nevertheless, surveying the years of his various periodical ventures, one sees that, after his miscellany period of *Bentley's* and *Master Humphrey's Clock*, he does respond as a journalist to some of the major issues of public debate of his time. His sympathies are continuously with the ordinary people, and he grows increasingly sceptical of the ability and will of government, its agencies and its supporting philosophies to enhance the common lot. Despite arguments to the contrary, he would appear not to have been a radical if, by a political radical, one means not merely an opponent of the present regime but one who is also the proponent of an alternative system which could somehow be made to work to the advantage of the disadvantaged majority.

These issues seem to be at the heart of Dickens's most political novel, *Barnaby Rudge* (1841). The story relates simultaneously the breaking of the relationship between fathers and sons and, in the account of the Gordon Riots of the 1780s which forms the climax of the novel, the violent disjunction between political authority and the population that refuses to recognise an authority which had been denied its competence, its right to recognition. It is often felt by critics that Dickens's attitude to the events he describes in this novel is confused and ambiguous. Consciously, it is said, he firmly takes

the side of authority and, unconsciously, his artistic imagination is fired by the power of the mob that tears down the fabric of the old order; burns, that is, the Maypole Inn and the Warren, and storms the prison of Newgate. Dickens has, without doubt, the analogy with the Chartist demonstrations and disturbances in mind just as, in writing *Middlemarch* from 1865 about the period of change between 1829 and 1832, George Eliot was responding to the prospect of the reforms of 1867.

Yet, in 1840, Dickens, as a sensitive man and observer of public affairs, might well be confused to the point of bewilderment in the face of the kinds of antagonistic certainties that confronted each other across the society of his day. In such situations, to make up one's mind and be decisive might well be the response of a less intelligent and less open-minded individual than Dickens was. Mr Gradgrind's abstract moral certainties are sincerely held, and are convincing — to himself.

In a speech delivered early in 1870 at Birmingham Dickens restated his political faith unambiguously to the effect that he had 'little faith in the people who govern us — please to observe "people" there will be with a small "p", but that I have great confidence in the People whom they govern; please to observe "People" there with a large "P".' He went on to quote a passage from Henry Thomas Buckle's *History of Civilisation in England* (1851–61), which is worth noting:

> They . . . may talk as they will about the reforms that government has introduced, and the improvements to be expected from legislation. But whoever will take a wider and more commanding view of affairs, will soon discover that such hopes are chimerical. They will learn that law givers are nearly always the obstructers of society, instead of its helpers; and that in the extremely few cases in which their measures have turned out well, their success has been owing to the fact that, contrary to their usual custom, they have implicitly obeyed the spirit of their time, and have been, as they always should be, the mere servants of the people, to whose wishes they are bound to give a public and legal sanction.

This statement assumes, as Dickens the journalist often appeared also to assume, that the 'wishes of the people' are identical with and not determined often by particular, conflicting interests. The novelist did not make the same assumption.

Opposite: Portrait of Angela Burdett-Coutts

Dickens and philanthropy

It was in terms practical rather than philosophical or intellectual that Dickens promoted the cause of reform. For thirteen years he was intimately concerned in, and may be said largely to have directed, an extraordinary and bold philanthropic exercise on behalf of a wealthy young heiress. She was Angela Burdett, the daughter of an early radical politician, who in 1837 inherited the fortune of her grandfather, the banker Thomas Coutts. *Oliver Twist* had attracted her father's attention when he read it in that year and it was soon afterwards that the young heiress and the young, successful author met at a dinner given by one of the partners in the bank. Miss Burdett-Coutts (she added her grandfather's name to her surname on her inheritance) became his intimate friend with whom he continued to exchange letters even after they drew apart on the failure of his marriage. After her parents' death, she attached herself to a number of men in turn, each of them remarkable in his own very different way. She even proposed marriage to the ageing Duke of Wellington, but it was to Dickens she turned for advice on the philanthropic uses of her fortune. In 1843 he pursued on her behalf the growing number of Ragged Schools and their problems. These schools had grown up on a totally voluntary basis among the children of the most poor in an attempt to give them a rudimentary secular education. Miss Burdett-Coutts gave the schools her support throughout her life, both directly and by aiding the work of Lord Shaftesbury, with whom Dickens also became friendly.

In 1846 together they planned the establishment of a Home for the rehabilitation of prostitutes and young female offenders, Urania Cottage, in Shepherd's Bush, opened in the following year. It was typical of Dickens's handling of such matters that he provided a piano for the inmates and persuaded his friend John Hullah to give them regular singing lessons.

Angela Burdett-Coutts lived at Holly Lodge, Highgate; her only companion, apart from her parrot and animals, a close friend who had originally been her governess. Details from this Highgate world inform the Highgate sections of *David Copperfield* and there is in the character of Agnes and her relationship with David a good deal that Dickens drew originally from the world of Miss Burdett-Coutts. The ambiguity of the status of the governess Hannah Browne, as she became, may have contributed to the character of Rosa Dartle.

Angela Burdett-Coutts shared the new, serious Evangelical faith and contributed largely to the establishment of the Church of England in the rapidly growing colonies. She interested herself continuously in schemes for emigration to the new countries, an interest which is also reflected in *David Copperfield*. But, again persuaded by Dickens, she directed her energies to the housing of the poor and, in the decade from 1860, became an unofficial health and housing local government to Bethnal Green. Columbia Square, a block of model dwellings in this district, was opened in 1862 and hailed in *Household Words*. It was Dickens who persuaded her that the buildings should be flats and not houses; a practical and important issue that came from his experiences as a lodger during his early life. He wrote in the article of 'passing strange boots on the way to bed . . . the smell of strangers . . . and the hats of men who despise them hanging in their hall'. Lodging letting, he judged, was 'the black art' of the nineteenth century, and the judgment opens that long vista of transients, precariously or temporarily housed in decaying rooms, who haunt his novels. Gas and water were laid on, and the top storey of the block was a huge laundry and drying space. Although the project, which grew even more ambitious later, no longer exists, it was a landmark in the history of philanthropic housing development. Dickens made sure that the work was well publicised in his magazine and spoke and campaigned for years on the related issues of sanitary reform, clean water and clean air on behalf of the submerged and rapidly growing population of London. His tireless activity in all these areas of social improvement is in itself an extraordinary achievement, full of compassion, imagination and a profound insight into the human problems created by a frenzied urban and commercial development without controls.

After he had separated from his wife, Dickens and Angela Burdett-Coutts scarcely met again. She had long been a close friend of the family and had paid for Charley's education at Eton. She twice attempted to effect a reconciliation between the partners without success. However, in 1855 W. H. Wills had, at Dickens's suggestion, become her secretary in addition to his post with *Household Words*, and the connection with her continuing philanthropic schemes was maintained through him. She died in 1906, and was long remembered by the inhabitants of the East End of London as 'the Queen of the Poor'.

Quite apart from his long and exacting commitment to Miss Burdett-Coutts's and other charitable functions, Dickens performed private acts of kindness and charity throughout his life. As well as the benefit theatrical performances for the families of friends who had died, he was generous with money and encouragement to a large number of fellow writers less successful than himself but who, he felt, nevertheless, belonged to the profession in which he had distinguished himself. As a public figure he was a constant target for begging letters of all kinds and lent his name and his unparalleled qualities as a public speaker to a number of charitable organisations, notably the Hospital for Sick Children in Great Ormond

Street in London, a fictional version of which made comfortable the last days of Betty Higden's little grandson Tommy in *Our Mutual Friend*.

Dickens's reforming zeal was the main practical response of a gifted and imaginative individual to the chaos of a changing society. It was a Nonconformist preacher who told his congregation: 'There have been at work among us three great social agencies; the London City Mission; the novels of Mr Dickens; the cholera.' The long series of thirteen major novels is the artist's effort to confront the chaos and find a way through it, using a wide range of strategies from comic deflation and satire to direct indictment. If the early works display a tendency to ascribe social and moral evil to the actions of wicked individuals, Dickens's mature vision is that of a world out of control, even though it appears to be 'nobody's fault' — the title he originally conceived for *Little Dorrit*.

That the novels are, as the preacher quoted above asserted, polemical is undeniable, yet they cannot be treated as descriptive reports on Dickens's individual experience, on the ideas that he encountered or on the larger social movements of his time. Although related, the reporter and the novelist are distinct figures, and in the novels the worlds of idea and experience are transformed in the writer's imagination by a fierce and excited creative energy into the rich shapes of fantasy, fable and story.

The ways in which London figures in the novels provide a good example of what I mean by a transformation into the rich and strange. Dickens has been continuously identified with London by later readers and exploiters of his imaginative findings. The great city is a real location in the changing, developing world of Britain in the nineteenth century. His experience of it, however, was neither only of a place that was undergoing soical strains in the process of change, nor simply as a source of material for an entertaining gallery of the various forms of social life waiting to be found there. London was a constituent element of Dickens's imagination and a necessary condition for the exercise of his art. Whenever he had to write in some other place, he felt its absence and longed for its bustling day-time streets and its secret nocturnal life. Dickens also inherited a long literary tradition of writing about London that stretched from the plays of Shakespeare and Ben Jonson to the essays of Goldsmith and Leigh Hunt. He made such good use of his inheritance that for later readers it is as though he recreated London in those shapes which still tend to conform with our experience or our imagination of it.

One may see something of the process by which life becomes art in the following letter of 1858 to Miss Burdett-Coutts. In it Dickens is reporting on a preliminary survey of a possible project among the very poor of London. He is fully aware of his tendency to turn the scene into what he calls an 'allegory', but in doing so he transfigures its features, the neglected child, the pale horse and the decaying surrounds, into a striking emblem of human and urban desolation:

JANUARY 7, 1853, 16 WELLINGTON STREET NORTH—STRAND; OFFICE OF *Household Words*

I have been down to this Saint Mark's District today, as a reasonably bad day on which to see it at its worst, and have looked well over it. It is intensely poor in some parts; and chiefly supported by river, wharf, and dock, employment; and by some lead mills. In one corner is a spot called Hickman's Folly (a Folly it is much to be regretted that Hickman ever committed), which looks like the last hopeless climax of everything poor and filthy. There is a public house in it, with the odd sign of the Ship Aground, but it is wonderfully appropriate, for everything seemed to have got aground there — never to be got off any more until the whole globe is stopped in its rolling and shivered. No more road than in an American swamp — odious sheds for horses, and donkeys, and vagrants, and rubbish, in front of the parlor windows — wooden houses like horrible old packing cases full of fever for a countless number of years. In a broken down gallery at the back of a row of these, there was a wan child looking over at a starved old white horse who was making a meal of oyster shells. The sun was going down and flaring out like an angry fire at the child — and the child, and I, and the pale horse, stared at one another in silence for some five minutes as if we were so many figures in a dismal allegory. I went round to look at the front of the house, but the windows were all broken and the door was shut up as tight as anything so dismantled could be. Lord knows when anybody will go in to the child, but I suppose it's looking over still — with a little wiry head of hair, as pale as the horse, all sticking up on its head — and an old weazen face — and two bony hands holding on the rail of the gallery, with little fingers like convulsed skewers.

4 Life into art: Dickens and London: 'that magic lantern'

'Why, Sir, you find no man, at all intellectual, who is willing to leave London. No, Sir, when a man is tired of London, he is tired of life; for there is in London all that life can afford.'

(Dr Johnson to James Boswell, 1777)

> Rise up, thou monstrous ant-hill on the plain
> Of a too busy world! Before me flow,
> Thou endless stream of men and moving things!
> Thy every day appearance, as it strikes —
> With wonder heightened, or sublimed by awe —
> On strangers, of all ages; the quick dance
> Of colours, lights, and forms; the deafening din . . .
> (W. Wordsworth: *The Prelude*, Book VII, 'Residence in London', 1850)

When, less than twenty years after Dr Johnson made his famous remarks, Wordsworth finally decided that he would dedicate his powers to poetry, he turned his back on London, the 'monstrous ant-hill', and, in the northern mountains of his native Lake District, sought out solitude and nature. In so doing, he was reaffirming a long tradition of literature to which, as we shall see shortly, even Dr Johnson belongs, and was at the same time establishing a strand of literary and aesthetic thinking that was to prove very powerful right through the nineteenth century. But in *The Prelude*, he expressed a view of the capital city that has an essentially modern flavour about it, for all the eighteenth-century associations that his words carry. Within the notion of the Sublime that shapes Wordsworth's awe and wonder at the immensity and monstrousness of the great city is carried a conscious sense of alienation from the scene. The multitudes of strangers who pass each other in the quick dance of its streets remain inscrutable to the poet. So many lives crowded together faced him with the problem of explaining those lives, one to another and all or any of them to himself. For Wordsworth, London remained a sublime spectacle of strangeness and impenetrable meanings, its total effect an assault on the senses. Yet, from the point of view of the anthropologist, it is precisely the presence of the stranger that distinguishes the city from all other forms of human settlement. Only here is the stranger's presence legitimate:

elsewhere, he is traditionally an object of hostility or, at best, of scorn to the local inhabitants.

The growth of nineteenth-century London

When Wordsworth quit London in 1799, its population numbered approximately 850,000. By the time Dickens was writing his first *Sketches* of London life and places thirty-four years later, more than one and a half million people lived in the capital. In each decade after 1841, by which time several railways were running to and from the city centre half a million more were added in what had become an explosion of growth. While in the first half of the century the population of England and Wales slightly more than doubled, London's grew two and a half times. The large majority of its inhabitants, therefore, were strangers to each other. Like Dickens and his family, they had been born elsewhere and brought up in a radically new and bewildering world.

'We who lived before railways and survive out of the ancient world, are like Father Noah and his family out of the Ark,' remarks a character in a novel by Thackeray, but it is Dickens who, foremost among modern writers, addresses himself to the experience of growing up and living in a close-packed urban world of strangers in those years of ceaseless change and transition. During that time the relationship between the words city, civility and civilisation, and between urban and urbane, that had characterised London life for Dr Johnson in the generation preceding Wordsworth's, were altered beyond recognition. It is in the actions and fictions of Dickens that we can chart much of the continuous and violent change of these years. In making use of his own varied experiences of London in his journalism, stories and novels, he makes the city available to literature as something more than a lurid, mysterious spectacle. To have been content to do so would have classed him with a kind of fiction that was already becoming popular. His readership, after all, consisted largely of those masses of human beings who, for whatever reasons, were being drawn into the cities from elsewhere in huge numbers. Instead, Dickens directs his readers' attention to their own experience and, by doing so, educates them into a new perception of the human and social changes that stemmed from the rapid and scarcely controllable growth of the capital city.

Dickens's London years

On the strength of memories of his Chatham childhood, Dickens liked to think of himself as a Kentish man and spent the last twelve years of his life nearby at Gad's Hill Place as a sort of local squire

and man of letters. Yet between 1822 and 1858 London was his permanent home and, even after that date, he still kept rooms for himself above the offices of *All The Year Round* in the Strand. There was, however, little other than the surrounding city that could be called permanent about his early London years up until his marriage in 1836. His father's Micawberish existence, dodging creditors and occasionally disappearing to hide from one financial crisis or other, entailed a life of forced removals from lodgings to lodgings, like a series of temporary encampments. These were just above or, as often, just below the line that divided the struggling middle classes from the poverty-stricken state in which the family frequently found themselves. Their months in the Marshalsea Prison were not the worst that they suffered. During those months Charles was lodged by himself in rooms, first in Little College Street with a Mrs Roylance who provided him with the outlines for Mrs Pipchin in *Dombey and Son*, and, later, in Lant Street in the district still called the Borough where the Marshalsea stood until it was closed in 1849. It had been demolished by the time Dickens wrote *Little Dorrit*. Later, as a solicitor's clerk and as a parliamentary reporter, he took different lodgings near his work or stayed with his parents wherever they happened to be camping. In 1835 he rented chambers for himself in Furnivall's Inn, but then took in his parents. He moved to Chelsea to be near his fiancée's family whose house lay just off the Fulham Road. The young couple were married in April 1836 by special licence at the grand new church of St Luke's in Chelsea and spent the first months of married life squeezed into the rooms in Furnivall's Inn. A growing income and the addition of a child made Dickens look for his first proper home since childhood days, and he decided on a twelve-roomed house near the British Museum. This house, 48 Doughty Street is now the headquarters of the Dickens Fellowship which publishes a regular journal of Dickens studies, *The Dickensian*. It is also a Dickens Museum and study centre, displaying a large collection of manuscripts, proof copies and texts annotated for his later dramatic readings.

Before the end of the year he was made a member of the Athenaeum Club and became a regular visitor to the receptions of the leading political and social hostesses of early Victorian London: Lady Holland at Holland House in Kensington and, less formally and more intimately, Lady Blessington at Gore House. He also dined with Angela Burdett (as she still was) in her mansion on the corner of Piccadilly and Stratton Street and rapidly became her closest confidant and adviser. From Doughty Street he moved to fashionable addresses until the purchase of Gad's Hill Place and his separation from his wife persuaded him to give up London.

Opposite: London and its environs, R Creighton, 1840

But, on the whole, it was not the London of fashion and high society about which he chose to write. Very little in the novels reflects the facts of his later life lived at the very centre of his age; to judge from *Dombey and Son* or *Little Dorrit* his imagination remained coldly unsympathetic to the society of political leadership and finance. It is a recurrent object of his most satirical mood, and his continuous subject matter is drawn rather from the London of his years between the ages of ten and twenty-one. In the course of his long solitary walks at all hours of the day and night, he came to know it better than anyone else. As his friends could confirm from their own knowledge, he knew in intimate detail the geography of London as it existed in the 1820s and 1830s before the city became the sprawl of suburbs that followed the building of the railways.

When he started work at Warren's Blacking Factory, it consisted of a decayed house on the north bank of the Thames. From there he would roam about the riverside, round the fruit and vegetable markets of Covent Garden or into the coffee shops along the Strand. From Camden Town in the north as far south as the Marshalsea Prison in the Borough, was an area he combed thoroughly during this time. Then, as solicitor's clerk and newspaper reporter, he gathered a close knowledge of the legal world of the courts with its associated huddle of Inns and chambers. Beyond this area, to the east of St Paul's Cathedral, lay the network of streets and alleys that make up the City of London with which he became equally familiar. Between these two districts lay Smithfield Meat Market and Newgate Prison and, nearby, the slums of Saffron Hill: locations ever since 1837 identified with the underworld of *Oliver Twist* (see Part Two, pp. 122–5). As is clear from many of the titles of the scenes in *Sketches by Boz*, Dickens was quick to perceive and exploit, for their humour and contrasts, those features of specialisation and segregation that have remained the most striking characteristic of nineteenth- and twentieth-century London. Their most obvious form is that of the contrast between rich and poor which the spectacle of the streets forces on the observer. In praising the *Sketches* Forster wrote that:

> Things are painted literally as they are ... the book altogether is a perfectly unaffected, unpretentious, honest performance ... containing unusually truthful observation of a life between the middle class and the low, which, having few attractions for bookish observers, was quite unhackneyed ground.

He is indicating what, already in these earliest pieces, is new and original in Dickens's writing. The contrasts of high and low life were already traditional in the literature of the city; they provide the form of, for example, Pierce Egan's *Tom and Jerry*. But it is Dickens's originality in his first published work to have captured precisely that margin, both human and physical, between the middle and the low; to have made visible the hitherto unremarkable and unperceived life that struggles to stay above or slides below the sharp line dividing respectability from poverty and criminality. These studies of scenes and characters are full of perceptions of this kind that were to be repeatedly deployed in different ways and to other ends throughout the later novels. Staggs's Gardens in *Dombey and Son* where the Toodle family live until it is swept away in the turmoil of the building of the new railway is a good example of a very precise evocation of the margin:

> Staggs's Gardens . . . was a little row of houses, with little squalid patches of ground before them, fenced off with old doors, barrel staves, scraps of tarpaulin, and dead bushes; with bottomless tin kettles and exhausted iron fenders, thrust into the gaps. Here, the Staggs's Gardeners trained scarlet beans, kept fowls and rabbits, erected rotten summer-houses (one was an old boat), dried clothes, and smoked pipes. Some were of opinion that Staggs's Gardens derived its name from a deceased capitalist, one Mr Staggs, who had built it for his delectation. Others, who had a natural taste for the country, held that it dated from those rural times when the antlered herd, under the familiar denomination of staggses, had resorted to its shady precincts. Be this as it may, Staggs's Gardens was regarded by its population as a sacred grove not to be withered by railroads; and so confident were they generally of its long outliving any such ridiculous inventions that the master chimney-sweeper at the corner, who was understood to take the lead in the local politics of the Gardens, had publicly declared that on the occasion of the Railroad opening, if ever it did open, two of his boys should ascend the flues of his dwellings, with instructions to hail the failure with derisive jeers from the chimney-pots.
>
> (*chapter 6*)

In Staggs's Gardens, the signs of the kinds of life lived there are rich with ambiguities. Located at the edge of the city, there is doubt whether its origins were rural or urban. Dickens employs the literary device of the catalogue of items to evoke heterogeneity and muddle. In turn, the incoherence suggests a life of improvisation and a not inept making-do with materials which happen to be lying about and can be pressed into some kind of secondary usefulness. The detail of the old boat turned summer house is used later to great effect in *David Copperfield*. The street and its description indicate the character and quality of the lives of its inhabitants and, in the novel, offer a sharp contrast to the domestic arrangements of Dombey. His

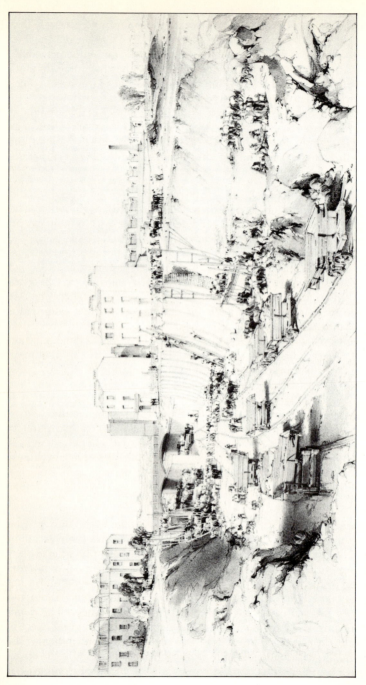

The Camden Town Railway cutting. Dickens incorporated this into Dombey and Son

house is blank to the outside world and stands in a street that bears an unsociable and 'dispirited' appearance. Staggs's Gardens and its inhabitants display more life and inventiveness than those streets where the wealthy live in their stifling exclusiveness.

In Dickens's descriptions of London, it is seldom a question of physical geography alone, even when its details are accurately remembered and faithfully reproduced. If he knew its streets and odd corners in all their wealth of detail, his friends attested to his equal attention to the forms of life the streets contained. Dickens was an expert mimic of the accents and idioms of Londoners of all kinds. His street scenes, beginning with those in the *Sketches*, are filled out with the dramas of the lives that are pursued in and through them. Styles of life hinted at or outlined — as the very title, *Sketches*, indicates — in these early essays are amply developed into full-scale portraits later. Among the most successfully evoked are the eccentric and slightly mad, the lonely, the degraded and the 'shabby-genteel'. The phrase recurs again and again in *Sketches by Boz*, sharply focusing the kinds of ambiguity that seem to inspire Dickens's literary imagination and invention. The wealth and subtlety of those ambiguities to which he is continually attracted are not necessarily to be explained as covert symbols of the anxieties and uncertainties of his own early life. They relate just as closely to a characteristic of city life which anyone may observe: its appearance of transitoriness. In Dickens's novels, houses, their inhabitants and whole streets can decay over time, can revive or, like Staggs's Gardens, be obliterated by equally ambiguous 'improvements'. Houses, like Mrs Clennam's in *Little Dorrit*, can collapse when they can no longer bear the weight of their own secretive past.

Ambiguity and transitoriness raise anxieties in the observer and relate in turn very closely to the inexplicability of city life of which Wordsworth complained. It is almost as though Dickens conceived his novels as the necessary explanations of the city's inscrutability. That he was fully conscious of the originality of his enterprise is made clear in the opening paragraph of 'Thoughts about People' from the *Sketches*:

It is strange with how little notice, good, bad, or indifferent, a man may live and die in London. He awakens no sympathy in the breast of any single person; his existence is a matter of interest to no one save himself; he cannot be said to be forgotten when he dies, for no one remembered him when he was alive. There is a numerous class of people in this metropolis who seem not to possess a single friend, and whom nobody appears to care for.

Characters from this numerous and negligible class abound in the novels: they are the humble clerks with secret histories who act as unlikely agents of benevolence or goodness. Newman Noggs in

Nicholas Nickleby and Panks in *Little Dorrit* are revealed as such. Wemmick, the lawyer's clerk in *Great Expectations*, is another example who is portrayed in considerable detail. His character and way of life are central to the major theme of the novel (see Part Two, pp. 146–7). Such characters are almost anonymous, they can melt into the endless crowds that flow over the streets. Their anonymity is shared by the professional seekers after hidden truths, like Nadgett the private enquiry agent in *Martin Chuzzlewit* and Bucket the police detective of *Bleak House*. As Bucket's name implies, the truths of life are hidden deep down: appearances are mysterious and illegible:

> A wonderful fact to reflect upon, that every human creature is constituted to be that profound secret and mystery to every other. A solemn consideration, when I enter a great city by night, that everyone of those darkly clustered houses encloses its own secret; that every room in every one of them encloses its own secret; that every beating heart in the hundreds of thousands of breasts there, is, in some of its imaginings, a secret to the heart nearest it Something of the awfulness, even of Death itself, is referable to this. . . . In any of the burial-places of this city through which I pass, is there a sleeper more inscrutable than its busy inhabitants are, in their innermost personality, to me or than I am to them?
>
> (*A Tale of Two Cities*, Book 1, chapter 3)

Dickens as novelist is like the detective figures in his novels in so far as he seeks to penetrate the mystery of appearances that is all that the city discloses to the onlooker. Many of the *Sketches* are designed from the point of view of the otherwise unemployed observer but, as he develops, so Dickens comes to take a more serious view of his task.

Dombey and Son marks an important stage in his artistic growth and provides evidence of his awareness of the nature of the task:

> Oh, for a good spirit who would take the house-tops off, with a more potent and benignant hand than the lame demon in the tale, and show a Christian people what dark shapes issue from amidst their homes to swell the retinue of the Destroying Angel as he moves forth among them! For only one night's view of the pale phantoms rising from the scenes of our too-long neglect, and from the thick and sullen air where Vice and Fever propagate together, raining the tremendous social retributions which are ever pouring down, and ever coming thicker
>
> (*chapter 47*)

In revealing the unknown life of the city, Dickens is revealing at the same time a moral and spiritual condition of which the signs are the sullen vapours that rise from it and the rain that falls ceaselessly upon it. The condition is one which, once identified, we ignore at our peril. Death, the Destroying Angel, is the ultimate threat, and, as can be readily understood from both of the foregoing passages, is closely related to the mysteries of individual lives.

The tradition of the city in literature

In making the association between the city and death, Dickens is invoking a central Christian belief. The contrast between the earthly city and the city of God can be traced back through the various forms of its literary expression to the writings of St Augustine, but the fictional form in which it was most readily available to Dickens as to his readers was that of *Pilgrim's Progress*. In Bunyan's allegorical fiction the two pilgrims, Christian and Faithful, must pass through the town of Vanity where is held a year-long fair at which only vanities are to be bought. Here the pilgrims are beaten and thrown into prison for refusing to purchase anything other than truth: the one item not for sale at the fair. Christian escapes to continue his pilgrimage in search of salvation, but Faithful is martyred at the stake.

Thackeray took the image of the fair at Vanity for the title of his best-known and most successful novel, although, as a panoramic satire of social manners, it owes more to Fielding's *Tom Jones* than to Bunyan's allegory of the earthly trials that are thrown in the way of him who would achieve spiritual and eternal life. In *Vanity Fair* London is present as the brilliantly lit, impressionistically described back-cloth against which the intrigues and actions of the groups of central characters are pursued in great detail. In Dickens's novels, from *Oliver Twist* on, it is as though London plays its own active role in the destinies of the characters. It seems inevitable that Oliver, the runaway, should meet the Artful Dodger and be led by him through the labyrinth of its streets to Fagin's den, the heart of evil and corruption. Noah Claypole, the older apprentice who had bullied Oliver during his time with Sowerberry the undertaker, unerringly takes the same path into a world of moral and spiritual evil, the features of which derive more directly from Bunyan than from Fielding. Like the thief and the receiver of stolen goods, the prostitute Nancy is a central figure in this drama of urban evil. Their careers could scarcely be followed anywhere other than in those places where strangers accumulate and Nancy, the thief's mistress, is haunted by signs of death in the streets as she anticipates that her betrayal of the gang will end in her own destruction.

From the opposite extreme of the moral scale, in *The Old Curiosity Shop*, Nell imagines at night that her grandfather's blood is seeping under the door into her room. She persuades him to flee with her in an attempt to escape the opportunities by which he is surrounded in the city to indulge his compulsion to gamble. As in *Oliver Twist*, the city in the later novel is described as a 'labyrinth' which corrupts and destroys.

The most explicit formulation of the notion that the city is a place of death and destruction is made in *Dombey and Son*. Harriet Carker, the housekeeper of her 'outcast' brother looks out through the rain and heavy mist towards the city from their home near the busy Great North Road, where it is neither town nor country but 'only blighted country and not town':

> She often looked with compassion, at such a time, upon the weary stragglers who came wandering into London, by the great highway hard by, and who, footsore and weary, and gazing fearfully at the huge towns before them, as if foreboding that their misery there would be but as a drop of water in the sea, or as a grain of sea-sand on the shore, went shrinking on, cowering before the angry weather, and looking as if the very elements rejected them. Day after day, such travellers crept past, but always, as she thought, in one direction — always towards the town. Swallowed up in one phase or other of its immensity, towards which they seemed impelled by a desperate fascination, they never returned. Food for the hospitals, the churchyards, the prisons, the river, fever, madness, vice and death — they passed on to the monster, roaring in the distance, and were lost.
>
> (*chapter 33*)

Dickens does not himself shrink from the contemplation of these objects of misery catalogued at the end of the foregoing passage, but the city viewed as a place of death does not represent the whole compass of his mode of dealing with the experience of city life. If such catalogues of its miseries recur in various combinations in his later novels, about the earlier work still plays the tradition of reflecting on city life which comes down to us from classical literature and which contrasts urban vice with rural virtue.

Town and country

The contemplation of the city, as an object of moral satire rather than as the worldly contrast to the ideal of the unworldly life, was shaped into literary form in the classical literature of Rome. Its forms were again directly borrowed and imitated in the eighteenth century in England. Samuel Johnson's poem *London*, written in 1738, is sub-titled *in imitation of the Third Satire of Juvenal*. In it the speaker proclaims his disgust at the violent overthrow of the traditional English pieties in the modern capital, from which virtue and decency have been exiled.

For who would leave, unbrib'd, *Hibernia's* Land,
Or change the Rocks of *Scotland* for the *Strand?*
There none are swept by sudden Fate away,
But all whom Hunger spares, with Age decay:
Here Malice, Rapine, Accident conspire,
And now a Rabble rages, now a Fire;
Their Ambush here relentless Ruffians lay,
And here the fell Attorney prowls for Prey?
Here falling Houses thunder on your Head,
And here a female Atheist talks you dead.
....

Grant me, kind Heaven, to find some happier Place,
Where Honesty and Sense are no Disgrace;
Some pleasing Bank where verdant Osiers play,
Some peaceful Vale with Nature's Paintings gay ...

A more savage picture of London Life is drawn in Tobias Smollett's *Humphry Clinker* (1771) in the letters which Matthew Bramble writes home during his stay there. Bramble assails the capital as a 'wilderness', and as 'a dropsical head [which] will in time leave the body and extremities without nourishment and support, luxurious, polluted —. . . a vile ferment of stupidity'.

In less virulent forms, *Sketches by Boz* and Dickens's early novels recapitulate the view of the city created by earlier satirical literature and are cast in the mould of the contrast between town and country. *Oliver Twist* and *The Old Curiosity Shop* portray an unconvincing idea of the contrast, and later critical judgment has confirmed John Ruskin's opinion reviewing the latter novel on its appearance, that, in *The Old Curiosity Shop*, Dickens appears to have run dry. 'It is evident that the man is a thorough cockney, from his way of talking about hedgerows, and honeysuckles, and village spires; and in London, and to his present fields of knowledge, he ought strictly to keep for some time. There are subjects enough in the *Sketches* which might be worked up into something of real excellence.'

Dickens's originality

The continued applicability of Ruskin's judgment forcibly suggests the limitations of Dickens's literary imagination. At the same time, however, Ruskin directs us to its strengths and its originality. If the early novels show a great deal of ineptitude in the banal generalisations in terms of which Dickens depicts a pastoral world inherited from his literary predecessors, they show also a growing awareness of the complexities and the bewildering variousness of modern city life. A strategy he uses several times is to record the impressions of the newcomer to the city. Chapter thirty-two of *Nicholas Nickleby*, and *Martin Chuzzlewit* in the chapters dealing with Tom Pinch's enforced flight to London and his settling in there, are both good examples of the technique; but it is in chapter nine of the latter novel, 'Of Town and Todgers', that we begin to perceive the complex inwardness of Dickens's imaginative response to the city. The opening paragraphs of the chapter — too long to quote here in full — are quite different in mood and tone from the 'many and many a pleasant walk' that, in chapter forty, Tom and his sister as sightseers take through Covent Garden or by the river wharves to watch the excitements of the departing steam ships. In a remarkable passage, Dickens evokes the 'drowsy and secret existence' of the locality of Mrs Todgers's boarding house and its inhabitants:

> Instances were known of people who, being asked to dine at Todgers's, had travelled round and round for a weary time, with its very chimney pots in view; and finding it, at last, impossible of attainment, had gone home again with a gentle melancholy on their spirits, tranquil and uncomplaining.

This little corner of London has been thrust aside and squeezed tight by new-fangled ways and changes that have overtaken the city all around, and has been left undisturbed to pursue its own form of life. The effect is that even those who fail to find it go away again calm in spirit rather than in frustrated outrage, such is its special atmosphere. Over time the area has become a perfect little town of its own, disturbed only by the occasional passage of a straying hackney-coach or lumbering waggon. Mrs Todger's house suits its surroundings. The ground-floor window is encrusted with the grime of a hundred years which holds together its cracked window-panes. There is a mystery about its cellars. They belong to someone else and, for all anyone knows, may be full of treasure. The truth of the origins of the house has been lost, but the roof-top commands a panoramic view of the roar and animation of the city which makes the 'hair' on the top of the nearby monument to the Great Fire of London stand on end with fright, and might tempt the viewer to cast himself down head-first into the 'wilderness upon wilderness'.

Todgers's had been spared the vertiginous bustle of modern city life and, in its interior, is practised by the lodgers and their visitors an energetic parody of the more graceful social life of an earlier age. Lodgers is, of course, the rhyming partner of Todgers and it is in the spirit of the broad comedy of the chapter that it should be so. The lodgers are characterised each by one distinguishing quality:

> They included a gentleman of sporting turn . . . a gentleman of a theatrical turn . . . and they included a gentleman of a debating turn, who was strong at speech-making . . . there was a gentleman

of a vocal turn, and a gentleman of a smoking turn, and a gentleman of a convivial turn. . . .

The list is both relentlessly repetitive and exhaustive, a sure sign, one might judge, of an overworked facetiousness. Yet it seems to me that what is presented in the gallery of types under Mrs Todgers's roof is not a striving after easy comic effect, feeble because unrestrained, so much as a hint of the flattening effect on character of an enforced and quite spurious notion of sociability. It is an effect engendered, at least in part, by the inmates' inadequate idea of the kind of social behaviour appropriate to such an institution, and in part by the institution itself. They have all been 'turned' into the one single characteristic that each can present to the others and to visitors such as the Pecksniff family, and by the employment of which each may claim some kind of individual identity.

It is Young Bailey in the role of satirical commentator who guides the reader's reaction and relates the entire chapter to the general theme of false appearance or hypocrisy, the satirising and exposure of which provides the framework of the novel. But at the same time, one's response is enriched and complicated by the energy of the chapter and by the author's brilliant pacing of the comic drama. While keenly enjoying the unfolding of the travesty of social life in his depiction, Dickens seems at the same time to be celebrating the expression of a genuine feeling of energy and conviviality. The atmosphere of the dinner held at Todgers's in honour of the Pecksniff family is quite unlike that of the society evenings depicted in the later novels. Compare, for example, the fashionable gathering at Merdle's in chapter twenty-one of *Little Dorrit*, or the dinner given by Podsnap in *Our Mutual Friend* (chapter eleven). In the later examples the satire is more concise, more impressive and sharply directed. It is not, however, as though Dickens was merely more at home on the margin of respectable society; the difference in mood and tone suggests that there was more life possible in the circle of Todgers's boarding house than around the ornately garnished tables of the wealthy.

Chapter nine of *Martin Chuzzlewit* seems to point simultaneously in several directions. Within the prevailing comic tone, it constitutes a satirical revelation of a secret form of urban life with all its pretentiousnesses. It points also towards those scenes of domestic cheerfulness and emphatic private celebration with which Dickens's writings and his life abound. The loyalty of a very large part of his continuing readership rests on the recurrent note of domestic jollification at moments of climax in his fiction. At the same time, however, the chapter seems to indicate a less frequently noted but equally important characteristic of his imagination. That is, it points to the relationship between individuals and the institutions they create for themselves in the social world. Such relationships seem, in Dickens's writings, always to have the same effect on the individual; by their oppressiveness they reduced him to a single dimension of existence.

Institutions of all kinds feature prominently and with remarkable frequency in most of Dickens's novels. A comprehensive list of them would be a long one, and would have to include schools, banks, workhouses, shops, solicitors' offices and courts of law, business houses such as Mr Dombey's, churches, prisons, government departments, gentlemen's clubs, varyingly hospitable public houses, circuses and theatres, hotels and lodging houses of all classes, down to the decayed slum of Tom-All-Alone's in *Bleak House* and the criminal haunt of Folly Ditch in *Oliver Twist*.

Formally constituted or informally created and inherited, institutions of the one kind or the other often provide a focus for the activities and reactions of the characters and, at the same time, can be felt as a positive presence constraining and distorting human life into a variety of unexpected shapes. In order to preserve anything of the flow of spontaneous life under such pressures, individuals are driven to exercising extraordinary and sometimes fantastic ingenuity. In *Bleak House* it is Chancery, and in *Little Dorrit* the Marshalsea which provide the central image that works on each of the characters and their varied destinies. Richard Carstone and Grindley, both suitors to the case of *Jarndyce* v. *Jarndyce*, are killed by their involvement in Chancery; Miss Flyte has been driven mad by it. Just so, William Dorrit, forced into prison by debt, has for so many years played out a protective fantasy of aristocratic patronage that he can never be released from it. In the same novel Arthur Clennam also is the prisoner of a secret hidden in a past not of his own making. His history has destroyed his freedom and autonomy, just as Dorrit has destroyed that of his younger daughter Amy in demanding the sacrifice of her life to his fantasy. When, at the very end of the novel, Clennam is released from the Marshalsea and he and Little Dorrit marry,

> They went quietly down into the roaring streets, inseparable and blessed; and as they passed along in sunshine and shade, the noisy and the eager, and the arrogant and the froward and the vain, fretted and chafed, and made their usual uproar.

They are survivors rather than victors and must be counted among all the 'blighted fruits' of the Marshalsea. Their future life, such as it may be, made up of 'sunshine and shade', will be completely private. To what that life may be, the roaring streets are utterly indifferent.

As a reformer in the fields of politics, morals and the environment, Dickens would be keenly aware of the relations between them. They were debated throughout the century and put into practice in schemes of model industrial villages or colonies that accompanied the growth of the factory system. What was a paramount necessity to the development of industry was the domestication and discipline of the work force. Robert Owen's mill village of New Lanark, founded in the same decade as Dickens was born, was only the earliest and perhaps best known of a number of similar endeavours, carried out particularly in the textile manufacturing area of the north of England. Owen shared the view that circumstances make men, whereas it is evident from a reading of any of his novels that Dickens was in no sense a determinist and believed rather in an original human character consisting of good or evil. Oliver Twist is impervious to experience because he illustrates the survival of 'the principle of goodness'. But, in the later novels, pressures and constraints exert their force upon the individual life to the detriment of human qualities. As his view of human nature develops from his early absolutist notions to take account of the effects of experience on the individual, so does his idea of the relationship of the individual and the city. In the later novels the city is no longer the monstrous death machine of *Dombey and Son*. Instead of a presiding Angel of Death, city life is perceived as being governed by its interlocking sets of institutions and customs. If danger and death still abound, these are no longer assumed to be the work of an immanent Destroying Angel, but rather the result of appalling conditions and the inevitable epidemic diseases that arise from irresponsibility and neglect on the part of constituted authorities. The world of *Little Dorrit* is, in the original tentative title, 'Nobody's Fault', because nobody in authority will face up to the responsibility.

Dickens's final London novel, *Our Mutual Friend* has no such central public institution. Instead, the characters' lives are related to 'money, money, money and what money can make of life'. The physical form which the abstract medium of currency and exchange takes is that of the dust heaps out of which old Harmon made a fortune that he left to his son John, who is presumed drowned. Dust and grit swirl thick and choking about the London of this novel. (In *Bleak House* it is mud and fog, in *Great Expectations* everything is cramped, dirty and crooked, and in *Little Dorrit* there is prevailing atmosphere of gloom and inhospitable dreariness that emanates from the prison.) The pursuit and exchange of money as currency is counterpointed by the surge and flow of the great tidal river that is London's dominant feature and the source of the city's growth as a mercantile and imperial capital city.

There is no doubt that Dickens overworks the Thames as a symbol in some of his novels. Polluted and unsavoury as its waters are in *Our Mutual Friend*, they still represent the opposite of the dust and are the waters of life; real life and real death to those who live by it. Nothing in this novel, however, or in *Dombey and Son*, matches the consummate artistry of chapter fifty-four of *Great Expectations* (see Part Two, pp. 150–3).

It is in an ironic paragraph in *Our Mutual Friend* that Dickens points to the possibility of a world ordered differently from the bleak social panorama that he depicts in these novels:

> Fearful to relate, there was even a sort of little fair in the village. Some despairing gingerbread that had been vainly trying to dispose of itself all over the country, and had cast a quantity of dust upon its head in its mortification again appealed to the public from an infirm booth. So did a heap of nuts, long, long exiled from Barcelona, and yet speaking English so indifferently as to call fourteen of themselves a pint. A peep-show which had originally started with the Battle of Waterloo and had since made it every other battle of later date by altering the Duke of Wellington's nose, tempted the student of illustrated history. A fat lady, perhaps in part sustained upon postponed pork, her professional associate being a learned pig, displayed her life-size picture in a low dress as she appeared when presented at Court, several yards round. All this was a vicious spectacle, as any poor idea of amusement on the part of the rougher hewer of wood and drawers of water in this land of England ever is and shall be. They *must not* vary the rheumatism with amusement. They may vary it with fever and ague, or with as many rheumatic variations as they have joints, but positively not with entertainment after their own manner.
>
> (*chapter 56*)

Throughout his novels there are scenes evoking ways of being together in human fellowship which suggest a notion of human society quite different from its oppressive, institutionalised forms that make up modern city life. Sometimes such scenes do portray institutions, but these are of a quite special kind, such as public houses (but not all, one must add), circuses and, as the passage quoted above confirms, fairgrounds. Most engaging perhaps, are those scenes drawn from the life of the theatre.

Dickens took his enjoyments seriously and robustly. From the theatre and the wide field of popular entertainment he drew a life-long pleasure as spectator and participant alike. In *Hard Times* he depicts Sleary's Circus as the life-giving antithesis of Mr Gradgrind's abstract schemes of education and life. Inadequate or incompetent attempts at entertainment seem especially to release the novelist's imagination into a celebration of what is informal and spontaneous, creative and enjoyable in human life. In Dickens's fiction the theatre becomes an ideal focus for pleasure: the theatre transforms life. In chapter forty-seven of *Great Expectations* Pip visits the theatre to watch Wopsle perform for the second time; this time in pantomime. The ironic, literal manner in which Dickens describes the events on stage comically emphasises the artistic poverty of the occasion and Wopsle's fall from the dramatic heights of *Hamlet*. Nevertheless, Pip is so absorbed that he fails to register the dangerous presence of the villian Compeyson sitting behind him in the audience. For those two hours he has totally relaxed the continuous vigilance needed for the effort to smuggle Magwitch successfully out of England.

Indeed, in contradiction of what can be read as an increasingly authoritarian set of utterances in his speeches and journalistic articles on the condition of England, on the treatment of prisoners and related topics of concern to him, the novelist's imagination, as it develops and deepens, reveals to us a view of human life that celebrates its creative and spontaneous forms. For these, the theatre provides the perfect analogy.

The ideal of home

What, as much as anything else, stamps Dickens as a Victorian writer is his characteristic insistence on the simple virtues of domesticity and family home life. The Victorian emphasis on the home is the product of a long and complex history of moral and social change, much of which is reflected in Dickens's own life. He does not invent the theme but is its most successful and influential promoter in imaginative terms. It is home and family life that cherish the individual sensibility and protect it from the damage inflicted on the individual by the larger world of society in 'that universal struggle to get a living' as the business of living is called in *Great Expectations*. A typical mid-Victorian expression of what lies behind Dickens's portrayal of families is that of John Ruskin, whom we may take to be representative of the period, writing in *Sesame and Lilies* (1865). In a passage discussing the place of women, he says:

> This is the true nature of home — it is the place of Peace; the shelter, not only from all injury, but from all terror, doubt and division. In so far as it is not this, it is not home; so far as the anxieties of the outer life penetrate into it, and the inconsistently-minded, unknown, unloved, or hostile society of the outer world is allowed by either husband or wife to cross the threshold, it ceases to be home; it is then only a part of that outer world which you have roofed over and lighted fire in. But so far as it is a sacred place, a vestal temple, a temple of the hearth watched over by Household Gods, before whose faces none may come but those whom they can receive with love, — so far as it is this, and roof and fire are types duly of a nobler shade and light, — shade as

of the rock in a weary land, and light as of the Pharos in the
stormy sea; — so far it vindicates the name, and fulfils the praise,
of Home.

(Lecture II. Of Queens' Gardens, Section 68)

Perhaps only Wemmick in *Great Expectations* lives in this state of total
divorce between home and society, but his home is a good deal
jollier and richer in fancy than the lofty, sacramentalised view of the
Victorian home that Ruskin would have us share. Dickens's characters simply enjoy themselves more in their private worlds and relationships when, that is, they are fortunate enough to possess these
and have the love and ability to create, like the Toodles of Staggs's
Gardens, a real home.

Theatres, circuses and domestic jollification in Dickens's fiction
are set over against modern, institutionalised city life and the
accompanying stresses and strains of a society in transition. The
strains arise because many of the institutions no longer correspond
to the realities of life, and many of the stresses are the result of
professional or occupational deformation. Even if, as Orwell
asserted, Dickens does not often appear to be interested in work as
such, many of the characters in his pages grow out of a job or
occupation. Almost as many, including a majority of the minor
characters, are also stunted by their occupation. Wemmick's
employer, Jaggers the lawyer, is a good example of such. It is spelled
out in the text that he was once different; more like Pip with similar
'poor dreams'. And it is a reflection on the world of *Martin Chuzzlewit*
and its universal hypocrisy that Montague Tigg can reverse himself
into the dashing, fraudulent Tigg Montague of the Anglo-Bengalee
Disinterested Loan and Life Assurance Company. More humbly,
Phil Squod, Trooper George's assistant at the shooting gallery in
Bleak House, survives a life which seems to consist entirely of being
blown up at intervals. The elements that make up Dickens's vision
of the life of a great city do not always cohere as purposefully and
to such powerful effect as they do in *Great Expectations*, but it is a
mistake to see him as primarily a reflector of the discrete and
heterogeneous surfaces of modern urban life. The surfaces of life and
its heterogeneity he can render superbly well and wittily, so that we
often have difficulty in holding apart Dickens's fictional London and
the London of Victorian England. But his vision is at once creative
and analytical, critical and celebratory. What he celebrates in
human life includes the simple traditional pieties of human love and
pleasure, and the joy in creativity that was the particular assertion
of the Romantic age which Dickens absorbed into his own experience. To see Dickens's characters as caricatures and grotesques is
not to see them at all. It is to fail to recognise the connections
between the kinds of lives that his characters invent for themselves

and the enveloping, shifting, murky world that they must inhabit. London and its scenes of teeming life was, as he came to realise only when he had been away from it, indispensable to the exercise of his creative gift. The extent to which he felt the importance of its presence to the very act of writing is made clear in his letter to Forster of 30 August 1846 from Lausanne while he was working on the early chapters of *Dombey and Son*:

> You can hardly imagine what pains I take, or what difficulty I find in getting on FAST. Invention, thank God, seems the easiest thing in the world; and I seem to have such a preposterous sense of the ridiculous, after this long rest, as to be constantly requiring to restrain myself from launching into extravagance in the height of my enjoyment. But the difficulty of going at what I call a rapid pace, is prodigious: it is almost an impossibility. I suppose this is partly the effect of two years' ease, and partly of the absence of streets and numbers of figures. I can't express how much I want these. It seems as if they supplied something to my brain, which it cannot bear, when busy, to lose. For a week or a fortnight I can write prodigiously in a retired place (as at Broadstairs), and a day in London sets me up again and starts me. But the toil and labour of writing, day after day, without that magic lantern, is IMMENSE!! I don't say this, at all in low spirits, for we are perfectly comfortable here, and I like the place very much indeed, and the people are even more friendly and fond of me than they were in Genoa. I only mention it as a curious fact, which I have never had an opportunity of finding out before. *My* figures seem disposed to stagnate without crowds about them.

Dickens explores the magic lantern for what it tells him of human life. After the moment of his imitative flights into pastoral nostalgia at the beginning of his career, he unfolds a series of insights into its physical and human geography that is progressively harsh and bleak; what he sees in the lantern's lighted pictures is a dramatic and colourful urban image, hostile to the traditional human sanctities and occasionally nightmarish. Even so, London becomes for Dickens the ground of the human condition on which he recreates the strands of interconnection and relationship underlying the appearance of muddle and incoherence. Unlike Wordsworth or Ruskin, he cannot wish it all away: unlike theirs, his vision of modern urban society is not alienated if, like theirs, it is not hopeful.

Our Mutual Friend conveys a mood of contemporaneity, as though, for the first time since *Dombey and Son*, Dickens were setting out to describe the present. Yet, in it, nothing of the great changes and developments that were taking place in London makes any showing. The new systems of sanitation, the first underground railway of 1864, the great Victorian Embankment of the following year, and

the driving of New Oxford Street straight through the criminal rook-
eries behind St Giles's Church: none of these important civic
measures, many of which he had long compaigned for, seems to be of
any importance to his themes. Instead, in describing the new national school building programme, he links it to a panorama of waste,
misrule and irresponsibility that can bring about only the destruction of fertility and cultivation:

The schools — for they were twofold, as the sexes — were down
in that district of the flat country tending to the Thames, where
Kent and Surrey meet, and where the railways still bestride the
market-gardens that will soon die under them. The schools were
newly built, and there were so many like them all over the country
that one might have thought the whole were but one restless
edifice with the locomotive gift of Aladdin's palace. They were in
a neighbourhood which looked like a toy neighbourhood taken in
blocks out of a box by a child of particularly incoherent mind and
set up anyhow; here, one side of a new street; there, a large
solitary public-house facing nowhere; here another unfinished
street already in ruins; there, a church; here, an immense new
warehouse; there a dilapidated old country villa; then, a medley
of black ditch, sparkling cucumber-frame, rank field, richly
cultivated kitchen-garden, brick viaduct, arch-spanned canal, and
disorder of frowziness and fog. As if the child had given the table
a kick and gone to sleep. ·

(*chapter 18*)

Part Two
Critical Commentary

5 Dickens and Childhood

The child and the importance of childhood experience to later life are at the centre of Dickens's concerns as an imaginative writer. He will continue to be read for his many other qualities as a novelist; for his humour, for his creation of a gallery of characters as memorable in their different ways as those of Shakespeare, and for the excitement of his elaborate and entertaining plots. But he is uniquely celebrated as the novelist of childhood. The emphasis scarcely needs to be made, yet is still worth bearing in mind if only because it forces on us the realisation that part of what he achieved as a writer was to impress the importance of childhood, not only on the novel intended for adult reading, but also on a whole society. Later critical responses to his novels have on occasion tended to suggest that his concern with childhood, impressive as it is, constitutes a limitation of his art. It is as though to be so totally engrossed in the topic of childhood, or so the argument seems to run, is not to be fully adult, to be unable to put away childish things. Another strand of the same argument reads the repeated handling of childhood in many of the novels as a compulsively repetitious return to his own childhood and to his view of his own parents as culpably negligent of their gifted and ambitious son. What, from the novels, is taken to be evidence for such views obliterates the necessary distinction between what the man suffers and what the artist creates. I would insist on the contrary that Dickens articulates in his fiction a view of childhood — perhaps it would be better to say views of childhood — which he inherits from the English Romantic poets and that, like theirs, these views represent an essentially adult concern. As he makes David Copperfield say:

> 'I believe the power of observation in numbers of young children to be quite wonderful for its closeness and accuracy. Indeed, I think that most grown men who are remarkable in this respect, may with greater propriety, be said not to have lost the faculty, than to have acquired it; the rather, as I generally observe such men to retain a certain freshness, and gentleness, and capacity of being pleased, which are also an inheritance they have preserved from their childhood.'
>
> (*chapter 2*, 'I Observe')

thereby stressing the continuity of experience from childhood to adult life.

The romantic child

In chapter four of his *Biographia Literaria*, Coleridge characterises genius in similar terms:

> To carry on the feelings of childhood into the powers of manhood; to combine the child's sense of wonder and novelty with the appearances, which every day for perhaps forty years had rendered familiar . . . is the character and privilege of genius, and one of the marks which distinguish genius from talents.

We recall that, in *Hard Times*, Mr Gradgrind, as part of his educational system for his own children, tells them, 'You are not to wonder.' What Coleridge emphasises about childhood is not a nostalgia for his own past, but rather a particular way of perceiving and experiencing for the first time that belongs only to childhood.

The same may be said, only more emphatically, of his companion and fellow-poet Wordsworth. Wordsworth returned to his own childhood in search of the sources of his deepest feelings and profoundest responses to experience. He entertained notions of the development of the human mind and of the nature and origins of knowledge derived from David Hartley's associationism and held, following Hartley and John Locke, that the new-born mind is a blank, a *tabula rasa*. Wordsworth's philosophical justifications for his views are less important than the fact that they put him in touch with his own experience and encouraged him to feel the importance of his earliest experiences to his later life, as is made clear in 'Lines composed above Tintern Abbey' and, most strikingly, in *The Prelude*. In these poems, although they tell equally of a development, the experiences of childhood are determining. 'The Child is Father of the Man'. The line, taken from a transparently lyrical statement of his faith in the relationship between man and nature, is used as the epigraph to the 'Immortality Ode', one of his best-known poems. The 'Ode' is a poem rich in the child's sense of the wonder of the earth and the loss of that sense in later life, but it is altogether unconvincing in its assertion of the compensations to the adult for that loss. The line is one which Dickens can interpret with an ironic literalness. He presumably knew it as he certainly knew other lines from poems of Wordsworth. Although he is no longer a child, Sam Weller stands in the relation of a father to his unworldly employer Mr Pickwick and to his own father. In the last completed novel, *our Mutual Friend*, Jenny Wren is the mother of her own father who is known by the name of Mr Dolls on account of his daughter's work as a dolls' dress-maker by means of which she supports him. 'Like his own father, a weak wretched trembling creature, falling to pieces, never sober.' Many girls in Dickens's novels are 'little mothers' to either a delinquent parent or to a neglected family of brothers and sisters. Little Dorrit, one recalls, is born in the prison where her family have languished for years under the burden of debt. Her father, William Dorrit, has, in that time, come to bear the title of Father of the Marshalsea and plays out a fantasy of the gentility of that position as an escape from a miserable reality. The whole duty of his younger daughter Amy is to sustain and protect him in his fantasy.

Wordsworth, in two powerfully resonant lines from the 'Ode,' wrote:

Shades of the prison-house begin to close
Upon the growing Boy,

as though, following the dimming of the 'visionary gleam', the process were inevitable. Childhood itself, in the same poem, is, to the contrary, full of 'delight and liberty'. But Amy Dorrit is not subjected to an inevitable process of loss and imprisonment. She had never experienced that simple creed of childhood, and the terrible constraints that act on her are there from the outset. They bring to mind William Blake rather than Wordsworth.

There is no evidence that Dickens had read Blake's *Songs of Innocence and Experience*, but it is here, more directly and fiercely than in the work of the other English Romantic poets, that we find close parallels with the children of the novels. Blake celebrates the child as an expression of natural, free and spontaneous human energy. In *Songs of Experience*, these energies are opposed by equally fierce constraints: the ties of parents, of church and of society's 'cold and usurous hand.'

My mother groan'd, my father wept,
Into the dangerous world I leapt;
Helpless, naked, piping loud,
Like a fiend hid in a cloud.

Struggling in my father's hands,
Striving against my swaddling-bands,
Bound and weary, I thought best
To sulk upon my mother's breast.

'Infant Sorrow' is a poem of intense compression. The words, with a Shakespearean economy and directness, enact a bitter contest of oppositions which ends in the damaging exhaustion of the infant's natural expressive energies. Dickens's novels are full not only of children unnaturally constrained by parents or guardians, but also of the damaged and distorted personalities that are the result of a constraining and distorting upbringing.

As in the poems of the English Romantics, the education of children is an integral part of his consideration of the topic. His pictures

94

of inadequate schools, whether brutal like Dotheboys Hall and Doctor Creakle's Academy, or totally misguided like Doctor Blimber's or Mr Gradgrind's establishments, are among his most savage and memorable satirical attacks on what he took to be inhuman aspects of nineteenth-century English life. Schooling equals denial and repression, whether systematic or terroristic, and what is denied is the child's world of the imagination. For Blake the child is a creature of 'Imagination' and 'Vision' which transcend that 'Outward Creation' that was the domain of Wordsworth, whom Blake continually reproached for his exclusive concern with nature and natural objects. Dickens's children do not see 'an Innumerable company of the Heavenly Host' in the sun, as Blake could claim to, but they do, or the favoured ones do, see fanciful pictures in the ordinary domestic fire grate.

What unites Dickens's and the various Romantic notions of childhood is a much older tradition that insists on the innocence of children, the tradition of Christian belief. In his will Dickens instructed his children always to be guided by the teachings of Jesus in the New Testament. He wrote the *Life of Our Lord* for his children while living in Switzerland in 1846 (it was only published in 1934), and echoes of Christ's words recur frequently in the novels together with references to the childhood of Christ and the injunction in Matthew: 'Except ye be converted, and become as little children, ye shall not enter into the Kingdom of Heaven.' Both the special perception that children possess in the poetry of Wordsworth and Coleridge, and the celebration of spontaneous expressiveness in Blake's often indignant vision of childhood meet in the Christian insistence with which the innocence of childhood is urged in their work. This is not in any way a sentimental insistence, but rather a means of focusing attention on the free and spontaneous expressiveness of all human life, and a warning of the ways in which individual, expressive experience is threatened in a new and rapidly changing world. What Wordsworth wrote in Book Five of *The Prelude*,

> These mighty workmen of our later age,
> Who, with a broad highway, have overbridged
> The froward chaos of futurity,
> Tamed to their bidding; they who have the skill
> To manage books, and things, and make them act
> On infant minds as surely as the sun
> Deals with a flower; the keepers of our time,
> The guides and wardens of our faculties,
> Sages who in their prescience would control
> All accidents, and to the very road
> Which they have fashioned would confine us down
> Like engines;

is a text vitally relevant to a central preoccupation of Dickens, and shows something of the continuity of thought between the earlier poets and the later novelists. Many of Dickens's characters have become 'engines' and, for 'prescient guide', we need look no further than Mr Dombey in his attempt to control the accidents of his son's life.

To look closely at Dickens's handling of childhood in his novels is to see much of what it was he inherited from the generation of Romantic poets who preceded him, and to approach very nearly what were his deepest concerns as an original imaginative writer in his own time.

The novels of childhood: Oliver Twist

From what I have written above I do not want it to be inferred that the subject of childhood is a theme, in the musical sense, upon which Dickens plays variations in different novels. Rather, I attempt to show in what follows that the growing child provides a focus for a developing preoccupation with human life and relationships. The preoccupation itself changes and becomes more profound in parallel with his developing art. It is a measure of the closeness of the subject to his concerns that his first novel to be designed as such, rather than arrived at by the accumulation of episodes, should feature a child as its eponymous hero.

Oliver Twist is peculiarly a figure without any character. He has no personality or child-like characteristics. Rather is he the vehicle of a certain kind of content and stands for one side of the argument that Dickens is conducting at the level of the surface of the story in what is, in many ways, a very consciously planned novel of ideas. What Dickens wanted to show in Oliver was 'the principle of Good surviving through every adverse circumstance, and triumphing at last', as he wrote in the Preface to the first complete edition. The idea is a very abstract and idealised one, which puts any indication of personality in Oliver in a strait-jacket. Set against it is the opposing principle of Evil, embodied in the underworld characters Fagin and Sykes and their Saffron Hill gang. The conflict is waged between goodness and evil, innocence and corruption, and provides the author with the form and rhythm of the book. Oliver oscillates between the upper and nether worlds in a regular pattern as the complicated story works itself out. And yet the story is too complicated and sufficiently interesting to sustain our attention or nourish our imaginations as readers. It is a secular version of John Bunyan's *Pilgrim's Progress* with Oliver surviving temptation to achieve at the end, not spiritual salvation, but a secure identity and a comfortable middle-class inheritance. The energies of the novel are discharged elsewhere; in the underworld activity of crime, robbery and murder set in the locations of Saffron Hill and Jacob's Island. For Dickens was entertaining other ideas than those represented in the progress through temptations of Oliver, the Parish Boy.

Oliver Twist was also written as an attack on a particular literary convention, the so-called Newgate novel of sensational criminal exploits which sentimentalised and romanticised the way of life of the criminal. In the Preface Dickens ranges himself with Fielding, Defoe, Goldsmith, Smollett, Richardson, Mackenzie and Cervantes as a novelist. At the outset of his career he claims his rightful place among them by asserting both that he has turned a realistic light on London's underworld and that the picture he has revealed is a truthful one. Lord Melbourne, Prime Minister at the time of its appearance, took it to be another Newgate novel and was only persuaded to change his opinion by the young Queen Victoria. However, the novel did shock many readers who were still applauding the comic exploits of Mr Pickwick. It also seems to me possible that, during the writing, Dickens had in mind William Hazlitt's essay on Jeremy Bentham in which Hazlitt presents a view of the criminal mind, opposed to that of Bentham that the criminal is amenable to reason and correction. The whole essay is worth reading for its close relevance in some of its details to the philosophical cast of Dickens's fiction; but of particular interest in the present context is what Hazlitt has to say in response to the idea of a calculation of interest which Bentham takes to be the spring of human action:

> What should Mr Bentham, sitting at ease in his armchair . . . know of the principles of action of rogues, outlaws and vagabonds? . . . If sanguine and tender-hearted philanthropists have set afoot an enquiry into the barbarity and defects of penal laws, the practical improvements have been mostly suggested by reformed cut-throats, turnkeys, and thief takers . . . if Newgate would resolve itself into a committee of the whole Press-yard, with Jack Ketch at its head, aided by confidential persons from the county prison or the Hulks, and would make a clean breast, some data might be found out to proceed upon; but as it is, the *criminal mind* of the country is a book sealed, no one has been able to penetrate to the inside!

Oliver Twist is an attempt to unseal the book of the criminal mind and is, at the same time, an attack on a Benthamite principle, the calculation of 'less eligibility' of the 1834 Poor Law Amendment Act, which I have outlined above on page 60. The two concerns do not entirely cohere, as the author's indignation at a serious social abuse gives way in the action to an imaginative exploration of two contrasting kinds of criminal mind; the reptilian deceit of Fagin and the brutal violence of Bill Sykes. Oliver's role, as we remember it from the story, is not that of the child who confronts Fagin in the condemned cell with the appeal to '. . . let me say a prayer. Do let me say one prayer. Say only one, upon your knees, with me, and we will talk till morning.' (Chapter 52) The passage is wildly improbable and quite unlike the early chapters in which the story of Oliver's sufferings is unfolded. At the beginning of the novel Dickens's satire is directed against the inhumanity of the conduct of the workhouse in its calculated hostility to the fact of Oliver's existence. His life is not merely unnecessary, it is an offence because it is a charge on public funds. He has no identity; his name was invented by Mr Bumble, the Beadle, and there is no indignity that he need be spared short of death at the hand of the chimney sweep to whom, for a moment, it is proposed to apprentice him. His dereliction is total; at the baby farm, at the workhouse under the Beadle's petty tyranny. It culminates in his apprenticeship as a child mourner to the local undertaker, where he is made to sleep among the coffins. He does not even know that he is an orphan, or what an orphan is, but forces the fact of his existence on the authority that denies it him by the simple device of asking for more to eat. As a result he is flogged on public occasions and put up for sale. His timorous and respectful, despairing yet courageous cry, 'Please, sir, I want some more,' has sunk deep into the English consciousness. Part of its power is that it is a sane and healthly response to the nightmare of undeserved and gratuitous suffering that Oliver somehow has to survive.

Oliver's innocence is obliged to survive if the character is to serve Dickens's other concern in the novel with the principle of goodness and the corrupting temptations of evil. From such promising beginnings as 'a Parish child — the orphan of a workhouse — the humble half-starved drudge — to be cuffed and buffeted through the world — despised by all, and pitied by none', his career might have been quite different. It might have been more like that of the convict Magwitch in *Great Expectations*, or nearer that of the Artful Dodger to whom it falls later in the novel to take up the protest made so powerfully on Oliver's behalf by the author in the earlier chapters. Like Magwitch, the Dodger is transported to a penal colony, which is presumably Australia, following his splendidly scornful performance in the face of what passes for justice at his trial. If the two major topics, that is the denial of innocence and the temptation of goodness, do not quite cohere, the novel is held together by a particular tone and style. It reads like a violent and primitive nightmare that the idyllic episodes and the ending do little to mitigate. I shall look more closely at the particular quality of the writing in Part Two, but it should perhaps be recalled just what an extraordinary achievement *Oliver Twist* was for a writer still only twenty-four, and how different an accomplishment from its equally successful forerunner, *The Pickwick Papers*.

Innocence and the world

I have suggested that I find little that is specific or persuasive about Oliver's settlement at the end of his story. Despite the long fever and illness brought on by his experiences, Oliver suffers no permanent damage as his author designed him to serve the particular ends which are stated in the Preface. It may also have been the case that Dickens himself wanted to think that all might turn out well in the end for the abused child. In a situation very similar to Oliver's, Smike the abandoned orphan of *Nicholas Nickleby* whom the hero befriends at the school where he is teaching, is denied his right to exist and ultimately dies of it. Smike's existence is literally denied by his father, the money-lender Ralph Nickleby. Nickleby had to keep secret the fact of his marriage for fear of losing his wife's property. The child of the marriage, who became Smike, had been sent to a boarding school in the north of England by Nickleby's agent who afterwards pretended that the child had died.

In turn, by a use of coincidence that seems to reassert connections that have been denied, Nicholas is sent to Dotheboys Hall by his miserly uncle Ralph, who is determined that the young man and his family shall not become a burden to him. Nicholas is to be an assistant to the school's brutal proprietor Wackford Squeers. He prevents Squeers from thrashing Smike by thrashing Squeers and takes Smike with him when he walks out, penniless and quite without prospects, to seek his fortune. From this point Nicholas is propelled through a series of picaresque adventures full of echoes of Fielding and Smollett before, by the aid of benevolence, he becomes a rich and famous merchant and can unmask the villainous Ralph by revealing to him the truth about Smike. Smike's knowledge of who he is, however, comes too late to save him from the wasting disease that is the consequence of his long years of neglect and harsh treatment. At his death he lies in an idyllic, pastoral landscape surrounded by his relations. He is too enfeebled by his experience of life to speak his love for his beautiful cousin, Nicholas's sister. It is as though in Dickens's next novel Oliver's sufferings and his special grace had been apportioned between two characters. Like Oliver, Nicholas has a special, invulnerable grace, and is acted upon rather than active in the pursuit of happiness and a comfortable accommodation in the world. But, if he is predetermined for success by the will of his author, it is the case that, when he does act, it is from motives of generosity and spontaneous good-heartedness. His special quality is constrasted with the vice of the uncle which leads directly to the latter's self-destruction. In many ways, by contrast and by coincidence, the woes and happinesses of human life are inextricably linked in *Nicholas Nickleby* and human benevolence cannot finally repair the waste caused by human vice and folly presented in Smike's life and death. The governing tone of the novel is comic but in his next novel of childhood suffering, Dickens sets out to reverse these proportions. In *The Old Curiosity Shop*, the comedy of Dick Swiveller's developing romance with the Marchioness is subordinated to the pathos of Little Nell's life of lonely responsibilities.

The Old Curiosity Shop

The novel began to form only uncertainly in Dickens's mind. His original intention was to write a short tale in several instalments to accompany the more miscellaneous articles and features that he was planning for his new weekly, *Master Humphrey's Clock*. The rapid drop in sales after the first issue soon persuaded him that his readers required a more sustained story from him and so he obliged them by enlarging the tale to occupy the whole of each number, glad enough to be embarked again on a story after chafing at the desultory character of the magazine he had designed for himself. Master Humphrey starts the novel off only to bow out awkwardly at the end of the third chapter. He was now redundant to Dickens's developing theme, although a great deal of the atmosphere with which his author surrounded the lonely, misshapen old clockmaker and his workshop remains in the setting of the novel. It is as though Dickens wants to exploit the contrast between the total innocence and goodness of the heroine and the atmosphere of the grotesque and the gothic by which her life is surrounded for the maximum aesthetic effect. As he wrote in the Preface to the first cheap edition, '. . . in writing the book, I had it always in my fancy to surround the lonely figure of the child with grotesque and wild, but not impossible companions, and to gather about her innocent face and pure intentions, associates as strange and uncongenial as the grim objects that are about her bed when her history is first fore-shadowed'.

At the same time, his plan is very consciously a moral one. 'Everything in our lives,' he writes in chapter fifty-three, 'whether of good or evil affects us most by contrast.' The force of this strategy drives him into trying to sustain throughout the novel a total and totally artificial separation between the two poles of the contrast, innocence and evil. Little Nell herself is propelled towards death by this very strategy. The world from which she has to flee is a world of torment to her and of irresistible temptation to her grandfather. Their wanderings lead them through a series of bizarre encounters each of which is intended to strengthen and justify Nell's desire to escape into a pastoral idyll. Here again, once arrived and safe, the life by which she is surrounded is offered in direct contrast to her young purity and innocence. It is, as we find in chapter fifty-three in the image of the exhausted well, a life which inevitably suffers exhaustion. Some passages in *The Old Curiosity Shop*, even whole chapters, are as fine as anything in Dickens, but it is impossible not to feel that the contrast which he set up for himself at the beginning simply does not hold up. There is, for example, nothing essential to the character of the story as it unfolds, in the 'grim objects' that stand about the shop owned by her grandfather where she lives. The objects are stage properties and the old grandfather, who gambles compulsively with the aim, as he thinks, of making the child's fortune, is too mechanically conceived ever to become credible to the reader. The material of what Dickens took to be his main conscious theme is similarly inert. As G. K. Chesterton wrote of the novel, what we object to is not the death of Little Nell, but her life. Again, she is an innocent whose virtue remains impervious to her experiences, although, like Smike, she dies of them. Yet it was Forster who had to point out to Dickens the inevitability of the child's death as the culmination of the tale. He was surely right as, for all its staginess, what holds the material together is the sense of death. Even the mourners at her grave-side, evoked not at all as individuals but as abstract and generalised personifications of age and youth, are more dead than alive as Dickens calls them up before us:

> And now the bell — the bell she had so often heard by night and day, and listened to with solemn pleasure almost as a living voice — rang its remorseless toll for her, so young, so beautiful, so good. Decrepit age, and vigorous life, and blooming youth, and helpless infancy, poured forth, on crutches, in the pride of strength and health, in the full blush of promise, in the mere dawn of life, together at her tomb. Old men were there whose eyes were dim and senses failing, grandmothers who might have died ten years ago, and still been old — the deaf, the blind, the lame, the palsied, the living dead in many shapes and forms, to see the closing of that early grave. What was the death it would shut in, to that which could still crawl and creep above it:
>
> (*chapter 72*)

That last sentence tells us what meaning it was that the author wanted to achieve in this paragraph of mournful iambics: the contrast between the dead child and the living who perhaps could have been more easily sacrificed. Yet the catalogue that precedes it evokes a procession of the halt, the blind and the enfeebled which also creates in the reader the effect of death rather than of life. Youthful life is perfunctorily acknowledged in a few platitudinous phrases in the passage, but forces its way to the surface elsewhere in the novel. Dick Swiveller is a lesser, comic Orpheus and the story of his successful rescue of the Marchioness from the underworld of Samson Brass's kitchen has elements of legend and fairytale to set off against the gloomy story of Little Nell. Dick possesses the gift of life and, by giving it to the Marchioness, creates for himself a wife and a life. While it would be difficult to argue similarly of Daniel Quilp, the monstrous dwarf, that he also represents life rather than death, he claims much more of the reader's attention than he would seem to warrant were he only to remain the gargoyle carved on the gothic edifice which Dickens originally intended should enshrine and sanctify Nell's innocence and passivity. Quilp is clearly a monster and not a human being, as his indifference to all sensations and sensitivities shows. He gulps down fiery liquids and can strike himself with as much violence as he ceaselessly offers others. Nevertheless, the tormenting imp does represent in his irrepressible frenzy a principle of life, its aggression and its sexuality, which Dickens suppressed in the materials and figures of his major action. Quilp's glee in mischief even when he is at his most sadistic is as uninhibited as his energetic career of malice. What he threatens, or so it has seemed to many modern readers, is the subversion of Dickens's conscious resolve which was, as he wrote to Forster when he had finished the writing:

> . . . to try and do something which might be read by people about whom Death had been, with a softened feeling, and with consolation.

The story of Dickens's own grief at having to write the ending is very well known: 'Dear Mary died yesterday when I think of this sad story.' He overwhelmed his readers in an extraordinanry flood of emotion at what must be thought of as a climactic moment, not only in Dickens's career, but also in the history of nineteenth-century English society. The success of the novel secured for him an international reputation and brought him into a powerful and intimate relationship with his readers which, for all the later fluctuations of his sales, he never again lost.

What nerve had Dickens touched on to provoke so sensational a response? Admittedly, to judge from Dickens and his friends, Victorian society laughed heartily and wept copiously, but the special quality articulated in the death of Nell seems to be, not so much an acknowledgement of the grief at child mortality which was a universal fact in that society, as a recognition of the irreconcilability of innocence and the world. Little Nell's death forced on readers the knowledge that, in the world of their experience, there was no place for her. She could only die, and with her was buried the myth of that idyllic, pastoral England the innocence of which

Dickens had celebrated in the pages of *The Pickwick Papers*. Such is the loss that was universally mourned in the work of a writer whose gift it was equally, as we shall see in the next chapter, to make conscious to his society the condition of modern, urban man.

Dombey and Son

When, in *Dombey and Son*, Dickens turns again to child death, it is with as great an effect but with very different purposes to be served. Paul Dombey is not an innocent child. Everyone around him knows his 'old-fashionedness'; he has a continuously observant knowingness in his relations with others which is more like children in the plays of Shakespeare than the child of the poems of the English Romantics. Furthermore, Paul's death occurs only a quarter of the way into the novel at the centre of which is the unyielding figure of Dombey Senior who must be brought to see that 'Dombey and Son is a daughter after all'. From the very moment of his birth, Paul's life had been dedicated to his father's ambition to have a son follow him, as he had followed his father, into the family business house.

> Those three words ['Dom-bey and Son'] conveyed the one idea of Mr Dombey's life. The earth was made for Dombey and Son to trade in, the sun and moon were made to give them light. Rivers and seas were formed to float their ships; rainbows gave them promise of fair weather; winds blew for or against their enterprises; stars and planets circled in their orbits to preserve inviolate a system of which they were the centre.
>
> (*chapter 1*)

It is a destiny in which Paul's older sister, Florence, has no role, and in which his mother is redundant, since she dies at the moment of his birth. From that moment, the natural flow of the child's life is channelled by his father's 'one idea' in conformity with the 'inviolate system' of the House of Dombey. Nature itself has no meaning other than to serve that system, and his father's plans and projects for him supplant reality. Feeble as he is, little Paul's flow of life is dammed and perverted by his father's pride. Despite the response that he can make to the show of love offered by his sister and by Polly Toodle, his wet-nurse and second mother, he grows, in as much as he grows at all, into a perverted kind of life:

> Thus Paul grew to be nearly five years old. He was a pretty little fellow though there was something wan and wistful in his small face, that gave occasion to many significant shakes of Mrs Wickam's head, and many long-drawn inspirations of Mrs Wickam's breath. His temper gave abundant promise of being imperious in after life; and he had as hopeful an apprehension of

his own importance, and the rightful subservience of all other things and persons to it, as heart could desire. He was childish and sportive enough at times, and not of a sullen disposition; but he had a strange, old-fashioned, thoughtful way, at other times, of sitting brooding in his miniature arm-chair, when he looked (and talked) like one of those terrible little Beings in the Fairy tales, who, at a hundred and fifty or two hundred years of age, fantastically represent the children for whom they have been substituted. He would frequently be stricken with this precocious mood up-stairs in the nursery; and would sometimes lapse into it suddenly, exclaiming that he was tired: even while playing with Florence, or driving Miss Tox in single harness. But at no time did he fall into it so surely, as when, his little chair being carried down into his father's room, he sat there with him after dinner, by the fire. They were the strangest pair at such a time that ever firelight shone upon. Mr Dombey so erect and solemn, gazing at the blaze; his little image, with an old, old, face, peering into the red perspective with the fixed and rapt attention of a sage. Mr Dombey entertaining complicated worldly schemes and plans; the little image entertaining Heaven knows what wild fancies, half-formed thoughts, and wandering speculations. Mr Dombey stiff with starch and arrogance; the little image by inheritance, and in unconscious imitation. The two so very much alike, and yet so monstrously contrasted.

On one of these occasions, when they had both been perfectly quiet for a long time, and Mr Dombey only knew that the child was awake by occasionally glancing at his eye, where the bright fire was sparkling like a jewel, little Paul broke silence thus:

'Papa what's money?'

The abrupt question had such immediate reference to the subject of Mr Dombey's thoughts, that Mr Dombey was quite disconcerted.

'What is money, Paul?' he answered. 'Money?'

'Yes,' said the child, laying his hands upon the elbows of his little chair, and turning the old face up towards Mr Dombey's; 'what is money?'

Mr Dombey was in a difficulty. He would have liked to give him some explanation involving the terms circulating-medium, currency, depreciation of currency, paper, bullion, rates of exchange, value of precious metals in the market, and so forth; but looking down at the little chair, and seeing what a long way down it was, he answered: 'Gold, and silver, and copper. Guineas, shillings, half-pence. You know what they are?'

'Oh yes, I know what they are,' said Paul. 'I don't mean that, Papa. I mean, what's money after all.'

Heaven and Earth, how old his face was as he turned it up again towards his father's

'What is money after all' said Mr Dombey, backing his chair a little, that he might the better gaze in sheer amazement at the presumptuous atom that propounded such an inquiry.

'I mean, Papa, what can it do?' returned Paul, folding his arms (they were hardly long enough to fold), and looking at the fire, and up at him, and at the fire, and up at him again.

Mr Dombey drew his chair back to its former place, and patted him on the head. 'You'll know better by and by, my man,' he said. 'Money, Paul, can do anything.' He took hold of the little hand, and beat it softly against one of his own as he said so.

But Paul got his hand free as soon as he could; and rubbing it gently to and fro on the elbow of his chair, as if his wit were in the palm, and he were sharpening it — and looking at the fire again, as though the fire had been his adviser and prompter — repeated, after a short pause:

'Anything, Papa?'

'Yes. Anything — almost,' said Mr Dombey.

'Anything means everything, don't it, Papa?' asked his son: not observing, or possibly not understanding, the qualification.

'It includes it: yes,' said Mr Dombey.

'Why didn't money save me my Mama?' returned the child. 'It isn't cruel, is it?'

'Cruel' said Mr Dombey, settling his neckcloth, and seeming to resent the idea. 'No. A good thing can't be cruel.'

'If it's a good thing, and can do anything,' said the little fellow, thoughtfully, as he looked back at the fire, 'I wonder why it didn't save me my Mama.'

He didn't ask the question of his father this time. Perhaps he had seen, with a child's quickness, that it had already made his father uncomfortable. But he repeated the thought aloud, as if it were quite an old one to him, and had troubled him very much; and sat with his chin resting on his hand, still cogitating and looking for an explanation in the fire.

Mr Dombey having recovered from his surprise, not to say his alarm (for it was the very first occasion on which the child had ever broached the subject of his mother to him, though he had had him sitting by his side, in this same manner, evening after evening), expounded to him how that money, though a very potent spirit, never to be disparaged on any account whatever, could not keep people alive whose time was come to die; and how that we must all die, unfortunately, even in the City, though we were never so rich. But how that money caused us to be honoured feared, respected, courted, and admired, and made us powerful and glorious in the eyes of all men; and how that it could, very often, even keep off death, for a long time together. How, for example, it had secured to his Mama the services of Mr Pilkins, by which he, Paul, had often profited himself; likewise of the great Doctor Parker Peps, whom he had never known. And how it could do all, that could be done. This, with more to the same purpose, Mr Dombey instilled into the mind of his son, who listened attentively, and seemed to understand the greater part of what was said to him.

'It can't make me strong and quite well, either, Papa; can it?' asked Paul, after a short silence: rubbing his tiny hands.

'Why, you are strong and quite well,' returned Mr Dombey. 'Are you not?'

(*chapter 8*)

In this splendid passage, father and son make a monstrous pair. Mr Dombey's life and world, rendered in metaphors of an arctic chilliness, are unnatural. From the first pages which recount the birth of his son and the death of his first wife, he is presented as incapable of dealing with the kind of life that manifests itself in feeling and spontaneity:

He was not a man of whom it could properly be said that he was ever startled or shocked; but he certainly had a sense within him that if his wife should sicken and decay, he would be very sorry, and that he would find a something gone from amongst his plate and furniture, and other household possessions, which was well worth the having, and could not be lost without sincere regret. Though it would be a cool, business-like, gentlemanly, self-possessed regret, no doubt.

(*chapter 1*)

And so the son, who shares something of the father's repellent inflexibility, is directed ironically into precisely that career, short-lived as it is, which will deny him the kind of life that is essential to childhood, and of which, in his feeble natural state, he stands in special need. At Brighton, where he is sent for the sea air and the good of his uncertain health, Paul is delivered into the hands of the 'ogress and child-queller' Mrs Pipchin, whose 'castle' stood 'in a steep by-street . . . where the soil was more than usually chalky, flinty and sterile' and for whom, finally, he is more than a match. His goblin stare unnerves her, and the unfeeling directness of his questions and observations routs her totally, so that she is obliged to leave him to the solitude which he prefers and which, until it is time for him to go to school, he shares with Florence.

The forcing house that is Dr Blimber's Academy occasions some of Dickens's most telling satire of nineteenth-century education. But the episode is at the same time poignant and rich in a poetic economy. After his first interview with Blimber Paul is left alone in the Doctor's study while his father is shown the school:

> And there, with an aching void in his young heart, and all outside so cold, and bare, and strange, Paul sat as if he had taken life unfurnished, and the upholsterers were never coming.
>
> (*chapter 11*)

Life unfurnished is what the Blimbers provide; stuffed with academic aridity and empty of warmth and imagination. What Paul knows when he knows nothing of Latin grammar is what Old Glubb used to tell him about the sea:

> 'He's a very nice old man, ma'am,' he said. 'He used to draw my couch. He knows all about the deep sea, and the fish that are in it and the great monsters that come and lie on the rocks in the sun, and dive into the water again when they're startled, blowing and splashing so that they can be heard for miles. There are some creatures,' said Paul, warming with his subject, 'I don't know how many yards long, and I forget their names, but Forence knows, that pretend to be in distress; and when a man goes near them, out of compassion, they open their great jaws, and attack him. But all he has got to do,' said Paul, boldly tendering this information to the very Doctor himself, 'is to keep on turning as he runs away, and then, as they turn slowly, because they are so long, and can't bend, he's sure to beat them. And though Old Glubb don't know why the sea should make me think of my mama that's dead, or what it is that it is always saying — always saying! We knows a great deal about it. And I wish,' the child concluded, with a sudden falling of his countenance, and failing in his animation, as he looked like one forlorn, upon the three strange faces, 'that you'd let Old Glubb come here to see me, for I know him very well, and he knows me.'
>
> 'Ha' said the Doctor, shaking his head, 'this is bad, but study will do much.'
>
> (*chapter 12*)

But Blimber's notions of education will not answer Paul's question about what the sea is saying, nor do anything but crush what little brain pupils, such as Mr Toots, originally possessed. Something of the answer to Paul's question is given in the novel by young Walter Gay, an orphan, brought up by his uncle the nautical instrument maker and his hook-handed companion Captain Cuttle. For Walter, the sea stands for mystery and adventure, danger and temptation, a challenge to his energy and imagination. It does not have for him that enjoyable terror that Paul has taken from Old Glubb; although Old Glubb's tales, if Paul has understood and reported them correctly, have at least stirred what childish imagination he possesses. It is a moment of intense pathos when, in reply to Dr Blimber's platitude, 'Shall we make a man of him?' Paul's reply is 'I had rather be a child.'

In this novel the child, or the idea of childhood, represents the whole of life that Mr Dombey has repudiated and replaced by pride and arrogance. Dickens announced that he wanted in *Dombey and Son* to do for pride what its predecessor, *Martin Chuzzlewit*, had done for selfishness. But, in examining the experiences and deprivations of little Paul, we catch a glimpse of what lies behind Dombey Senior's frozen stiffness, and it is a measure of the quality of Dickens's imaginative insight into the growing Victorian world of money and finance that he obliges us to look behind the appearances of pride and wealth. Dombey, as Dickens has created him, fears the expressive life which, for the romantic writer, is most purely exemplified in the lives of children, and has converted into the objective relationship of hard cash all natural human expressiveness and warmth of feeling. He cannot, and it is a small example, bring himself to utter the words 'my love' to his wife at the birth of his son,

'He will be christened Paul, my — Mrs Dombey — of course.'

and his second marriage is a business transaction. Edith Grainger is like himself, cold and haughty. She never was a child, as she reports, but only the instrument of her mother's dealings in the marriage market. The marriage broker, Major Joey Bagstock, is an intensely wrought portrait of the loathsome aggressively masculine man who may well be sexually impotent: an appropriate companion to the emotionally frozen Dombey.

It is as well for Florence that her own mother was never quite a Dombey. She represents that fund of warmth and love which is proper to human relationships as these are exemplified in the novel in the relationship between parents and children. Although Paul dies early in the novel, its imaginative centre is located in that relationship which has been denied by Dombey. Instead he has immured himself within a substitute world of money and business as an escape from the responsibility for relationships, from the contingencies of life and from time and accident to which all life is subject. He is defeated by the inner world where he took himself to be so secure through his wife's act of revenge, and it is only when he has been stripped of everything he possesses and is contemplating suicide that his restoration can begin. Florence is its necessary agent. The closing paragraphs are set on the sea shore where he walks with Florence and her children years later when, 'the white-haired gentleman likes best to see the child free and stirring . . .'

Dombey and Son represents a new seriousness in Dickens's creative development. The novel is written on a single theme, planned in advance and, although he changed his original intention that Walter Gay should trail away towards dissipation and ruin, it is free of the improvisation that he had often been driven to in his earlier work. He wrote it consciously 'with the drag on', curbing his exuberant inventiveness, achieving thereby a new, graver tone. Nevertheless, the final effect is uneven; he was writing in different places, Geneva and Lausanne, Paris and London, and interrupted himself in order to produce his Christmas Book for 1846, *The Battle of Life*. The reader can scarcely fail to notice the inadequacy of those chapters which deal directly with the career of Edith Dombey. The very theme of revenge suggests the melodramatic exaggerations with which Dickens surrounds her, and which are absent from the most effective passages and chapters elsewhere in the novel. Despite the occasional unconscious slide at moments of high pathos into something very like Wordsworthian blank verse, the central theme of Dombey's domestic relations is evoked with an astonishing range of supple and restrained prose and descriptions of poetic intensity. I have chosen one short passage for particular comment (see page 120–1) which shows at the same time Dickens's achieved mastery of the technique of stream-of-consciousness. At heightened moments the reader is inside the mind of little Paul, and, perhaps equally worthy of note, inside the mind of Carker as he flees from his pursuer Dombey towards his death.

Incidents from common life: David Copperfield

I have suggested above that the world of Dombey is essentially domestic, the novel an evocation of private feelings and personal relationships. Dickens's novel is a quite unparalleled celebration of the everyday and the domestic, the transformation of the incidents of common life into great art. It is as though, in *David Copperfield*, Dickens had set out deliberately to follow Wordsworth's prescription for his own poetry: 'to choose incidents and situations from common life, and to relate or describe them, throughout, as far as was possible, in a selection of language really used by men, and at the same time, to throw over them a certain colouring of imagination'. The novel is rich in metaphors and similes drawn from common experience; Yarmouth, for example, would have been nicer to David's very young eyes on his first visit with Peggotty 'if the town and tide had not been quite so mixed up, like toast and water'. The other major source of metaphor is that characteristically Dickensian well of imaginative nourishment, the world of fairy-tale and the oriental stories from *Tales of the Genii*. In his pursuit of Dora's love what he must do, David affirmed to himself, was to 'take my woodman's axe in my hand, and clear my own way through the forest of difficulty, by cutting down the trees until I came to Dora'. After the shattering of his first love for Dora and his affection for Steerforth, David contemplates the blank and waste of 'the whole airy castle of my life'.

David Copperfield remained Dickens's 'favourite child', and George Orwell reports that when he first read it, at the age of nine or so, he felt that the first hundred pages must have been written by a child. Many readers have assumed since Forster first revealed the close parallels in his *Life* that the book is a thinly-disguised autobiography and that David is the young Charles Dickens who, like his author, survives inauspicious beginnings to become a famous and distinguished author. Forster quotes from the autobiographical fragment Dickens wrote for him a year earlier in order to show just how close the parallels are. Yet it seems to me that if one does read *David Copperfield* as romanticised autobiography, one then misses the whole fictional and imaginative experience. Dickens's own view, expressed in a letter to Forster, was that he had achieved in the writing an ingenious and 'very complicated interweaving of truth and fiction'.

Forster's own view of the novel distinguishes David from his author most forcefully, and then goes on to see it as an account of David's life in which, as we read, we rediscover our own childhood and make for ourselves a secret accompanying autobiography. This universalising experience alone should convince us that what we are reading is a product of invention and not a personal history. For the rest, Forster draws attention to the marvellous cavalcade of characters and emphasises the appearance of spontaneity that is a great part of the peculiar charm of the novel. He also makes an important point when he asserts that 'the incidents arise easily, and to the very end connect themselves naturally and unobtrusively with the characters of which they are a part . . . but unity of drift or purpose is apparent always, and the tone is uniformly right'. The purpose he conceives somewhat narrowly and moralistically as a lesson in the value of self-denial and patience, the strengthening of our generous emotions and the protection of the domestic virtues; whereas it seems to me that Dickens's imaginative vision is wider than that which would limit it to the development of the character of the narrator.

The first person recollection of a past history is a valuable formal fictional device which Dickens employs to stunning effect. Yet it is not a single history which is recollected in the unfolding of the novel. Central to the structure of *David Copperfield* is the simple arrangement of the leading characters. Three male children are brought up by doting mothers. None of them has a proper father. The structure is completed, in a fashion as symmetrical as anything in Jane Austen's fiction, by balancing them against three girls, each brought up by a doting father or, more properly in the case of Little Emily, by a doting substitute father. Each imperfect relationship is characterised by an unqualified love on the part of the parent. It is as though, following an exploration in *Dombey and Son* of the consequences of the denial of love, Dickens has now turned his attention to its affirmation in an abundant variety of forms. Again, each of the three young men is drawn from each of the three social classes. Steerforth (as his name implies) has wealth, position and power and the unqualified support of his mother in their employment. Uriah Heep, in contrast, has been severely schooled in the exercise of humility and propitiation of all those who 'are higher' in the social 'heap'. There are risks involved in the attempt to spell out the symbolism inherent in fictional names; yet no names in fiction are neutral, and certainly no writer has contributed more than Dickens to the common language by way of the names he fixed with inexhaustible appropriateness to a host of his fictional characters. Grimwig, Fang and Bumble are names in the tradition of the comedy of Shakespeare and Ben Jonson, but as Dickens develops so the names, especially those of his comic characters, become less allegorical, more allusive and poetic. *Oliver Twist* is particularly rich in this respect. The Biblical Uriah was the husband of Bathsheba, whom the King seduced. The King was David, and, co-incidental as it may be, Dickens's juxtaposition of the two names does suggest the sexual rivalry that exists between them; a rivalry the roots of which David Copperfield has difficulty in acknowledging in himself.

The symmetry is completed when we realise that the three young women with whom they become involved are equally distributed to roles within the three social classes. That the arrangement could scarcely be unconscious leads me to speculate further that, in making it, Dickens was posing the question of what life chances were possible to the young man of each class; or perhaps, having settled finally on the name and framework of David's life and development, the question posed itself in a different way. What, the question might run, would this boy's chances have been had he been born into the upper or the lowest class? Steerforth and Heep then become fantasy projections of David's own self, embracing those aspects of the self that David would consciously repudiate.

Even if, in one's experience of reading the novel, the scheme I am suggesting is scarcely apparent and of little importance to the way in which one reads, it does at least have two important consequences. Firstly, it frees the reader to consider the work as a product of the novelist's creative imagination and not identify too closely the narrating voice of the adult David with that of Charles Dickens the writer. The importance of making the distinction is that it confirms one's sense that Dickens does not always endorse David's judgment of an event or another character. The clearest example of David's frequent misperceptions is the case of Tommy Traddles who, if anyone is, is the model in the novel of hard-working patience and endurance finally rewarded. To see as much, however, the reader is obliged to stand off, as Dickens surely did, from David's continuously patronising tone when he recalls his friend. The second consequence is that the arrangement does suggest a way of connecting the child and the adult David. Many readers have found unsatisfactory David's settlement into the life of the distinguished novelist with the wise and virtuous Agnes, more angel than woman, for his second wife. It is perhaps not surprising that we hear so little about what it might be like to be a novelist. Dickens's attention at the end of the novel is directed elsewhere, to answering in fact, the question that my view of the structure of the novel suggests he set out from: what chances in life inhere in the different social classes? David is set between the extremes of Steerforth and Uriah Heep, both of whom are invested with a great deal of their author's creative power. Steerforth enjoys too much freedom of the will, which is an essential element of his Byronic attractiveness. Nothing he does repays David's admiration and adoration, yet, even when he has betrayed the trust that everyone who comes across him is drawn into offering him, David, in chapter thirty-two admits freely that 'if I had been brought face to face with him, I could not have uttered one reproach, I should have loved him — still —'.

The circumstances of Steerforth's death make no difference to the feeling, even though that which helped to make him so attractive has destroyed him. Heep, on the other hand, is an Oliver Twist who has suffered the consequences of an early long suppression. Humility has become for him a way of dealing with the world, a source of pride and vengeful power as he explains to an unwilling David in chapter thirty-nine. '"Be 'umble, Uriah," says father to me, "and you'll get on. It was what was always being dinned into you and me at school; it's what goes down best. Be 'umble," says father, "and you'll do" and really it ain't done bad.' The reader, like David finds Heep, with his clammy chill and serpentine calculation, an object of loathsome fascination. We rejoice in the comedy of his unmasking by Micawber. David's character, however, is not fixed in the same way. As the narrator and the leading character who questions with his opening words whether he is to be the hero of his own story, he is a combination of nature and accident, and therefore kept deliberately by his author more open to the influences of experience and of other characters. By nature he seems timid and, even though he takes an intuitive dislike to his mother's new suitor, Mr Murdstone, trustful. The trait, as Betsy Trotwood scornfully points out at her first comic appearance for the birth, is inherited from his father who had called his house The Rookery on the evidence of the nests alone. We see it at work when he allows the waiter to eat his dinner at the inn where the coach stops that is taking him to school, and again, at school where one of his first acts is obligingly to hand over all his money to Steerforth for a feast. Otherwise he is the wax on which experience seals its impression; a history which encompasses the extreme contrast of paradisial love and a total denial of his right to an autonomous existence by his mother's second husband.

Wonderfully evocative as they are, the early chapters of the novel never transgress the ordinary and limited possibilities of everyday existence. It is the extraordinary visualisation and dramatic rendering which give them an unparalleled vivacity and charm. They require little in the way of commentary except perhaps to indicate that they encompass the varieties of love and its denial. Nevertheless, it is the case that many of these kinds of love fail to secure and enhance life adequately. David's mother, unlike his nurse Peggotty, is not much more than a doll-like figure of vanity. '"What was it they said, Davy? Tell me again . . . it was never bewitching," she said, laughing. "It never could have been bewitching, Davy. Now I know it wasn't!"' Her love is quite unable to spare David Mr Murdstone's idea of firmness and discipline. What refuge he has is with Peggotty and the small collection of books upstairs which 'kept alive my fancy and my hope of something beyond that time and place . . . reading as if for dear life'. Thus Dickens makes the case for fantasy and imagination as essential nourishment for a child. They enable David to survive and, later, in the company of Mr Dick at Dover and Canterbury, are kept alive by the games they play and by their kite flying.

Again, Mr and Mrs Micawber certainly love each other loyally and devotedly, yet it in no way serves to stem the comic haplessness of their married life. Similarly, Rosa Dartle's repressed passion for Steerforth provides only violence and injury. David's marriage to Dora, a child-wife very like his child-mother, is a fairy tale of great enchantment in its tender and humorous unfolding. Yet when David once begins to discipline himself to the serious task of his life as a writer, the enchantment begins to fade. What destroys it is the series of scenes he witnesses between his old schoolmaster from the settled Canterbury days, Dr Strong, and his wife Annie, which seems to present him with the troubling possibility of marital infidelity. Dr Strong is an old, preoccupied scholar with a young, attractive wife. At this point Dickens comes near to breaking the dramatic illusion that the narrating voice has created around us when he repeats insistently the phrase Mrs Strong uses in her explanation 'There can be no disparity in marriage like unsuitability of mind and purpose'. Until that moment in the novel, the novel's meaning has been carried by character and incident, but the insistence on the phrase and the one which follows it when Annie thanks her husband 'for having saved me from the first mistaken impulse of my undisciplined heart', forces on David, and on the reader, a new perspective on his existence. With it comes an acknowledgement of his own undisciplined heart in his marriage and in his affection for Steerforth. The death of Dora, the unmasking of Heep and Steerforth's drowning in the storm off Yarmouth all coincide. David is wearing mourning for his wife as he goes to tell Mrs Steerforth the news of her son's death.

It is now that Dickens completes his not altogether satisfactory answer to the question of life chances. Through breakdown and a very Wordsworthian restoration among the mountains of Switzerland, David is brought to see that his love for Agnes is more than fraternal admiration and affection for her angelic qualities. (It should be noted that Wordsworth's *Prelude* was first published in July 1850 as Dickens was writing the later parts of *David Copperfield*. If it is only a coincidence, then it is a quite remarkable one. My own feeling is that Dickens read the poem when it appeared.) The personal qualities that enable one to survive the loss of childhood fantasy and innocence in order to achieve maturity and success are those which Forster has listed for us and which Dickens has appended to Agnes, although perhaps not in a fashion which would quite convince us.

The after-image of *David Copperfield* that the memory retains is not of its ending and the working out of Dickens's serious purposes, but of its earlier chapters which follow in detail the apparently random and picaresque adventures of the younger David. What stay in the mind are the scenes of his mother's total but ineffectual love, of Jane Murdstone's cruelty and aggression which, as Dickens hints powerfully, stem from her sexual frustration; of Salem House and the humiliation of the blacking factory, of the wonder and mystery to the child of the varieties of adult relationships. The marvellous strengths of the novel lie here and in those moments which fire the child's fantasy. Perhaps the most memorable example of these is his first sight of the Peggotty home at Yarmouth, the captivation of which is that it is a 'real boat which had never been intended to be lived in, on dry land'. This is its 'charm' and the idea of living in it is 'romantic'. It is like 'Aladdin's palace, roc's egg and all'. From Dickens's description and David's first reaction to it, it would appear that Phiz's illustration showing the boat upside down must be wrong. The charm can only be complete if the boat *could* sail away, as indeed it does in a later dream that David has of Uriah as a pirate sailing it away. The significance of the novel resides in such occasions rather than in any prescriptive catalogue of virtues such as Forster offers; the beginnings of the moral life are located firmly in fantasy and early experience.

Childhood and the later novels

Bleak House and *Little Dorrit*, although they are not novels about childhood, should be noted in this chapter. It may well be the case that the writing of each was triggered by Dickens's contemporary preoccupations; the condition of the law in the former, the inefficiency of government administration in the latter. At the same time, however, they do show a continuity with and development of the concerns that Dickens had explored in *David Copperfield* in that they are concerned with the growth of the self from earliest experiences into relations with others in the larger society. In both novels the personal past and the past of society bear heavily on the present. The plot of each pivots on the recovery of information buried in the past which is essential to the life of the central character and which has always been withheld. The disclosure of the information reveals the cause of the history of suffering and unhappiness.

That her birth is a mystery connected with her overwhelming sense of isolation is clear to Esther Summerson from the beginning of her portion of the narrative of *Bleak House*. In chapter three she relates briefly the story of her upbringing until the moment at which the novel properly begins in the Court of Chancery, where the endless suit of *Jarndyce* v. *Jarndyce* is being heard. Despite Esther's denial that she has any particular literary competence — she knows she is not clever — Dickens makes every word tell forcefully in a complete and concise account of the early history of this dispossessed child. In other respects she is presented as an ordinary girl. David Copperfield, in the first sentence of his narrative, suggests that we should not look upon him as a hero, and that the action which follows is unlikely to be heroic in any conventional literary sense but, in Esther's case, the difference between her history and that of any other ordinary girl is determining. She has been brought up by her godmother, her aunt as it soon turns out, who has assumed the all-too apposite name of Miss Barbary, to be conscious of her isolation and of a terrible, unexplained restraint that lies on her. She is made to feel 'guilty yet innocent' by her godmother's revelation to her on her birthday that:

'Your mother, Esther, is your disgrace, and you were
hers. The time will come — and soon enough — when
you will understand this better, ... Forget your mother
and leave all other people to forget her who will do
her unhappy child that greatest kindness . . . submission,
self-denial, diligent work, are the preparations for
a life begun with such a shadow on it. You are
different from other children, Esther, because you

were not born, like them, in common sinfulness and
wrath. You are set apart.'

Like that of the Murdstones, this gloomy puritanical theology denies
to the girl her right to exist, but its parade of goodness persuades
Esther that she herself must be bad. She reacts to her sense that her
existence is her own fault by deliberately submitting herself to the
exacting programme of submission and self-denial that her
godmother prescribes for her: 'to do some good to someone, and to
win some love to myself if I could'. It is almost as though in
portraying Esther Summerson, Dickens has set out to give a plausible motivation to a life very like that of Agnes Wickfield in *David
Copperfield*. For they are very similar; they both discipline themselves
to putting up with the role, which is imposed on them, of little
housekeeper, jangling a bunch of household keys at the waist. Some
critics have thought as little of Esther's credibility as of Agnes's, but
it seems to me that her motivation is firmly and economically established and that her deliberate choice of that particular strategy for
survival is vindicated by her final achievement of happiness against
the odds.

We are continuously reminded that it is a conscious strategy by
the string of alternative names that others affix to her as though she
were their object. Esther is not herself, nor is she allowed to be. The
objectification has already begun in the treatment she receives from
her godmother and from the housekeeper, Mrs Rachel, as she is
removed from her home after her godmother's death. The letter
from the legal office, with its clipped instructional tone and visualised abbreviations that Dickens is careful to reproduce exactly in
appearance, reflects not merely legal whimsicality but also this same
attitude of treating persons as though they were things. We shall see
in the commentary on *Great Expectations* that the conversion of
persons into objects or instruments is central to Dickens's indictment of a whole emerging society. If further evidence were needed
of what Esther's choice cost her, then it is to be found in the
confusing dreams she suffers during her weeks of illness with the
fever that is being spread through the land:

At once a child, an elder girl, and the little woman I have been
so happy as, I was not only oppressed by cares and difficulties
adapted to each station, but by the great perplexity of endlessly
trying to reconcile them ... I am almost afraid to hint at that
time in my disorder ... when I laboured up colossal staircases,
ever striving to reach the top.

Dare I hint at that worse time when strung together somewhere
in great black space, there was a flaming necklace, or a ring, or
starry circle of some kind, of which *I* was one of the beads? And

when my only prayer was to be taken off from the rest, and when it was such inexplicable agony and misery to be a part of the dreadful thing?

(chapter 35)

The nightmare of not belonging to oneself is remarkably similar to a dream that Pip has in *Great Expectations* during his breakdown (see Part Two, p. 152). But Esther survives to marry Allan Woodcourt, the doctor who is to become 'a medical attendant for the poor . . . an appointment to a great amount of work and a small amount of pay; but better things will gather about it, it may be fairly hoped' as Mr John Jarndyce, her later guardian, first reports the matter to her. Esther's life in the future, as in the past, will be dedicated to the service of others. Therein lie her happiness and her fulfilment, although to reduce her life to a sermon on the virtue of self-denial is to be blind to the context of life and other lives in which it is portrayed. The fate of Miss Flite is a marvellous counter-example.

Bleak House, with its divided narration, reaches out to wider extremes of society than Dickens had attempted in any previous work. The extremes are held together by the case in Chancery and the related, governing mystery of Esther's origins. They include the aristocratic great house in Lincolnshire, seat of Sir Leicester Dedlock, and the slums of London. Tom-all-Alone's is a slum property in the case and the source of the disease which many die of and which disfigures Esther. Jo, the crossing sweeper who inhabits the slum, is at the very edge of this social panorama:

> dirty, ugly, disagreeable to all the senses, in body a common creature of the streets, only in soul a heathen. Homely filth begrimes him, homely parasites devour him, homely sores are in him, homely rags are on him: native ignorance, the growth of English soil and climate, sinks his immortal nature lower than the beasts that perish. Stand forth, Jo, in uncompromising colours From the sole of thy foot to the crown of thy head, there is nothing interesting about thee.

Jo, whom Allan Woodcourt's professional and humanitarian instincts attempt to rescue from a death in utter dereliction, is Dickens's bleakest childhood portrait; an uninteresting and negligible element in the 'condition-of-England question' that the novel surveys, yet one which raises Dickens's voice to an angry and impressive indignation. There are other neglected children in the same novel; notably the young Smallweeds who seem never to have been children, and the younger brother and sister of Charley, whom Esther and Mr Jarndyce rescue from a life of drudgery. Mrs Jelleby works for philanthropic schemes on behalf of the heathen natives of Borrioboola-Gha to the neglect of her own young family. Philanthropists like Mrs Pardiggle who work on home ground are no better either to their own children or to the victims of their ministrations. It is a sorry and indignant catalogue, but there is one curious portrait in this novel that provides a sour commentary on a tendency, not always easy to overcome, to sentimentalise children and Dickens's attitude to them and their experience. Bearing in mind the quotation from *David Copperfield* on p. 92 at the beginning of this chapter, the figure of Harold Skimpole represents in this novel the child who has refused to grow up. Skimpole, a beneficiary like Esther of Mr Jarndyce's goodness, is an intelligent, amusing, gifted entertainer. Whether or not he was taken, as many contemporary readers thought, from Dickens's friend Leigh Hunt the essayist, poet and mentor of John Keats, Skimpole is a brilliantly conceived and executed contrast to Esther's chosen discipline of submission. Skimpole rejects any notion of responsibilities, even for himself, transforming them into occasions for light-hearted and often genuinely witty aesthetic contemplation. Trained as a doctor, he was too lazy to practise, having 'no head for detail' and acts, therefore, as a foil to Allan Woodcourt. Esther finds Jo and brings him home in a state of high fever. Skimpole is all for putting him out:

> 'My dear Jarndyce . . . I am a child. Be cross to me, if I deserve it, but I have a constitutional objection to this sort of thing. I always had, when I was a medical man. He's not safe, you know. There's a very bad fever about him.'

> *(chapter 31)*

It is Inspector Bucket, the detective who finally solves the mystery of Esther's birth, who also finally places Skimpole for her, and for us readers:

> 'Whenever a person proclaims to you "In wordly matters I'm a child", you consider that person is only a-crying off from being held accountable, and that you've got that persons's number and it's Number One.'

Skimpole is the amateur artist, the dilettante. The final contrast is, of course, with Charles Dickens who not only considered himself, as a writer, an entertainer of a large admiring audience, but also held himself accountable for what he wrote.

In nothing that he did, it seems to me, did he accomplish in his fiction more than in his profound exploration of the condition of childhood and the consequences of the denial of the child's autonomous right to exist 'free and stirring' in body and imagination. If *David Copperfield* is his most enchanting evocation of the subject, *Great Expectations* is the occasion, as we shall see, of his most radical critique of a society seen through the experience of a child.

6   Dickens's prose style

As much as anything else in his work, the continuous vitality of Dickens's prose style speaks clearly on behalf of what at the end of the previous section I called the flow of individual life in his novels. One only has to note, as an example, the way in which the most minor character in terms of the action is distinguished by an individual speech pattern, an idiosyncratic idiom which belongs only to that character and is never repeated. To have achieved as much argues both an extremely flexible style that can recreate such discriminations, and an interested and shrewd observation of human beings. Although it is a mark of distinction of which he can deprive his heroes and heroines, Dickens's characters are identified and take their place in the world of the novel to which they belong through their language. Sarah Gamp and Flora Finching are perhaps only the most memorable examples of a whole genre. But beyond the dramatisation of speech, Dickens is capable of a remarkable variety of effects, and his writing is not often as slack as in the passage quoted on page 101 from *The Old Curiosity Shop*.

Many of the best effects are extended; they can be deployed over whole chapters. I have had occasion several times to refer to chapter nine of *Martin Chuzzlewit* and would point to Podsnap's conversation with the foreign gentleman over dinner in chapter eleven of *Our Mutual Friend* as an equally great comic achievement despite the total lack of action. Dickens can also seize hold of a minor character by means of a single thematic simile and pursue it through a play of variations on it which can occupy the whole of that character's space in the novel. Pancks, the rent-collector in *Little Dorrit*, acts out the part of steam tug-boat to his pompous, rack-renting employer Casby. Only rarely does Dickens confine his wit-play to the limits of a single sentence, as in 'a narrow alley leading to the river, where a wretched little bill, FOUND DROWNED, was weeping on the wet wall' (Little Dorrit), or in the description of Mrs Gradgrind: 'like an indifferently executed transparency of a small female figure, without enough light behind it' (*Hard Times*). When he does so limit the humour, the effect is that of poetic wit.

Dickens's tendency, however, as many critics have noted and found fault with, is the opposite. Especially in his descriptions, he piles elaboration on top of exuberant exaggeration to the point at which, in the overflow of invention, objects, houses, even whole landscapes can seem to take on a life of their own. It is a quality of the writing present in the earliest examples of his work. In *Sketches by Boz* it is inseparable from a certain archness and facetiousness which, between them, betray the self-consciousness and unen-livening deliberateness of the humour. More frequently than one might think, however, occur genuine flashes of an energetic and spir-ited inventiveness, which is captured in the tone and style of a successful rhetoric of colloquial informality.

> We love to walk among these extensive groves of the illustrious dead, and to indulge in the speculations to which they give rise; now fitting a deceased coat, then a dead pair of trousers, and anon the mortal remains of a gaudy waistcoat, upon some being of our own conjuring up, and endeavouring, from the shape and fashion of the garment itself, to bring its former owner before our mind's eye. We have gone on speculating in this way, until whole rows of coats have started from their pegs, and buttoned up, of their own accord, round the waists of imaginary wearers; lines of trou-sers have jumped down to meet them; waistcoats have almost burst with anxiety to put themselves on; and half an acre of shoes have suddenly found feet to fit them, and gone stumping down the street with a noise which has fairly awakened us from our pleasant reverie, and driven us slowly away, with a bewildered stare, an object of astonishment of the good people of Monmouth Street, and of no slight suspicion to the policemen at the opposite street corner.

> (*Sketches by Boz*: 'Monmouth Street')

The style reveals a self-conscious effort to parody that of elevated reflection. The phrase 'these extensive groves of the illustrious dead' burlesques the tone of classical speculation become cliché. Yet, from among all the sprawl of the final uncontrolled sentence, springs a flash of Dickens's characteristic power in the imagining of 'half an acre of shoes have suddenly found feet to fit them, and gone stumping down the street'. The phrase has its appropriate alliter-ative rhythm, a typical exaggeration borrowed from an unexpect-edly different area of experience in 'half an acre of shoes' and a great deal of energy in the placing of the homely, colloquial verb 'stumping'.

Whatever one thinks of Dickens as a descriptive writer — and many critics continue to find fault with his elaborations and exuber-ances — he demonstrates continuously great power and range beyond the comic purposes of much of his writing. The storm scene in which Ham and Steerforth are drowned (*David Copperfield*, chapter 55) is a good example, but he is also equally capable of altogether subtler tones and moods, as the two following contrasting passages clearly show.

> For all that the child observed, and felt, and thought, that night — the present and the absent; what was then and what had been

— were blended like the colours in the rainbow, or in the plumage of rich birds when the sun is shining on them, or in the softening sky when the same sun is setting. The many things he had had to think of lately, passed before him in the music; not as claiming his attention over again, or as likely ever more to occupy it, but as peacefully disposed of and gone. A solitary window, gazed through years ago, looked out upon an ocean, miles and miles away; upon its waters, fancies, busy with him only yesterday, were hushed and lulled to rest like broken waves. The same mysterious murmur he had wondered at, when lying on his couch upon the beach, he thought he still heard sounding through his sister's song, and through the hum of voices, and the tread of feet, and having some part in the faces flitting by, and even in the heavy gentleness of Mr Toots, who frequently came up to shake him by the hand. Through the universal kindness he still thought he heard it, speaking to him; and even his old-fashioned reputation seemed to be allied to it, he knew not how. Thus little Paul sat musing, listening, looking on, and dreaming; and was very happy.

(Dombey and Son, chapter 14)

The passage is controlled by the wave-like rhythm of the prose and resembles the music that plays outside little Paul's reverie. Like the music, the reader moves in and out of the mind of the child as Dickens creates the movement of a mind between present and past, mingling the two in the scarcely perceptible transitions of tense. It is not often that Dickens uses exotic imagery, but the simile of the rainbow colours and richly plumed birds supplies the place of objective description, and leads into the feeling of suspended time that is carried throughout the piece by the recurrent present participles. The passage is a fine example of Dickens's marked interest in unusual states of mind, and his ability to convey them in fiction.

My Lady Dedlock has been down at what she calls, in familiar conversation, her 'place' in Lincolnshire. The waters are out in Lincolnshire. An arch of the bridge in the park has been sapped and sopped away. The adjacent low-lying ground, for half a mile in breadth, is a stagnant river, with melancholy trees for islands in it, and a surface punctured all over, all day long, with falling rain. My Lady Dedlock's 'place' has been extremely dreary. The weather, for many a day and night, has been so wet that the trees seem wet through, and the soft loppings and prunings of the woodman's axe can make no crash or crackle as they fall. The deer, looking soaked, leave quagmires, where they pass. The shot of a rifle loses its sharpness in the moist air, and its smoke moves in a tardy little cloud towards the green rise, coppice-topped, that makes a background for the falling rain. The view from my Lady

Dedlock's own windows is alternately a lead-coloured view, and a view in Indian ink. The vases on the stone terrace in the foreground catch the rain all day; and the heavy drops fall, drip, drip, drip, upon the broad flagged pavement, called, from old time, the Ghost's Walk, all night. On Sundays, the little church in the park is mouldly; the oaken pulpit breaks out into a cold sweat; and there is a general smell and taste as of the ancient Dedlocks in their graves. My Lady Dedlock (who is childless), looking out in the early twilight from her boudoir at a keeper's lodge, and seeing the light of a fire upon the lattticed panes, and smoke rising from the chimney, and a child, chased by a woman, running out into the rain to meet the shining figure of a wrapped-up man coming through the gate, has been put quite out of temper. My Lady Dedlock says she has been 'bored to death'.

(*Bleak House*, chapter 2)

Here again, the control of mood is masterly. Dickens's description creates a Tennysonian melancholy (Lincolnshire was Tennyson's home county) by the details such as that of the deer who 'leave quagmires, where they pass,' and the smoke from the muffled gunshot that 'moves in a tardy little cloud' with the effect that all movement is all but arrested. The mood is defined by the language, its rhythm and phrases such as 'sapped and sopped,' 'soft loppings', and suggests the lifelessness and depression of the ancient Dedlock family which is conveyed by the description of appearances saturated by the incessant rain. The brief contrasting sketch of domestic happiness and warmth serves economically to reinforce the dominant mood.

Whatever Dickens may have meant when he insisted to Forster that he intended to be 'realistic' in his fiction, he certainly did not mean by using the word that he thought of himself as a literalist. He defended his style by asserting that, in order to distinguish literature from a literal account, the reader had to be made aware of the palpable presence in the writing of the author's 'fancy', his imagination. Perhaps Dickens's greatest gift is an exuberantly inventive sense for comedy. Its possession is not the most important for a writer of narrative, and Dickens often reports to Forster during composition that he is obliged to restrain his fancy. The gift is everywhere in evidence throughout his work from the earliest to the last, unfinished *Edwin Drood* but, at the same time, by looking more closely at the writing itself, one can be persuaded that he did develop as an artist and that his development manifests itself in his style. To try to show as much let us take two not totally dissimilar pieces of writing, early and late. Each describes a journey through London. Oliver Twist, in chapter twenty-one of the novel, is being hastened through the streets early in the morning by Bill Sikes on their way to commit a robbery.

THE EXPEDITION

It was a cheerless morning when they got into the street; blowing and raining hard; and the clouds looking dull and stormy. The night had been very wet: for large pools of water had collected in the road: and the kennels were overflowing. There was a faint glimmering of the coming day in the sky; but it rather aggravated than relieved the gloom of the scene: the sombre light only serving to pale that which the street lamps afforded: without shedding any warmer or brighter tints upon the wet house-tops, and dreary streets. There appeared to be nobody stirring in that quarter of the town; for the windows of the houses were all closely shut: and the streets through which they passed, were noiseless and empty.

By the time they had turned into Bethnal Green-road, the day had fairly begun to break. Many of the lamps were already extinguished; a few country waggons were slowly toiling on, towards London; and now and then, a stage-coach, covered with mud, rattled briskly by: the driver bestowing, as he passed, an admonitory lash upon the heavy waggoner who, by keeping on the wrong side of the road, had endangered his arriving at the office, a quarter of a minute after his time. The public-houses, with gas-lights burning inside, were already open. By degrees, other shops began to be unclosed; and a few scattered people were met with. Then, men and wowen with fish-baskets on their heads; donkey-carts laden with vegetables; chaise-carts filled with live-stock or whole carcases of meat; milk-women with pails; and an unbroken concourse of people, trudging out with various supplies to the eastern suburbs of the town. As they approached the City, the noise and traffic gradually increased; and when they threaded the streets between Shoreditch and Smithfield, it had swelled into a roar of sound and bustle. It was as light as it was likely to be, till night came on again; and the busy morning of half the London population had begun.

Turning down Sun-street and Crown-street, and crossing Finsbury-square, Mr Sikes struck, by way of Chiswell-street, into Barbican: thence into Long-lane: and so into Smithfield; from which latter place, arose a tumult of discordant sounds that filled Oliver Twist with surprise and amazement.

It was market-morning. The ground was covered, nearly ankle-deep, with filth and mire; and a thick steam, perpetually rising from the reeking bodies of the cattle, and mingling with the fog, which seemed to rest upon the chimney-tops, hung heavily above. All the pens in the centre of the large area: and as many temporary ones as could be crowded into the vacant space: were filled with sheep; tied up to posts by the gutter side were long lines of beasts and oxen, three or four deep. Countrymen, butchers, drovers, hawkers, boys, thieves, idlers, and vagabonds of every low grade, were mingled together in a dense mass; the whistling of drovers, the barking of dogs, the bellowing and plunging of oxen, the bleating of sheep, the grunting and squeaking of pigs; the cries of hawkers, the shouts, oaths, and quarrelling on all sides; the ringing of bells and roar of voices, that issued from every public-house; the crowding, pushing, driving, beating, whooping, and yelling; the hideous and discordant din that resounded from every corner of the market; and the unwashed, unshaven, squalid, and dirty figures constantly running to and fro, and bursting in and out of the throng; rendered it a stunning and bewildering scene, which quite confounded the senses.

Mr Sikes, dragging Oliver after him, elbowed his way through the thickest of the crowd; and bestowed very little attention on the numerous sights and sounds which so astonished the boy. He nodded, twice or thrice, to a passing friend; and, resisting as many invitations to take a morning dram, pressed steadily onward, until they were clear of the turmoil, and had made their way through Hosier-lane into Holborn.

From the opening use of the pathetic fallacy as a way of establishing the dreariness of the empty urban streets between night and day, the author's unfolding strategy is clear and simple. He orchestrates his effects so that they rise and accelerate from the 'few country waggons slowly toiling' to the discordant crescendo of the tumult of Smithfield Market. The passage moves by means of a gathering together and accumulation by numbers. Syntactically, the movement is similar: no detail is allowed to stand in the way of the growing weight of sensations falling on the boy. The grammar breaks down into a catalogue of unrelated items. Everything is directed towards the climax in Smithfield where, amid cries, animals, filth and rough animation, Oliver's senses are subjected to a violent assault. Again, in the last long sentence of the Smithfield paragraph, the structure quickly falls into a catalogue of confusions. (In passing, one might note how frequently novelists of many different kinds respond to the discontinuities and confusions of the appearance of the big city by making long, discrete lists. It is a characteristic response.) The effect on the reader is both crude and powerful; he is being hustled along just as brusquely as Oliver.

To complete Oliver's disorientation, Bill Sikes drags him through the thickest of the crowd; but what stands against the danger of total loss of control by writer and reader alike is the very carefully laid geography of the scene. The reality of the surrounding streets

(Sikes's route could be checked by a little map-reading) at once suggests that Sikes knows what he is doing, and contrasts forcibly with his attempt to destroy by means of the experience any sense Oliver might have of his own reality or identity.

At the end of the Smithfield paragraph, however, we seem to lose sight of Oliver altogether in the last clause: 'a stunning and bewildering scene, which quite confounded the senses'. Not Oliver's, but rather those of the Boz-like observer at this point. Dickens is here generalising about that kind of urban experience.

The river journey in chapter fifty-four of *Great Expectations* offers the reader an altogether much greater sense of artistic control, and a splendid example of the literary imagination at work.

The air felt cold upon the river, but it was a bright day, and the sunshine was very cheering. The tide ran strong, I took care to lose none of it, and our steady stroke carried us on thoroughly well. By imperceptible degrees, as the tide ran out, we lost more and more of the nearer woods and hills, and dropped lower and lower between the muddy banks, but the tide was yet with us when we were off Gravesend. As our charge was wrapped in his cloak, I purposely passed within a boat or two's length of the floating Custom House, and so out to catch the stream, alongside of two emigrant ships, and under the bows of a large transport with troops on the forecastle looking down at us. And soon the tide began to slacken, and the craft lying at anchor to swing, and presently they had all swung round, and the ships that were taking advantage of the new tide to get up to the Pool, began to crowd upon us in a fleet, and we kept under the shore, as much out of the strength of the tide now as we could, standing carefully off from low shallows and mud-banks.

Our oarsmen were so fresh, by dint of having occasionally let her drive with the tide for a minute or two, that a quarter of an hour's rest proved full as much as they wanted. We got ashore among some slippery stones while we ate and drank what we had with us, and looked about. It was like my own marsh country, flat and monotonous, and with a dim horizon; while the winding river turned and turned, and the great floating buoys upon it turned and turned, and everything else seemed stranded and still. For now the last of the fleet of ships was round the last low point we had headed; and the last green barge, straw-laden, with a brown sail, had followed; and some ballast-lighters, shaped like a child's first rude imitation of a boat, lay low in the mud; and a little squat shoal-lighthouse on open piles, stood crippled in the mud on stilts and crutches; and slimy stakes stuck out of the mud, and slimy stones stuck out of the mud, and red landmarks and tidemarks stuck out of the mud, and an old landing-stage and an old roofless building slipped into the mud, and all about us was stagnation and mud.

We pushed off again, and made what way we could. It was much harder work now, but Herbert and Startop persevered, and rowed, and rowed, and rowed, until the sun went down. By that time the river had lifted us a little, so that we could see above the bank. There was the red sun, on the low level of the shore, in a purple haze, fast deepening into black; and there was the solitary flat marsh; and far away there were the rising grounds, between which and us there seemed to be no life, save here and there in the foreground a melancholy gull.

As the night was fast falling, and as the moon, being past the full, would not rise early, we held a little council: a short one, for clearly our course was to lie by at the first lonely tavern we could find. So they plied their oars once more, and I looked out for anything like a house. Thus we held on, speaking little, for four or five dull miles. It was very cold, and a collier coming by us, with her galley-fire smoking and flaring, looked like a comfortable home. The night was dark by this time as it would be until morning; what light we had, seemed to come more from the river than the sky, as the oars in their dipping struck at a few reflected stars.

At this dismal time we were evidently all possessed by the idea that we were followed. As the tide made, it flapped heavily at irregular intervals against the shore; and whenever such a sound came, one or other of us was sure to start and look in that direction. Here and there, the set of the current had worn down the bank into a little creek, and we were all suspicious of such places, and eyed them nervously. Sometimes, 'What was that ripple?' one of us would say in a low voice. Or another, 'Is that a boat yonder?' And afterwards, we would fall into a dead silence, and I would sit impatiently thinking with what an unusual amount of noise the oars worked in the thowels.

At length we descried a light and a roof, and presently afterwards ran alongside a little causeway made of stones that had been picked up hard by. Leaving the rest in the boat, I stepped ashore, and found the light to be in the window of a public-house. It was a dirty place enough, and I dare say not unknown to smuggling adventurers; but there was a good fire in the kitchen, and there were eggs and bacon to eat, and various liquors to drink. Also, there were two double-bedded rooms — 'such as they were,' the landlord said. No other company was in the house than the landlord, his wife, and a grizzled male creature, the 'Jack' of the little causeway, who was as slimy and smeary as if he had been low water-mark too.

The movement of the passage is strongly marked by the movement and change of the tide from ebb to flow. The progress of the oarsmen and their passengers is noted by the changes in the surrounding landscape as they glide from the Port of London, past the woods and hills behind Gravesend towards the flat monotony of the marsh country of Pip's childhood. As they put London behind them, the escape party loses the busy commerce of the river; 'two emigrant ships', 'under the bows of a large transport with troops on the forecastle looking down at us' and pass a fleet of ships making use of the tide to gain the port. The last craft they pass, in contrast to the big ships at anchor, are 'shaped like a child's first rude imitation of a boat'. They have travelled from the constructed world to that of Pip's rough and primitive beginnings. The abundance of features noted and the richness of detail suggest Pip's anxious watchfulness, but the 'squat shoal-lighthouse . . . crippled in the mud on stilts and crutches' images in its decay the melancholy futility of the enterprise. The incantatory repetition in the rest of that sentence marks the only pause in the flow of the narrative and serves to underline the inevitable dissipation of their effort. When night falls the 'galley-fire smoking and flaring' in the passing collier reminds them of 'home' left irrecoverably behind, and their resting-place with its attendant Jack and associations with smugglers confirms in the reader the sense that Pip has outlawed himself in his undertaking to help Magwitch escape to the Continent.

The entire passage sustains a continuous dramatic tension and the reader is drawn through an evolution of emotions from the airy briskness of the start of the journey to that final 'low-water mark'. The writing is finely judged and concise; free, except in the sentence about the omnipresent mud, from rhetorical elaboration. Rather, the prose possesses a calmly ordered simplicity and intensity, perfectly articulated in:

> The night was as dark by this time as it would be until morning; and what light we had, seemed to come more from the river than the sky, as the oars in their dipping struck at a few reflected stars.

Dickens wrote nothing finer than the prose of *Great Expectations*.

7 Great Expectations: a commentary

All other swindlers on earth are nothing to the self-swindlers.

(chapter 28)

I

Dickens launched *All the Year Round*, his third weekly periodical, in April 1859 with the first instalment of *A Tale of Two Cities*. The story became one of his most popular, although Forster complained somewhat of its lack of humour. When the occasion arose in the following year for his next novel, Dickens was able to assure him that the new story, to be about the same length and also divided into three parts, would be 'exceedingly droll. I have put a child and a good-natured foolish man in relations that seem to me very funny.' The occasion was provided by the failure of the leading serial with which Dickens, as editor, tried to follow the great success of Wilkie Collins's *The Woman in White*. This was Charles Lever's *A Day's Ride, A life's Romance* which was losing readers at an alarming rate, and so Dickens set about *Great Expectations* in October 1860. The first instalment appeared in the first December issue in good time for Christmas.

Like *David Copperfield* it is written in the first person and is the story of the narrator's early life, told in retrospect. The connections between the two novels are not fortuitous. 'To be quite sure I had fallen into no unconscious repetitions, I read *David Copperfield* again the other day, and was affected by it to a degree you would hardly believe.' The precaution he notes in his letter to Forster indicates Dickens's awareness of the continuities of his concerns as a novelist: to some extent the later novel is a reconsideration of material he had already explored in the form of the autobiographical memoir. But, whereas the earlier work appears many-stranded, loosely woven and open-textured, suggestive of the spontaneous and accidental character of life itself, the experience of reading the later novel is that of yielding to a single, powerful and urgent current. It has what is unusual in Dickens's work, a single plot and, coming after the panoramic scale of *Bleak House* and *Little Dorrit*, a very small canvas. The action moves backwards and forwards over a very limited geography, between the village on the edge of the North Kent marshes and London by way of the local market town. It is an intimate landscape, restricted and confining in a manner characteristic of the novel as a whole, well matched to the severe constraints of weekly serial publication.

The story is bold and stark in outline, made up of elements that

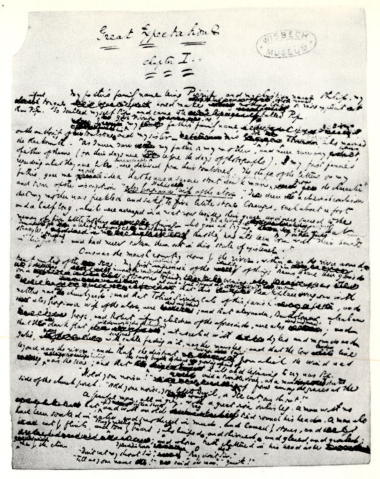

Page one of the manuscript of Great Expectations

seem to echo the world of folk-tales with its cast of a convict, a
strange rich old lady, a blacksmith and the blacksmith's boy who
is promised a large fortune if he will transform himself into a
gentleman. Although Pip's expectations are thrust on him, the
fantasy of 'Great Expectations' or great wealth must have been a
common one in the nineteenth century. Like Little Emily aspiring
to that of lady in *David Copperfield*, Pip aspires to the status of
gentleman even before Mr Jaggers, the great lawyer from London,
tells him of his good fortune. In *Bleak House*, Richard Carstone dies
when his hopes for the outcome of the Jarndyce case fail to materi-
alise. The mysterious paths of large inheritances and the entangle-

ments that follow from lost or misplaced wills wind the spring that sets in motion a large number of novels written in the period.

The plot as narrated by an older Pip recollecting turns on a single reversal of fortune: the *peripeteia* of classical tragedy. When Pip learns that the source of his wealth is not the rich old recluse Miss Havisham but the convict who once terrorised him out on the marshes at Christmas when he was a child and forced him to steal food and a file from his own home, he is filled with revulsion. Magwitch, the convict, has returned from the penal colony to which he was transported for life in order to see the London gentleman his money has made, although to do so is to risk the death penalty if he is discovered. When Pip understands something of the convict's story and past life, he bends all his efforts into smuggling the old man out of England to the Continent, even though he has rejected all claim to his benefactor's wealth. His efforts fail. The convict is recaptured at the very moment of making good his escape, is injured, tried and sentenced to death. He dies before the sentence can be carried out. His wealth is forfeit to the Crown but, as he lies dying, Pip is able to tell him that he has a beautiful daughter who is a lady and whom Pip loves. Estella was the proud girl he had known when he was taken as a boy to play at Satis House for Miss Havisham's amusement. With Magwitch and Miss Havisham dead and the connectedness of the past made clear, Pip suffers a terrible breakdown. His sister's husband, Joe Gargery, the blacksmith who had brought him up as a child, nurses him back to health. The only thing that Pip had been able to do with his fortune was to help his friend, Herbert, to establish himself in a shipping firm. Pip joins Herbert abroad and only returns home after a number of years. In the ruins of Satis House he again meets Estella. She tells him that, like himself, she has suffered much and they leave together.

Despite the bold, easy flow of the narrative and Dickens's evident mastery of both subject and style, the writing is muted and restrained in its most important effects rather than exuberant and expansive in his most characteristic manner. The mastery and control are evident from the opening sentences.

> My father's family name being Pirrip, and my christian name Philip, my infant tongue could make of both names nothing longer or more explicit than Pip. So I called myself Pip, and came to be called Pip.

The music is subdued, rendered by the assonance of the short 'i' vowels enclosed in the plosive consonants; the prose is tough and sinewy, and, like the subject itself, stripped of any excess. The reminiscence of Blake's 'Chimney Sweep', from *Songs of Innocence*, may be unconscious or coincidental, but by the time the reader has arrived at the end of this first, brief paragraph, he has already

The cottage at Chalk, near Gravesend. This may have been the original for the Gargery dwelling. See A Dickens geography, page 176

committed himself to the world of the novel. We are plunged immediately into the action that governs the entire movement of the novel, Pip's reversal of fortune, but, at the same time, the first chapter is full of quite remarkable resonances. It all happened a long, unspecified time ago 'long before the days of photographs'. What is here recalled to memory is the manner in which Pip first

131

Graves of the children of the Comport family, Cooling churchyard where Dickens often used to walk. See A Dickens geography, page 173

comes to realise that he is alive and that he is conscious of being alive, while his parents and little brothers are dead around him in the graveyard. To be alive and conscious is to be possessed of fancy or imagination; for, from the style of the engraved letters on his parents' tombstones, Pip 'unreasonably' creates their characters, just as, from inadequate evidence and impressions, the novelist creates an imagined living world. Pip is the author of his world, a world of 'trying to get a living ... in that universal struggle —'. The catalogue of names of the family dead that Pip rehearses is also suggestive. Those of his little brothers are full and rotund names; their identities are perfected and are part of Pip's first impression of the 'identity of things'; whereas that of their remaining, lonely living brother expresses in its brevity only a potential — a potential for growth. *Great Expectations* is a dramatised exploration of the meaning of human growth and of the pressures that distort the potential of the ordinary individual in the process of growing up.

The evening is also 'raw', and the landscape a 'wilderness' stretching out across the marshes towards the river which is nothing more than a 'low leaden line beyond' and to the 'savage lair' of the wind which is the sea. Dickens creates a landscape of chaos before the world was given shape, before civilisation, and we soon learn that the local pronunciation of marshes is 'meshes'; they are not easily to be escaped.

I have suggested that the opening paragraphs are full of poetic resonances which one might miss if one's response to them is directed only by Dickens's controlling tone which is delicately humorous; but there can be no mistaking the issues that are brought vividly into play by Pip's terrifying encounter with the convict. To arrive at self-consciousness is simultaneously to arrive at the consciousness of guilt. The convict starts up from among the graves:

> A fearful man, all in coarse grey, with a great iron on his leg. A man with no hat, and with broken shoes, and with an old rag tied round his head. A man who had been soaked in water, and smothered in mud, and lamed by stones, and cut by flints, and stung by nettles, and torn by briars; who limped, and shivered and glared and growled; and whose teeth chattered in his head as he seized me by the chin. 'Oh! Don't cut my throat, sir,' I pleaded in terror. 'Pray don't do it, sir.'

The figure appears to be scarcely human as it surges out of the primitive elements of earth and water. Even nature is hostile to his condition and his history. The convict then turns the child upside down on a tomb-stone, an action that concentrates the whole ensuing history of their relationship into the moment of Pip's seeing the steeple under his feet. Seated precariously on a high tomb-stone, his very life is threatened and in the balance. Terrified almost out of that life, he is utterly helpless to resist his attacker and seeks an apparently useless refuge in politeness and propitiation. It is the condition of childhood, of which the convict takes every desperate advantage in his violent demand for food and file, even to the characteristic adult invention of the secret and more threatening companion. Pip's last glimpse of the man, if such he is, catches him limping away across the featureless land under an angry line of sky towards the gibbet, the one object that stands out from the surrounding featurelessness, as though to hook himself up there again.

The whole is a remarkable opening chapter in which the tide of Dickens's meaning is swiftly conveyed by very simple dramatic and pictorial means with an effect that is at once grim and comic. Chapter two confirms Pip in his guilt. His sister makes him feel guilty that he exists at all and that he is an unnecessary burden she has been forced to carry.

'I'd never do it again I know that. I may truly say I've never had this apron of mine off since born you were. It's bad enough to be a blacksmith's wife (and him a Gargery) without being your mother.'

Her husband, Joe Gargery the blacksmith, is powerless to protect Pip from her brutal and unfeeling upbringing 'by hand'.

Mrs Joe's apron, we are told, is a coarse one 'having a square impregnable bib in front that was stuck full of pins and needles' which she parades as a badge of her drudgery. But her drudgery is self-imposed, and for the reader her apron becomes a badge of defence against human contact, love and warmth. The pins and needles signal a self-punishing aggressiveness that contrasts forcefully with Joe's mild, good-natured simplicity and unqualified friendship. It is Joe, however, who betrays Pip into punishment for appearing to have bolted a slice of bread which in an agony of guilt he has secreted down a trouser leg for the convict out on the marshes. The punishment is to have a pint of Tar-water poured down his throat, a medicine that always made him 'conscious of going about, smelling like a new fence'. Consciousness in the paragraph describing Tar-water finds its echo in the first word of the next paragraph — conscience. To be conscious is to be conscious of guilt, and so it is that as Pip prepares to steal the food from his own home, he learns that the prison hulks, those 'wicked Noah's Arks', are waiting for him, moored in the river across the marshes. As he rifles the Christmas stores in the pantry, the very stair boards call after him and the hanging hare seems to reproach him. However, he takes some brandy and tops up the bottle from a jug which he fetches from the kitchen. He is in great haste and, although he does have time to tell us about the little glass bottle into which he pours off the brandy, omits to tell us what was in the jug he took from the kitchen. We only learn that it was Tar-water when Uncle Pumblechook drinks it and falls into a paroxysm of choking at the end of the family Christmas dinner. The incident makes a splendidly comic comment on the medicine and on the medical treatment of children, but it also makes a comment on Pip. Or on Dickens as author. Either it is Dickens who deliberately conceals what is in the kitchen jug for the sake of the delayed comic effect, or it is Pip whom, as we already know, Tar-water made smell like a new fence. He could scarcely have failed to be conscious of what he was doing when he substituted it for the brandy. 'I didn't know how I had done it, but I had no doubt I had murdered him somehow.'

No doubt, we are pleased to see Pumblechook, the measure of whose selfishness and pretentiousness we have already taken, get what he deserves, and it is just possible to feel that Dickens sacrifices artistic coherence to local comic effect. Yet the novel strikes us as

A prison hulk of Deptford

seamless, effortlessly controlled and coherent, so that the lapse seems plausible. Pip as narrator, on the other hand, is the central consciousness within the novel, who spends a great deal of time reflecting in a confessional mood of self-dissatisfaction on his states of mind at particular crises in his story.

There are, however, occasions on which Dickens deliberately makes us stand right outside Pip and judge him. Perhaps the most striking commentary on Pip's progress is offered by Trabb's boy, who is a near relation to Young Bailey in *Martin Chuzzlewit* with the same ferocious penetration of pretension or hypocrisy. Trabb's boy's parody in the public street of Pip, the new-made gentleman in his fine new suit of clothes, is more than Pip can tolerate. Yet the reader takes it that the incident represents a cautionary comment about Pip, rather than about the coarse and common character of the life that Pip had escaped. Again, in chapter seventeen when Pip confides in Biddy his discontentedness at the forge and his ambition to be a gentleman, we stand aside from him when he asserts that he might have been happy as he was and would ask Biddy to marry him:

'I should have been good enough for *you*; shouldn't I, Biddy?'
    Biddy sighed as she looked at the ships sailing on, and returned

for answer, 'Yes; I am not over-particular.' It scarcely sounded flattering, but I knew she meant well.

Biddy clearly meant nothing of the kind.

Then, in chapter forty-four, Miss Havisham, in response to his accusation that she allowed him to continue to believe that she was his benefactor, flashes at him: 'You made your own snares. *I* never made them.' In chapter eighteen Pip did indeed, on receiving from Mr Jaggers, the lawyer, the announcement of his great expectations, jump to the conclusion that 'My dream was out; my wild fancy was surpassed by sober reality; Miss Havisham was going to make my fortune on a grand scale.' The words that he uses here — 'dream', 'wild fancy' and 'grand scale' — should provoke in the reader some caution about the way in which Pip reacts to the promise. His mistake, it could be argued, is natural and understandable; but more importantly, it satisfied the fantasy he had been nourishing, a fantasy served from the outset by his sister and by Pumblechook. Perhaps in diluting the brandy with Tar-water, he did have Pumblechook in mind as the intended victim. Perhaps Pip suppressed a desire to murder his great-uncle that he could not bring himself to acknowledge in himself. To suggest as much would entail the further view that Pip, in being unable to admit to certain feelings while eagerly confessing to others, feeds the fantasies approved by the adult figures in his life. It would then follow that the initial double guilt he feels for having stolen and for existing at all, is the secret agent of society's power over the individual, acting to suppress the original self in favour of a false self, a 'self-swindler' that is, of whom society can approve because he has sought its approval.

If the foregoing sounds too speculative or too tenuous a way of suggesting that Dickens requires the reader to resist the seductiveness of Pip's account of his early life, there is a further piece of evidence in the final paragraph of chapter thirty-eight.

In the Eastern story, the heavy slab that was to fall on the bed of state in the flush of conquest was slowly wrought out of the quarry, the tunnel for the rope to hold it in its place was slowly carried through the leagues of rock, the slab was slowly raised and fitted in the roof, the rope was rove to it and slowly taken through the miles of hollow to the great iron ring. All being made ready with much labour, and the hour come, the sultan was aroused in the dead of the night, and the sharpened axe that was to sever the rope from the great iron ring was put into his hand, and he struck with it, and the rope parted and rushed away, and the ceiling fell. So, in my case; all the work, near and afar, that tended to the end, had been accomplished; and in an instant the blow was struck, and the roof of my stronghold dropped upon me.

Dickens's work abounds in references to folk literature of all kinds, including fairy stories and the *Tales from the Arabian Nights*. This story, from *Tales of the Genji*, was very well known to him because it was the one he had dramatised when he was still a little boy. In the context of the novel Pip seems to want us to infer that he is the innocent victim of a dreadful plot at the moment of his success. In the original story, however, the slab set into the ceiling above the bed of state was the idea of the Sultan's Vizier when it was learned that the country was about to be invaded by their enemies. It is the culprit, the leader of the invading army who is the object of the plot. Rather than bring war and misery to the people by resisting, the Vizier advised the Sultan to retreat to the mountains and leave behind a magnificent pavilion with the great bed in its centre to entice the enemy leader. The plan works. The slab falls and destroys its intended victim when, miles away in the safety of the mountains, the Sultan cuts the rope that holds the slab in place. He is then happily restored to his people and his land.

Dickens evidently remembered the story rather better than Pip who adapts it, inappropriately if not unnaturally, to his own view of his situation.

I have gone a long way round to make a case that the older Pip is not altogether a reliable narrator and that it would be a mistake to assume that he is continuously truthful or that it was possible for him to be so. He is a more complex character than David Copperfield, like him as he is in constitution and character; ambitious, timid and sensitive. Just as David is not always in his author's confidence (in, for example, his judgement of Steerforth), neither is Pip, with more serious consequences for what we take the novel to be about. Even though we know him to be innocent, Pip *feels* guilty by reason of his existence and becomes a criminal through terror. These are his qualifications for entry into a society composed largely of guilt and criminality.

Crime and the graveyard are the limits of his first horizons. David's earliest memories of his view of the world beyond his domestic paradise also includes a graveyard, where his father is buried, but his early world is more richly populated than that of Pip's limited existence. There is never a suggestion that David, even when his author and therefore the reader seem to judge him and his actions adversely, misrepresents himself on any occasion, whereas Pip, on the other hand, seems to be betrayed from the first moment of consciousness into self-suppression and insincerity. He is not one of Dickens's children of grace; he has, unlike David, neither talent nor qualification other than his desires. Like Esther in *Bleak House*, he is guilty yet innocent. His testimony dramatises a very modern consciousness, oppressed and self-repressing. It is on that account alone the more valuable to us.

Nevertheless, if we compare the family Christmas dinner with the meal he brings to the convict on the marshes, it is clear from these early chapters that Pip is also alive to human feelings. Despite its celebratory significance, Pip is the victim of everyone except Joe at the dinner. Instead of love and relationship, there is only an unrelaxed and unaccustomed formality. Pip is made miserable instead of happy. Pumblechook treats him like an animal, musing on what his destiny might have been had he been born a pig and not a boy. For Pumblechook there exists perhaps little enough difference between boys and pigs: 'Dunstable the butcher ... would have whipped you under his left arm, and with his right he would have turned up his frock to get a penknife from out his waistcoat-pocket, and he would have shed your blood and had your life.' At least the violence with which the convict threatened Pip was born of desperation, and Pip seems able to appreciate the fact as he watches him eat and ram the food down his throat, like a dog. Pip is moved to pity the man's desolation and say:

'I am glad you enjoy it.'
'Did you speak?'
'I said I was glad you enjoyed it.'
'Thank'ee, my boy. I do.'

Thus a relationship is established between them. Pip becomes, as indeed he is to be, 'my boy' to the convict and a little later, in chapter five, the man in turn becomes 'my convict' to the boy. The point is confirmed at the end of chapter five when the man confesses to having taken a pie and other food from the blacksmith's. Joe's response is to affirm: 'God knows you're welcome to it ... We don't know what you have done, but we wouldn't have you starve to death for it, poor miserable fellow-creature. — Would us, Pip?' The embrace of Pip in this humane and forgiving response is natural and unobtrusive, yet Pip is bound to take a long journey through his great expectations, through disillusionment and suffering in order to appreciate its justice. Joe's response is an acknowledgement of the human predicament in a situation — the retaking of the fugitives on Christmas day — of utter indifference to humane considerations. The chapter ending evokes the sense of a brutal repression of life that colours the rest of the novel:

By the light of the torches, we saw the black Hulk lying out a little way from the mud of the shore, like a wicked Noah's Ark. We saw the boat go alongside, and we saw him taken up the side and disappear. Then, the ends of the torches were flung hissing into the water, and went out, as if it were all over with him.

Chapter five closes on a profound note of finality, but right up to the moment of Magwitch's reappearance in his chambers on a stormy night in London years later, Pip is reminded from time to time of his earlier induction into the world of crime.

His own development, however, seems to point in the opposite direction. Until he is to be apprenticed to Joe at the forge, he does odd jobs about the village and goes to school where his beginnings in learning are full of struggles and collisions with the alphabet and the nine figures. His first 'hilly' attempt on his slate at a letter produces in Joe an astonished reaction. 'I say, Pip, old chap' cried Joe, opening his blue eyes wide, 'what a scholar you are. An't you?' The blacksmith's notion of scholarship is purely external and uncritically admiring.

> 'Give me,' said Joe, 'a good book, or a good newspaper, and sit me down afore a good fire, and I ask no better. Lord' he continued, after rubbing his knees a little, 'when you *do* come to a J and a O, and says you, "Here, at last, is a J-O, Joe," how interesting reading is'

Neatly dovetailed into the comedy are the serious encouragement of Pip's aspiration, already stirring consciously, to be educated and Pip's own awakening realisation of the superiority that attaches to learning. From Joe's enjoyment of reading, Pip derives the assurance that 'Joe's education, like steam was yet in its infancy'.

Similarly, Magwitch proudly takes it as a token of Pip's achieved status that he can read foreign languages that Magwitch cannot understand. For himself, however, Joe prefers to be 'a little inconwenienced' than to assert an independence of his wife by trying to get an education. He explains as much to Pip in his account of his life, a story of much harsher conditions than Pip must suffer. He is 'dead afeerd of going wrong in the way of not doing what's right by a woman', and Pip gains for him a new admiration out of this explanation.

But the association of education and power has been made and it is sealed by the return of Mrs Joe from town with the news that Miss Havisham has asked Pumblechook to provide a boy to come and play at Satis House. '"And of course he's going. And he can play there, ... or I'll work him ... for anything we can tell, this boy's fortune may be made by his going to Miss Havisham's ..."'. The deepest irony of the novel is that his fortune is made, yet not by Miss Havisham. Instead it is provided by the hunted 'dung-hill dog' Magwitch. We already see, however, in the conjunction of education and fortune, the shaping of Pip's career.

His first experience of Satis House and its inhabitants is that everything is 'so strange, and so fine — and melancholy —'. He associates Miss Havisham with waxworks and skeletons and, after their first encounter, fancies for a moment in the chill of the deserted brewery yard that he sees her white figure high above him in the air, hanging from a beam. Miss Havisham and her bizarre surroundings evoke a rich and poetic resonance in Pip and the reader alike. Light and life are excluded, time has been arrested at one moment in the past and all animation is suspended in the imperceptible and inevitable decay that can only end in death. Pip's first acquaintance with a higher social class than his own is an acquaintance with the atmosphere of death by which the life of that class is permeated. For the first time he is made to feel ashamed of being 'a common labouring-boy', of calling the knaves Jacks, and of possessing 'coarse hands' and 'thick boots'. He catches shame like an infection from Estella, a pretty girl who is called in to play cards with him for Miss Havisham's diversion. What more appropriate game than 'beggar my neighbour'? Estella and the card-game are called for because Pip cannot perform to order that one activity most natural, in Dickens as in William Blake, to children which can only be performed spontaneously. The very idea of the word 'play' involves spontaneity and cannot be commanded. But Miss Havisham explains that she sometimes has sick fancies:

'. . . and I have a sick fancy that I want to see some play, play, play, play'

Pip is keenly aware of the conflict, just as his awareness of the capriciousness of his sister's upbringing of him had induced in him a 'perpetual conflict with injustice'. To the conflict which already works in him has now been added at this first encounter with Estella, contempt, humiliation and shame, thus confirming the sensivity and moral timidity to which he confesses.

But that is not all that he takes away from his first experience of Satis House. Miss Havisham's world is, after all, strange and fine and, even if she does treat him insolently by bringing him his food to eat outside and laying it down on the stones for him as though he were a dog, Estella is beautiful. Satis House has enlarged his imagination as we learn from the marvellous invented description of the occasion he gives afterwards to Pumblechook and his sister, and in his later confession to Biddy of his dissatisfactions:

It was summer-time, and lovely weather. When we had passed the village and the church and the churchyard, and were out on the marshes and began to see the sails of the ships as they sailed on, I began to combine Miss Havisham and Estella with the prospect, in my usual way.

The experience has also confirmed him in his aspirations to gentility. Furthermore, the occasion allows him to feel superior to the bullying Pumblechook who, it transpires, has never in fact set eyes on his landlady. Yet the elaboration of the lie by flags and swords is not merely a kind of childish revenge. The lies do suggest at the same time that Pip has neither grasped nor understood the strange and disturbing novelty of the experience and is unwilling to share it with others because it has spoken to his innermost secret being.

His sister is sure that Pip will benefit from the connection. Miss Havisham would 'do something' for him, and she favours 'property' over Pumblechook's speculation that it might take the form of an apprenticeship to 'some genteel trade — say, the corn and seed trade, for instance'. Joe is reprimanded for his caution in suggesting that it might only be one of the dogs who fought for the veal cutlets. It is 'before the fire goes out' that Pip confesses his invention of the scene to Joe. Throughout the novel the warmth of the forge fire is contrasted with other forms of heat and light. Satis House is ill-lit by candles; and the light of day is excluded. Estella's fieriness is cold, like both the distant stars her name represents and the jewels she wears. Dickens's continuous employment in *Great Expectations* of the symbolic resonances of what appears to be purely naturalistic description is unobtrusive yet quite remarkably uniform.

The same may be said for the continuous juxtapositions that carry forward the action and give it significance. An immediate and very relevant example can be drawn from chapter ten which follows Pip's introduction to Satis House. As the result of his visit he reaffirms his determination to 'get on in life' (which, as we recall from the first page of the narrative is a 'universal struggle') and persuades Biddy to teach him all she knows. On the same day in the Three Jolly Bargemen he meets the mysterious stranger who takes aim at him with a half-shut eye as though aiming an invisible gun, and gives him two 'fat sweltering one-pound notes'. The notes and the accompanying gesture are a reminder of Pip's complicity in crime and guilt which he will not be able to escape. His efforts to do so only serve in the end to bring him face to face with the reality of his relationship with Magwitch, the 'dung-hill dog'. Similar reminders come at him repeatedly in the course of his progress. He tries to brush the dust of Newgate Prison off his feet before meeting Estella in London. Then, as Herbert sees him off on the coach to visit Estella and Miss Havisham, he agains sees, this time in fetters, the mysterious man who gave him the two pound notes and who is to ride behind him on the journey.

Such reminders signal to the reader rather than to Pip both the close and continuous presence of the moment of the earliest association of the identity of things with guilt and criminality, and the continuity of the criminal world with the life of that other upper socially-approved world of money and status. Among the many hints and signals given throughout the novel, the object with the most powerful associations is the leg-iron from which, in chapter three, Magwitch freed himself with the aid of the file Pip stole from the forge. In chapter sixteen it is the remarkable piece of evidence that Joe picks up and identifies after it has been used in a savage attack on his wife. Pip's 'reasonable' inference is that it was probably his convict's leg-iron and that the attacker may well have been Orlick or the mysterious stranger at the Jolly Bargemen. However, it is an inference that he arrives at only after his first reaction which was that he 'must have had some hand in the attack'. When he first hears the news, his head is full of Mr Wopsle's reading of George Lillo's tragic melodrama *George Barnwell, or the London Merchant* in which Barnwell is persuaded by his mistress, Millwood, to rob his employer and murder his uncle, for which crimes they are both hanged. First produced in 1731 it is an early play concerned with everyday commercial life and Dickens refers to it in several works. An early allusion occurs in 'Horatio Sparkins' in *Sketches*, where it clearly indicates a son's thoughts of murdering his father. Mr Pickwick and Sam Weller both display knowledge of it. Here, in chapter fifteen, the use of the play is extended over half a chapter. It exemplifies Wopsle's absurb pretensions to being an actor, a career he pursues in London in a parodic echo of that of Pip, and it provides yet another occasion for Pumblechook's bullying intimidation of the child. A degree of redundancy belongs properly to all comic art, but the juxtaposition of the melodrama of murder, the blackness of the night, the guns sounding from the Hulk, the presence of Joe's journeyman, Orlick, on the walk back from town who can confirm that prisoners have escaped, and the breaking of the news of the savage attack on Mrs Joe, added together, create a profounder atmosphere of unease than might be appropriate, to comedy.

It is in this atmosphere that Pip feels guilty at the news, and confesses at the beginning of chapter sixteen:

> With my head full of George Barnwell, I was at first disposed to believe that *I* must have had some hand in the attack upon my sister, or at all events that as her near relation, popularly known to be under obligation to her, I was a more legitimate object of suspicion than anyone else.

I do not take Pip to be reacting, as any innocent person might, to an accusation of guilt. No one had accused him. But I do infer that the option of feeling innocent is not available to him. He may well have had thoughts of killing his sister in order to put an end to her injustice and his miseries. As in the case of the Christmas incident with Pumblechook and the Tar-water in the brandy, he is not going to confess to such thoughts if he had been entertaining them.

The mystery of the attack and the reappearance of the leg-iron is explained readily enough in chapter fifty-three in which, in answer to an anonymous summons, Pip goes by night to the sluice-house by the lime-kiln on the marshes. On his arrival he is surprised, caught and bound up by Orlick who has lured him there in order to kill him. What is remarkable about the way in which the chapter is written, however, is neither Orlick's confession that it was he who dropped Pip's sister 'like a bullock' with the leg-iron he had picked up on the marshes, nor the powerfully dramatic rendering of the scene from within a consciousness suffering the extremity of pain and the imminence of a violent death. The mysterious core of this finely imagined chapter is surely Orlick's accusation that it is Pip who is ultimately responsible for his sister's death:

> 'Old Orlick's a going to tell you something. It was you as did for your shrew sister . . .. Now you pays for it. You done it; now you pays for it.'

It is as though Pip must be forced to acknowledge, by violence if necessary, at once his total isolation as an individual and his implication in the common guilt. The primitive and brutal Orlick is the agent of that dark knowledge which rises from the marshes. Insofar as Dodge Orlick has any character it is one made up of skulking evil, featureless and unqualified like the marshes he haunts. For all the pure malevolence of his intentions what Orlick has to say to Pip is profoundly true, and marks an important stage in the long and painful process of Pip's struggle towards a freedom from the constraints and fetters of the society he had so long been growing willingly towards.

Repeated references such as those to the leg-iron or to convicts which I have pointed to in the foregoing, together with the juxtaposition of incidents which comment directly on each other and are entailed in Dickens's use of the form of the first person dramatic narrative, constitute the method of the novel. It is significant that considerations of method rise directly out of any attempt to deal with the subject matter and plot of the novel and lead us back again into the important questions that surround the meaning of the novel. *Great Expectations* is a novel remarkable for the closeness of the fit between method and meaning, subject-matter and significance. It might seem to follow, therefore, that there could be little dispute about its meaning. Recent critics, however, have disagreed widely and interestingly on what its meaning might be. Much depends on the reader's own experience of reading the novel, and my own is such as to suggest that Pip's reports of his feelings and reactions are not always as reliable as his descriptions of places and events. As a consequence, it seems less important to decide whether he is a sympathetic character or a mere snob than to attempt to understand, by taking hold of Dickens's method, that we can see more of Pip's character and world than he sees. He is driven by a fear of guilt and shame to try to rise in a society he could scarcely be expected to understand. The more he struggles against them, the more he is enmeshed in them until he is forced into facing them and making the choice between the status to which he has aspired and the life of the outcast Magwitch.

II

What kind of society is it that Dickens evokes in the novel and towards which Pip aspires? What are the growing individual's relations with it? We begin to glimpse something of the answers to such questions in the chilly comedy of the family Christmas dinner which, even without the secret terror of his encounters with the convict on the marshes, was an occasion of misery for the child. Then later, as he moves beyond the confines of the forge and the marshes, he is overcome by the utter strangeness of Miss Havisham and her surroundings. Pip reports everything he sees at Satis House, including his hallucinated vision of Miss Havisham hanging from a beam high up in the long-neglected brewery. But in doing so, he fails to make for himself the obvious inference that it is a world fixed in the past and everywhere in decay; a world of death. He is drawn towards this world by the accidental collision with the pantomimic pale young gentleman with whom he fights and whom he knocks down. That, on this occasion, he should feel 'but a gloomy satisfaction' in his victory and think of himself as a 'savage young wolf' (one recalls the phrase when, in the sluice-house later, Orlick also calls him 'wolf' and 'young wolf') shows vividly to what extent he has already come to share society's view of that self. Further, that Estella, whom the fight had excited, should offer her cheek for him to kiss as a reward ensures that he will continue to be attracted towards her if only because the kiss inflames his feeling of worthlessness beside her. By this point in his progress his education in guilt and shame is complete. To escape them he takes the route that society approves.

The immediate response to the announcement of his great expectations is Pumblechook's 'May I? _may_ I?' which is splendid fun as a display of self-abasing ingratiation that Pip, to his credit, finds intolerable. It perplexes him that Trabb, the tailor, must also take new measurements for his grand new clothes, since he already has them, but he is assured that, 'it wouldn't do under existing circumstances, sir — it wouldn't do at all'. It is as though Pip must be made to see that he is already a different person.

Wearing his new clothes, he pays a last call on Miss Havisham whom he twice refers to as his 'fairy-godmother'. It as as though Dickens wants to emphasise the illusion that Pip is swayed by; Jaggers spoke only of an unknown benefactor. Miss Havisham, however, uses the occasion for her own ends by allowing her cousin

Sarah Pocket, who is present as an agent of a family anxious to inherit Miss Havisham's wealth, to infer that she is in fact Pip's benefactor. Pip takes it that his wild fancy has been confirmed, thus rendering unbearable to him his ultimate disillusionment.

However, it is only once Pip has established himself in London that the reader is invited to take the full measure of the society of wealth and status for which Pip is being educated. His first impression of the place is both that its immensity was scaring and that it was 'rather ugly, crooked, narrow and dirty'. Mr Jaggers's office is located at its very heart in Little Britain. The street was a real street in Dickens's time which still exists, but one cannot help but admire the ironic, if unforced, appropriateness of the name to Dickens's subject. In close proximity lie huddled together St Paul's Cathedral, Newgate Prison, and Smithfield Market. Again, the juxtaposition is unforced and geographically accurate but it makes a powerful comment on society's arrangements. The first object he is shown is the gallows yard in the prison and the Debtors' Door and is given to understand that 'four on 'em would come out at that door the day after tomorrow at eight in the morning, to be killed in a row'. The site and the explanation give him a 'sickening idea of London'.

Jaggers's office is no better: his black horse-hair chair is like a coffin and the casts of two swollen faces on a shelf are those of clients who were hanged. When Pip finally sees Jaggers, the lawyer is surrounded by clients and supplicants whom he terrifies, just as his name had terrified Pip's coachman into accepting the correct fare. Jaggers dominates Pip's experience of London. He is all-powerful in the law, manipulating and bullying it as he chooses or as he is paid. The whole world, as it seems, is frightened of him and he even bullies his lunch-time sandwich. Yet he wields his power utterly irresponsibly. When he goes home he washes his hands carefully in scented soap and is free of any connection with his office world, although he seems to inhabit no other nor to possess a private life nor a private self. As Pip's guardian, he refuses all personal responsibility, remarking only of the arrangements made on Pip's behalf 'of course you'll go wrong somehow, but that's no fault of mine'. That his private nature coheres almost entirely with his professional character is made clear on the occasion in chapter twenty-six of the invitation to Pip and his friends to dine with him at home. In a telling gesture, he scrapes his work out of his nails with his penknife and, after bluntly telling his guests to go, retires once again behind a clean towel to wash his hands of them. During the dinner itself, he takes particular note of the most disagreeable of Pip's companions, expertly raises a disagreement and a contest of physical strength among them and ends it by forcing his housekeeper to display her scarred, powerful wrists.

The dinner is not only a confirmation of what the reader has already been directed towards in the character of Jaggers but, at the same time, one in a series of meals in this novel that are eaten without enjoyment, without genuine hospitality or any expression of the warmth of human relationship. The most significant of these is the untouched wedding feast which has lain for years spread on the large table at Satis House, serving only spiders and mice with nourishment. Jaggers's idea of hospitality contrasts totally and comically with that of his clerk, Wemmick. Pip's first impression of Wemmick is that, with his pillar-box mouth and his general demeanour at the office, he is of the same, closed kind as his employer. Yet like Pip, he was new to London once, and has taken on a professional protective disguise. Wemmick survives the world of London by having perfected a total separation of his social and private selves. He is twins in effect, and Pip soon meets and comes to recognise the hidden, Walworth twin. At home in Walworth, life is full of spontaneous warmth of feeling and ingenious playfulness that has transformed a cottage in a garden plot into a bower and a defended castle with moat and drawbridge. It is as though in the description Dickens is enjoying an extended pun on the meanings of the word 'retreat'. 'So, sir . . . if you can suppose the little place besieged, it would hold out a devil of a time . . . ' Wemmick's private world is full of fantasy but it is a fantasy of siege conditions, the house is in need of defence, against presumably, the encroachments of the outer social world which seems to Wemmick to threaten his private world of family and feasting. Even that most social of ceremonies, his wedding, in which the private and public selves appear as one, must be conducted surreptitiously in a denial of its public and social aspects. To Pip's surprise, Mr Jaggers has never seen Walworth to admire it. 'No; the office is one thing, and private life is another. When I go into the office, I leave the Castle behind me, and when I come into the Castle, I leave the office behind me. If it's not in any way disagreeable to you, you'll oblige me by doing the same. I don't wish it professionally spoken about.' At the office it is as though the gaiety and ceremony of the Walworth Castle had never existed. The constraints under which Wemmick serves Jaggers appear again as he accompanies Pip back across the river to his place of business. 'By degrees, Wemmick got dryer and harder as we went along, and his mouth tightened into a post-office again.'

The remainder of Pip's circle of acquaintance in London is narrowly circumscribed. It consists of the Pocket family and the small group of young men who like himself have come to study with Mr Matthew Pocket, a 'serious, honest and good' man always 'zealous and honourable' as Pip reports. Mrs Pocket, on the other hand, carries through life a conviction that she should have been a duchess. The fixation on the aristocracy for which she has failed to qualify by marriage excuses her any responsibility for the domestic

arrangements. Her children are therefore 'tumbled up' by an assort-
ment of incompetent servants whom Mr Pocket can scarcely afford.
His goodness and seriousness disqualify him from the rewards of
success and status which society offers. The same may be said of his
son Herbert, the pale young gentleman of the childhood boxing
match, who is now to be Pip's companion and social mentor. At the
very beginning of their friendship Pip twice records an odd impression he has that Herbert, for all his 'looking about' for a future in
shipping insurance, will never be successful or rich.

Nevertheless, Herbert and his father are gentlemen and Herbert's
induction of Pip into his new role in society is gentle, humouring
and quite free of jealousy. Pip feels that Herbert also knows the
source of his fortune, but that he has been put at ease on the subject
since Herbert, despite the relative poverty of his father, displays
nothing of the remainder of the family's assiduous toadying to Miss
Havisham. Furthermore, Dickens gives us through the mouth of
Herbert a disquisition on the qualities of the gentleman. According
to Herbert it is a principle of his father's that 'no man who was not
a true gentleman at heart, ever was, since the world began, a true
gentleman in manner. He says no varnish can hide the grain of the
wood; and that the more varnish you put on, the more the grain will
express itself.' (chapter 22). Without appearing to break the
dramatic surface of the writing in this novel, Dickens is at times
surprisingly direct in his address to the reader. It is clear from the
passage that Dickens is giving assent to the idea of a gentleman that
Herbert expresses. At the same time it is made equally clear that
to be a gentleman and to be socially successful are incompatible
ambitions. It is part of Pip's better nature that he feels his deficien-
cies in a way that makes him stick to his studies. His better nature
is also supported by his friendship with Herbert and with the
Walworth side of Wemmick, but these friendships are not enough
to prevent his sliding into debt, dissipation and a life composed of
trivialities in the company of a club called the Finches of the Grove.
The Finches, apart from his fellow private students, remain anonymous, but confirm for the reader a sense of the aimlessness of the
way of life of the set of wealthy young men.

During this period of Pip's young life, it is the interruptions to his
nullifying routine that demand our attention. It is, after all, a lull,
a period of waiting until the moment when his benefactor should
reveal his identity. First, there is the visit from Joe announced in
Biddy's respectful letter. That it is not a success is the result of Pip's
inability to break through Joe's notion of the deference due to
gentility. Pip would rather his old friend and play-mate had not
come at all and, despite feeling remorseful about it, is greatly
relieved to see the back of him. The visit is punctuated by the refusal
of Joe's hat to remain on the mantelpiece where he felt obliged to

put it. The comedy with the hat is a sign of the unnatural constraint that Pip imposes on the situation by his unwillingness to relax. Between them, Joe and Pip perform an unmanageable balancing act and have difficulty in maintaining the roles they have forced upon themselves. It was Pip's place to accept Joe for what he was, not for what Joe, in the awkwardness of his novel situation, thought was required of him. After Joe's departure, Pip hesitates before going down to call him back, long enough for Joe to have disappeared. Pip's confession of his hesitation recalls that similar delay he reports to us earlier of wishing to get down from the coach that first carried him away from Joe and the forge towards London and his new life of great expectations. He delays long enough to make a return impossible. On each occasion one can see a very different kind of explanation for the delay from the one Pip offers. He it is who breaks away; Joe merely releases him and will accept no compensation for the loss of his apprentice.

More in tune at this time with the ambitions he nurses are Pip's resumed relations with Estella, whom, in his own words, he has fastened to the innermost life of his life. It is on the coach journey to see her again at Miss Havisham's that he is forcefully reminded of what he is trying to escape by fastening his dreams to Estella, when the convict breathing down his neck on the top of the coach provokes in him a vague and undefined fear that he describes as the revival of the terror of childhood. It is the central irony in the novel that the harder he attempted to suppress his original guilt and shame of which his undefined terror is the symptom, the nearer he comes to being forced to acknowledge them. Estella plays an important role in the socially approved life that Pip thinks he is making for himself when, all the while, she is a convict's daughter and, like Pip, the instrument of another's desire for revenge on that society.

The society from which Pip seeks approval is revealed as one in which power derives from status and wealth where the possession of either of these distinctions divided man from man. Personal survival lies not in seeking its approval or in embracing it, but in escaping it. Pip's liberation from the miseries of his past comes not from society nor from his fantasy of a destined life with Estella in a restored Satis House, but from those past experiences which he has striven most to keep hidden: the earliest sources of his feelings of guilt and shame. Like Pip, who hides things from the reader and from himself, society hides much and represses more. In the telling gesture of its most powerful representative, Jaggers, it washes its hands of human responsibility and of all that relates human beings to each other.

Magwitch's sudden reappearance out of the darkness and depths of the stairway, and his disclosure to a stunned and bewildered Pip that he and not Miss Havisham is his benefactor, is the pivot on which the plot and the meaning of the novel both turn. After the initial shock, however, the reader is better placed than Pip to appreciate the importance of Magwitch's story in relation to the point that Pip has reached in his long, deluded journey towards approval by a society the nature and qualities of which he has never been able to judge out of his own experience. The deliberate choice of Magwitch, the extreme victim of his society, as the example of the human life which constitutes the most radical critique of that society, is a brilliant stroke on Dickens's part. It is also a stroke aimed with the simplicity and directness of a fairy tale. That the Magwitch who returns to shock Pip is no longer the grotesque figure who terrorised him out on the marshes is a trivial objection to Dickens's strategy for the character. The manipulation of the reader's response to the wretched felon from a sharing of Pip's and Herbert's revulsion from him to a sympathetic appreciation and pity for a human being is imperceptible yet firmly controlled by the writer. Dickens might well have had before him the example of the outcasts and solitaries who make their painful ways across the bleak landscapes of Wordsworth's poems. Not necessarily, however, as behind both poet and novelist sound strong echoes of the tradition of the Christian beatitudes with their consolations for the poor and the disinherited of the earth.

In *Great Expectations* the career of the transported felon stands in diametrical opposition to that of Pip who is transported effortlessly towards the centre of a society which has denied ever more harshly the other's right to maintain life in himself. What is apparent from the account of his life which Magwitch gives Pip and Herbert in chapter forty-two is that, at the beginning of their lives, Pip and Magwitch were interchangeable. Each might have followed the other of the two destinies that such a society offers: one is brought up to be, in his own words, 'a warmint', the other a gentleman. In the music of the opening paragraph of the novel, the note of reversibility in Pip's name may have escaped attention. Philip Pirrip is a palindromic name; things could go either way for him. It is an ingenious aspect of the plot that Dickens should make the felon the creator of the gentleman as an act of revenge upon society, but it is at the same time something more. By arranging the plot in such a fashion the author also demonstrates the inherent and indissoluble links between society and social approval on the other hand and criminality and guilt on the other.

In making these connections, the role of the lawyer Jaggers is crucial. It is he who holds together the two poles of the novel. He acts equally, and equally irresponsibly, on behalf of the wealthy eccentric lady and the transported convict. The plot-lines of this story: Magwitch's use of Pip for revenge on society and Miss Havisham's similar use of Estella, are in the keeping of a lawyer who remains secretive, will admit nothing and treats what everyone else says or does as admissible evidence. Jaggers's intimidating presence is a denial of the possibility of justice in a world where even the law is another victim of the stab of his accusing forefinger or of his deliberate hesitation during a gesture made with a large white handkerchief. Jaggers serves ends which are manifestly unjust to the human beings he has to deal with. 'I'll have no feelings here. Get out.' These are the words with which he throws a supplicant out of the office at the end of chapter fifty-one. His power is based on his bullying refusal to recognise that part of others that makes them human. The law's discrimination between Magwitch and the arch-villain Compeyson is equally inhuman and, on being recaptured and sentenced to death, Magwitch receives his sentence as only one among thirty-two men and women who are sentenced to death at the same time. It is the example of Magwitch and the experience of making the escape attempt solely on his behalf that rescue Pip from a future that might well have been similar to that of Jaggers for whom the world is divided into those who beat and those who cringe.

Once conviced that 'his boy' really is faithful and intends to help him get out of the country, Magwitch appears to Pip to 'soften' and lose all trace of the 'lowness' that he has pathetically tried to suppress in the presence of gentlemen. In the course of the brilliantly written chapter fifty-four (see p. 125), as the boat carries them to their rendezvous with the steamship bound for Hamburg, Magwitch dips his hand in the water and smiles:

> 'We'd be puzzled to be more quiet and easy-going than we are at the present. But it's a flowing so soft and pleasant through the water, p'raps, as makes me think it — I was a thinking through my smoke just then, that we can no more see to the bottom of the next hours, than we can see to the bottom of this river what I catches hold of. Nor yet we can't no more hold their tide than I can hold this. And it's run through my fingers and gone, you see'
> Holding up his dripping hand.

> 'But for your face, I should think you were a little despondent,' said I.

'Not a bit on it, dear boy It comes of flowing on so quiet, and of that there rippling at the boat's head making a sort of a Sunday tune. Maybe I'm a growing a trifle old besides.'

Magwitch has finally relaxed the force of his will that drove him through the years of penal exile against all the odds in his determination to do well by the boy who gave him the food on the marshes all those years before. The moment marks his liberation from everything, including society itself, that has driven him through a life of desperate hardship and deprivation. His discernment of a Sunday tune in the rippling flow of the water that carries them along is appropriate to his perception of the religious character of his new-found insight. Pip receives it from him only after the escape attempt has failed and Magwitch is lying mortally wounded in the bottom of the police galley. Pip comes to realise that:

> my repugnance to him had all melted away, and in the haunted wounded shackled creature who held my hand in his, I only saw a man who had meant to be my benefactor, and who had felt affectionately, gratefully and generously towards me with great constancy through a series of years. I only saw in him a much better man than I had been to Joe.

In his new freedom Magwitch has succeeded in doing what in all his earlier determined attempts he had failed to do. He had, in the confusion of the moment of his re-taking, managed finally to kill Compeyson, his oppressor and pursuer. Lying in the bottom of the boat he can now say:

> 'I'm quite content to take my chance.'

Magwitch is at last his own man. He has achieved his freedom through the agency of the child Pip to whom he has indeed become a second father now that he has abandoned the role of benefactor. The symbol that confirms the relationship is that of the hand which Pip holds in his own, in the boat, and throughout the subsequent trial. Pip remains by his side in the prison hospital until his death where Magwitch notes what is best of all:

> 'You've been more comfortable alonger me, since I was under a dark cloud, than when the sun shone. That's best of all.'

But Pip's liberation is still not immediate. The first result of Magwitch's death and his rejection of Wemmick's practical advice

151

to secure Magwitch's 'portable property' is his collapse and break-down. He tells of a feverish dream he suffers:

> that I confounded impossible existences with my own identity; that I was a brick in the house wall, and yet entreating to be released from the giddy place where the builders had set me; that I was a steel beam of a vast engine, clashing and whirling over a gulf, and yet that I implored in my own person to have the engine stopped, and my part in it hammered off . . ..
>
> *(chapter 57)*

Which suggests the violence of the struggle to recover his own identity and break free of the self-swindling social object he has become. He recovers only with the aid of Joe, with whom, in the course of recuperating, he re-experiences all the stages of his earliest life in which Joe had tended him, carried him about and helped him to walk by himself.

> He would sit and talk to me in the old confidence, and with the old simplicity, and in the old unassertive protecting way, so that I would half believe that all my life since the days of the old kitchen was one of the mental troubles of the fever that was gone.

'Unassertive' and 'protecting' suggest at once the contract between Joe Gargery and Mr Jaggers. If, as I suggested earlier, society offer only two alternative roles, gentleman or convict, then Joe had rejected both. He was not, one recalls, to be badgered by the bullying lawyer and he refused to address the cadaverous Miss Havisham, not because he was stupidly ignorant, as Pip in his embarrassment had thought, but because he could not see Miss Havisham as a living person. Joe's successful path through the universal struggle had been the path of truth and love and the playfulness of the message 'what larks'. It was a path that demanded the strength of self-denial, but he has remainded his own man and is ultimately rewarded in his marriage to Biddy and the birth of his child. Biddy has even taught him to read and write. To Joe as to Biddy, Wemmick's essentially urban compromise, to turn himself into twins, would have been a moral impossibility. Wemmick's strategy for survival is that of the pragmatist who knows that the world's evils are not to be overridden, only circumvented and accommodated.

Pip's final insight is that he cannot go back in his release from 'arrogance and untruthfulness'. The setting of his attempt to return is idyllic:

> The June weather was delicious. The sky was blue, the larks were soaring high over the green corn, I thought all that country-side

more beautiful and peaceful by far that I had ever known it to be yet.

But the idyllic setting is not arranged for him, it is for Biddy and Joe on their wedding day. Pip can only go on and take the chances that his better nature offers him. For, in all the distortion that has imposed itself on him by his own efforts as much as the efforts and examples of others, something of an original, better nature has clung to him, fostered in his relationship with Joe and Herbert. What released him was a conspicuous self-forgetfulness that prompted him to rescue Magwitch and to save Miss Havisham from the fire on the occasion when his declaration of his hopeless love for Estella forces on her an acknowledgement of the crime she has committed against the girl in educating her to gain revenge on the male sex.

It is an extraordinary achievement on Dickens's part that Pip never quite loses our sympathy and that, in his final sacrifice of all hopes for himself in the service of others, he exemplifies what Dickens seems to assent to in the idea of the true, unvarnished gentleman. Pip might well have failed. The success of his secret strategy to pay for Herbert's position in Clarriker's shipping firm fills his eyes with 'tears of triumph' that he can scarcely restrain. Triumph is what Magwitch feels in his 'lowness' at the thought that he has done well enough to own the brought-up London gentleman he has made of Pip. It is only when Pip no longer has the money and begs it of Miss Havisham, refusing anything for himself, that the dangerous temptation of power is resisted. Our sympathy with Pip is based on no special pleading by his author. He represents neither a privileged principle of Good nor victimisation by deliberate moral or psychological villainy. His claim on us is based on nothing more than the common humanity that, whether individually or collectively we know it or not, we all share.

V

What then, are we to make finally of the changed ending? Pursuing the notion of taking his chance, it would seem that the original intention to end with an accident encounter two years later between a wiser Pip and an Estella who had suffered 'outrageous treatment' from her husband, Drummle, and had re-married a country doctor on his death, was, as Forster thought, 'more consistent with the drift, as well as the natural working out of the tale'. It was Bulwer Lytton who suggested the revised published ending which unites Pip and Estella. As a result, Dickens added 'as pretty a little piece of writing as I could, and I have no doubt that the story will be more acceptable through the alteration'.

Had Dickens not felt the strength of his friend's objections and advice, he would surely have left the ending as it was (see Appendix B). But the reconsidered ending is not only a pretty piece of writing and its appropriateness is not merely a matter of aesthetic satisfaction. That Estella, of all people, should be the daughter of Magwitch brings home to Pip, if Orlick in the sluice-house had failed to do so, that his implication in criminality is not unique but is common to all human beings.

In the added final paragraph he takes her hand as he had taken Magwitch's among the ruins of his former life. The time of day, the rising of the mist and the unbalanced syntax of the final sentence taken together suggest an ambiguity and an exhaustion with 'all passion spent' that qualify what might easily have become a conventional happy ending. I do not think that Dickens at a late stage in his career could have brought himself to the point of tacking that kind of conventional reassurance on to a novel which, in every other respect, enacts the struggle of the self to realise and break away from the corrosions of guilt that are rooted in a society based on a denial of the right of the individual self to exist.

That the self should only find itself by losing itself is a traditional Christian paradox. *In Great Expectations* it is a truth learned by hard experience and suffering. It is what Mrs Joe learns only by being almost battered to death. In her idiocy and in dumb show she tells what she has learned by her embrace of her assailant Orlick. Her last words – 'Joe', 'Pardon', and 'Pip' — must be words of love.

That Pip can make little of the incident between Orlick and Mrs Joe should not surprise us; he still has a long road to travel before he perceives anything of what the author invites the reader to see in the novel.

In what I have written about *Great Expectations* it is not difficult to catch resonances of the ideas of Thomas Carlyle (see the quotation from *Past and Present* on pp. 61–2). At the same time, in the form that the novel takes, that is, in the retrospective autobiography of a man who has been, in part at least, a self-swindler and unknown to himself in humanly important ways, one hears echoes of William Blake's *Songs of Experience*. From the evidence of the novel, Dickens seems to share with Carlyle an anger that a society of money should have usurped the place of a community made up of an intricate and delicate web of human relationships, and with Blake a sense that such a condition has not simply fallen like a plague upon men. To learn that men have colluded in their own and others' suffering is to hear, with Blake, 'the mind-forg'd manacles' of his bleak poem 'London'.

Great Expectations may not be Dickens's most important novel or his greatest achievement. There is considerable disagreement about what those might be as about where the flaws lie in his best work. But there is little dissent from the judgement that this novel remains his most powerfully conceived and executed achievement and that it is a masterpiece.

Part Three
Reference Section

Dickens's illustrators

Dickens's novels in their mode of instalment publication with illustrations belong firmly in a popular tradition whose greatest representative in the previous century was William Hogarth the satirist. His series of dramatic moral tableaux, *The Rake's Progress* and *Marriage-à-la-Mode* were universally reproduced. Dickens had Hogarth prints on his walls at Gad's Hill Place and it has frequently been suggested not only that Hogarth's moral and satirical view of society was an important influence on the development of his creativity, but also that he took characters and their appearances from Hogarth's illustrations. The dress of, for example, Bill Sikes, would appear to owe more to Hogarth than to Dickens's observation.

The Victorian period marks the high-point of book illustration as an art in England. Gustave Doré, the French graphic artist of great distinction, thought it worth his while to establish a gallery in London from which to sell his work all over the world. Doré's etchings of London, more than the work of all others, resemble in mood and spirit Dickens's dark scenes of London life, but the illustrations to Dickens's novels seem to raise a number of problems for the modern reader less dependent than was his earliest audience on visual support for the imaginative written word. Even though Dickens was able to command the talents of many of the best-known names of his age to make illustrations for him, it seems to me that they fail more often than not to enhance what Dickens depicts in words. Nevertheless, there is plenty of evidence from the writing itself that Dickens visualised the characters, scenes and incidents in his novels and stories, and frequently emphasised the pictorial character of the occasion. As his art develops it becomes less true that the depiction embodies obviously satirical elements and exaggerations that might be easily rendered in visual terms. The change is discernible in much of the writing of *Dombey and Son* which he undertook, as I have noted elsewhere, with a new seriousness and a restraint of his exuberant comic sense that results in a gain not so much in realism as in poetic intensity of a quality and richness almost impossible to render visually. What one notices about the illustrations from *Dombey and Son* onwards is, as often as not, their failure to come near the special quality of the writing both in detail and mood. While 'Phiz' was preparing the illustrations for this novel, Dickens was particularly anxious that Dombey Senior should not be represented as an object of satire, and remained disappointed with his illustrator's notion of what was appropriate for Mrs Pipchin. Dickens's reaction indicates what one feels to be true about

A Doré engraving: Waterloo arches

159

Warm reception of Pecksniff from Martin Chuzzlewit

the illustrations to his works: the earliest are the best and the most memorable for being the most appropriate to Dickens's early comic, satirical mode.

His first illustrator was GEORGE CRUIKSHANK who made the etchings for *Sketches by Boz* and *Oliver Twist*. Cruikshank came directly out of the eighteenth-century tradition as, at the beginning of his career, he worked for James Gillray, the political cartoonist of the Regency period. Gillray had been a pupil of Hogarth. HABLOT K. BROWNE ('Phiz') was not yet twenty-one when he succeeded Robert Seymour as the illustrator of *Pickwick*. He was immediately successful in a way which suggests another important visual source of Dickens's imagination; namely, the tradition of the popular theatre. As I have indicated elsewhere (see pp 55–7), much of the dialogue of Dickens's novels up to and including sections of *Dombey and Son* is conceived in theatrical terms. This is no less true of the action of the novels of the same period. *Martin Chuzzlewit* is particularly theatrical in conception, as well as in execution, in that a major strand of the plot concerns false appearance and its unmasking at the last. Chapter fifty is paced as though it were a staged disclosure scene, the climax of which is old Martin's blow with his stick which knocks Pecksniff down. As Phiz's illustration depicts, in his fall Pecksniff knocks two books from the table; Molière's comedy *Tartuffe*, a dramatic study in hypocrisy, and Milton's *Paradise Lost*. Even though, since Pecksniff notes that it was the knob of the stick that found his head, the stick is drawn the wrong way round, the gesture of Old Martin posed in the centre and surrounded by his family and their friends is overtly stylised, and the whole picture represented as though it were a *tableau vivant* on a stage. The remainder of the chapter concerns explanations interrupted by the unlikely entrances and exits of Sweedlepipe and a spinning Young Bailey, and Sarah Gamp. To everyone Old Martin dispenses praise or blame in the manner of the final scene of popular comic plays. One notes the similar features of the illustrations that depict the dismissal of Tom Pinch by Pecksniff and the reading of the note from Moddle to Charity Pecksniff, his intended bride, from whom he has fled in misery. As Dickens's art gains in dramatic power so the obviousness of the theatrical surface diminishes, thus making redundant illustration of the kind in which Browne excelled. And for all the later experimentation with other illustrators who worked sometimes in collaboration with Browne, or who superseded him after the completion in 1859 of *A Tale of Two Cities* for *Household Words*, none seemed better able to perceive or follow the direction in which Dickens was moving.

GEORGE CATTERMOLE was brought in with Browne to illustrate *Master Humphrey's Clock*. He therefore worked on *The Old Curiosity Shop* and *Barnaby Rudge*, introducing a strong element of romatic gothic fantasy to both novels which helped to emphasise the sentimentality of Little Nell's death scene and to fantasticate the Maypole Inn, the original of which was the King's Head at Chigwell, in Essex. From the accompanying illustrations it is clear that Cattermole fantasticates what Dickens intensifies.

For the Christmas books, Dickens habitually used several illustrators, as though to add value for money. Of these, who included his close friends DANIEL MACLISE and CLARKSON STANFIELD, the painters, only JOHN LEECH seems to me to share anything with that earlier tradition out of which Cruikshank and Phiz developed that is sympathetic to the mood and tone of the writing. Leech was one of the foremost of Victorian cartoonists in his own right, and was

The Maypole Inn, George Cattermole's illustration to Barnaby Rudge

for many years *Punch's* leading visual commentator. His first published work, *Etchings and Sketchings by A. Pen Esq.*, containing sketches of 'cabmen, policemen, street musicians, donkeys, broken down hacks and many other oddities of London life', which appeared in 1835, suggests a close affinity with the world of *Sketches by Boz*. Among other distinguished artists employed to illustrate the Christmas books were JOHN TENNIEL, best known as the illustrator of Lewis Carroll's two books of *Alice's* adventures, and EDWARD LANDSEER. After *Great Expectations* Dickens turned to a younger generation of painters, MARCUS STONE, whose work added but little to *Our Mutual Friend*, but whose father made three plates for *The Haunted Man* and had been a close companion of Dickens, and the younger LUKE FILDES. Fildes replaced Wilkie Collins's brother as illustrator of *The Mystery of Edwin Drood*, and introduced an inappropriately contemporary documentary style of drawing which showed nothing of the line of caricature and fantasy inherited by his predecessors.

The novels of many of Dickens's younger contemporaries were illustrated, but *Middlemarch* by George Eliot which began to appear in 1871 did without, and, for all the visual and poetic quality of his imagination and his visual training as an architect, Hardy did not use illustrators for publication in book form. Dickens's readers may make what they will of the tradition of Dickens illustrations. He

Fezziwig's dance from A Christmas Carol, *John Leech*

certainly outgrew the need for them. In a late novel conceived pictorially and dramatically as I take *Great Expectations* to be, the reader scarcely notices their total absence. Further, although some recent scholars maintain that the often highly complex illustrations were essential to the interpretation of the novels, and especially for the imperfectly educated, it should be noted that the cheapest editions, aimed at the poorest readers, all the time appeared without the familiar illustrations and were usually understood.

Dickens and his circle: short biographies

Dickens's friendships constitute a remarkable feature of his many-sided life. He enjoyed the companionship of painters, actors and politicians; figures in professional and fashionable public life. Many of them can be followed in his continuous and voluminous correspondence with them or in the lists of guests assembled at his own or others' receptions and festive gatherings. He also shared a mutual admiration with the leading literary figures of his day. Taken together, they would make up a social history of much of the intellectual life of the Victorian age since, whilst still very young, he was taken up by an older generation which had been intimate with the most notable literary figures of the turn of the century and, in later life, cultivated the acquaintance of younger men of talent, some of whom survived well into the twentieth century. From so distinguished a company I have thought it best to make only a selection, but one which would be interesting for the light thrown on the range of lives and activities in the period and for the different ways in which other lives reflect that of Dickens himself. I have omitted some of the most distinguished names, such as Thackeray and Tennyson, in favour of some who were either closer to him, or who have had less consideration from later readers although they may well have been at the forefront of serious and popular attention in their own day.

DICKENS, JOHN (1785–1851). Dickens's father was a clerk in the Navy Pay Office until 1828 when he resigned to become a parliamentary reporter for the *Morning Herald* and his brother-in-law's *Mirror of Parliament*. Later he worked for his son on *Household Words*. Seldom out of debt, his reckless conviviality was a continuous charge on Charles, as were the habits of a number of his family. None of his other children prospered: of Frederick (1820–1868), a clerk in the Secretary's office of the Custom House, Dickens said that 'it was a wasted life'. Alfred (1822–1860) could not manage money matters and at his death left his widow and five children for his brother Charles to support. Frances (1810–1848) was a talented singer who died young. Tiny Tim in *A Christmas Carol* and Little Paul Dombey may have been suggested to Dickens by his sister's delicate, deformed child. Despite everything in the way of family troubles, Dickens retained a great affection for his father if not for his mother. The authentic Micawberish air breathes through the following extract from a letter John Dickens wrote to 'Miss Coutts and Co.' optimistically hoping to persuade the bank to let him have money in his son's name. '. . . contemporaneous events place me in a difficulty which without some anticipatory pecuniary effort I cannot extricate myself from'. Mr Micawber owes a great deal to John Dickens, and was surely created out of love as much as out of exasperation.

The impression one gains from the Dickens family life, which consisted mainly of a series of forced moves from one set of cheap lodgings to another, is of the precariousness of Dickens Senior's grip on the lower rungs of the social ladder of which the growing classes of petty functionaries and tradesmen were beginning to take hold. The novels are full of such individuals and families, struggling in isolation to rise or to survive and occasionally falling off the bottom into degradation and misery.

CARLYLE, THOMAS (1795–1881). The career of this Scottish essayist and historian requires more notice in connection with Dickens and his intellectual background than these notes can afford. His singular voice, deliberately pitched after the manner of an Old Testament prophet crying in the wilderness, booms out across the Victorian period and leaves very few of his contemporaries unmoved by it. Carlyle's basic beliefs match those of Dickens, in that they were shaped by the earlier generation of Romantics. Carlyle was an admirer of Goethe and a student of German transcendental idealism. His first important work was a *Life of Schiller* (1823–4). *Sartor Resartus* (1834) is a fictionalised autobiography in which a powerful personal crisis is solved by rejecting modern, materialist and rational explanations of man in favour of an unquestioned faith in the unseen, and an assertion of the superiority of spiritual life over material existence. Above all, he asserted the unassailable primacy of the individual: 'the History of the World is the Biography of Great Men'. It was his *History of the French Revolution*, published in 1837, that established him at the forefront of intellectual life. He and Dickens met first in 1840, and it was he who supplied Dickens with the background historical material for *A Tale of Two Cities* — a cartload of books sent round from the London Library of which, in 1841, Carlyle was a founding member.

His direct influence on Dickens's work, notable in *The Chimes* and *Hard Times*, which was dedicated to him, can be traced through his essays on politics and his devastating attacks on theories of political economy in *Chartism* (1839), *Past and Present* (1843) and his *Latter-day Pamphlets* (1850). Despite the influence, I do not take Dickens to be a Carlylean in his major novels even when their tone of voice can sound very similar. They were very different in personality and in mood as writers, Carlyle's being most frequently directly ethical and moral with, towards the end of his long life, a tendency to a strident irritability. Carlyle's individualism turned too readily to an authoritarianism which is quite alien to the mood and tone of Dickens's major imaginative work.

It is too often assumed that, in the question of influence in their relationship, the influence always works from Carlyle to Dickens. Their friendship was long enough and continuously close enough for it to have been mutual. The best parts of Carlyle's later, most bitter essays, are occasionally brightly illuminated by flashes of a kind of wit and humour that seems to owe much to Dickens and mitigates the crude harshness of Carlyle's often unpalatable message, to a society hell-bent, in his view, on destroying itself by shooting the Niagara Falls of democracy. Dickens would not have made that kind of judgment of the value of the lives of ordinary human beings. Nevertheless, the powerful attraction between them can be read from Carlyle's words written after their first encounter:

> . . . a fine little fellow . . . clear blue eyes that he arches amazingly, large protrusive rather loose mouth, a face of most extreme *mobility*, which he shuttles about — eyebrows, eyes, mouth and all — in a very singular manner while speaking. Surmount this with a loose coil of common-coloured hair, and set it on a small compact figure, very small, and dressed à la D'Orsay rather than well — this is Pickwick. For the rest, a quiet, shrewd-looking, little fellow, who seems to guess pretty well what he is and what others are.

> (Quoted in J. A. Froude, *Thomas Carlyle, A History of his Life in London 1834–1881*, published 1884)

COLLINS, WILLIAM WILKIE (1824–1889) replaced Forster to a considerable extent as Dickens's closest literary confidant soon after he began to contribute to *Household Words* in 1855. He is best remembered as the author of *The Moonstone* and *The Woman in White*. Both novels show the influence of Dickens in the matter of characterisation and, inevitably, perhaps, the inferiority of Collins's conception. His eccentrics seem, in their eccentricities, far less organically related to their roles in the action and illuminate the particular genius of Dickens in this respect. His influence on Dickens in the making of plots of intrigue, on the other hand, was doubtless considerable (see T. S. Eliot's essay of 1927; 'Wilkie Collins and Dickens', in *Selected Essays*).

Called to the Bar in 1851 Collins preferred the literary life. He and Dickens collaborated on a number of stories for *Household Words* and *All the Year Round*, including *The Lazy Tour of Two Idle Apprentices* and 'No Thoroughfare', as well as on *The Frozen Deep*. Collins wrote a number of other less well-known novels, but it was the above-named works that established him as the originator in England of the detective novel.

His brother, CHARLES AUSTEN COLLINS, was a painter connected with the Pre-Raphaelite Brotherhood who exhibited at the Royal Academy. In 1860 he married Kate Dickens against her father's wishes, as he was never in good health, and later wrote essays and a few novels. He designed the cover for the instalments of *The Mystery of Edwin Drood* but had to give up illustrating the novel almost immediately as he was too ill to continue. He died in 1873.

D'ORSAY, ALFRED GUILLAUME GABRIEL, COUNT (1801–1852). At the time of his first visit to England in 1821 for the coronation of George IV, D'Orsay was a tall aristocratic young officer in the French Army. Everyone he met was struck by his graceful bearing, handsome face and charming manners. In the following year in France he met Lord and Lady Blessington and subsequently became engaged to Lord Blessington's daughter by his first marriage who was still only fifteen when she was married. He resigned his army commission despite the urgencies of the Spanish campaign and toured Italy with the Blessingtons. There he met and sketched a portrait of Byron, who described him as a 'cupidon déchainé . . . our ideal of a Frenchman before the Revolution'. After the death of Lord Blessington in 1829 the Countess and D'Orsay set up a salon in London which attracted a wide circle of the artistic and fashionable world. Dickens was introduced into it by Talfourd and, like other young writers such as Harrison Ainsworth, began to model his appearance on D'Orsay's dandiacal fashionability. Dickens named his fourth son (born 1845) Alfred D'Orsay Tennyson. He was known as 'Skittles' to the family. Bulwer, equally a dandy, was also very much at home at Gore House.

D'Orsay was an artist and sculptor of considerable talent. Apart from profile sketches of Dickens and many other figures in the arts and literature and fashion, he delighted the ageing Duke of Wellington with a portrait of him; his statuettes of Napoleon and Wellington were reproduced widely.

His relations with Countess Blessington were a subject of scandal, but they lived scrupulously separately until, in 1849, he had to flee to Paris to escape his creditors at the moment when Lady Blessington was declared a bankrupt. She followed him there and died soon after. He set up a studio and embarked on a series of portrait busts and a colossal statue of Napoleon of whom he was a life-long admirer. He died in France in 1852. There is a handsome equestrian portrait of D'Orsay by Sir Francis Grant in the National Portrait Gallery, London.

FORSTER, JOHN (1812–1876) was Dickens's first biographer and, for many years, his closest friend and literary adviser. The story of his relations with Dickens, especially in literary matters, is told at length in Part One, but he was equally importantly engaged elsewhere as a literary figure of the first half of the Victorian Age. What he wrote as a schoolboy in Newcastle appeared in print and he expressed a passion for the theatre while still very young which made him a friend of Charles Lamb. Forster studied law in London in preference to going to Cambridge, and met Leigh Hunt who, as he later acknowledged, influenced him all his life. He soon became dramatic critic on the *True Sun*. At the age of twenty-two he moved into his famous chambers at fifty-eight, Lincoln's Inn Fields (the model for lawyer Tulkinghorn's chambers in *Bleak House*). For many years he was in the employment of the Commissioners of Lunacy, in a post which allowed him time to write. He wrote history and biography and was a prolific and serious reviewer. He also proof-read for Dickens. For some time he was editor of Leigh Hunt's periodical *The Examiner*, and followed Dickens for a few months as editor of the *Daily News*. Apart from his *Life of Dickens*, his most successful work was a *Life of Goldsmith* at which he laboured for many years. Loud-voiced, stern and serious in appearance, (he may have lent something of this side of his character to Mr Podsnap in *Our Mutual Friend*), he was in fact a gentle and tender friend who included among his acquaintance the most distinguished intellectual figures of the time.

At his death he left unfinished a biography of Swift and gave his library of eighteen thousand volumes (including a Shakespeare First Folio), manuscripts including those of nearly all of Dickens's novels, paintings and a splendid collection of drawings to the Victoria and Albert Museum in South Kensington, London. The Forster collection is a valuable source of material relating to Dickens's life and work.

LAYARD, SIR AUSTEN HENRY (1817–1894). Born in Paris and brought up in Italy, Layard was the son of a member of the British Ceylon Civil Service and it was as he was travelling there overland that he first encountered the civilisation of Asia Minor. He stayed a year in Persia and then in Turkey, where he began to explore what he was convinced was the site of the ancient city of Nineveh. His excavations lasted for ten years from 1841 and, in their later stages, were supported by the British Museum. His accounts of the work at Nineveh and Babylon won him an international reputation.

Layard and Dickens met in Naples in 1853 where each discovered in the other a profound concern with the social problems of their time. Layard was on his way back from witnessing the battle of the Alma in the early stages of the Crimean War and returning to England to give evidence to the committee of enquiry into the conditions of the British Army at Sebastopol. As a result of this experience, and as he was Liberal MP for Aylesbury, he formed the Administrative Reform Association with Dickens as a founding member. They remained close friends until Dickens's death. Chapman and Hall published their correspondence in the three-volume selection of Dickens's letters which they made between 1879 and 1882. Layard was a world traveller and writer on art as well as an archaeologist. During his lifetime he received a large number of public distinctions.

LYTTON, GEORGE EARLE LYTTON BULWER, FIRST BARON LYTTON (1803–1873) probably became a prolific novelist from the need for money. He wrote verse as a child and later, during an adolescence and early manhood that have about them a Byronic atmosphere not unlike that which surrounds the short life of Steerforth in *David Copperfield*. He was strongly under the influence of his mother who opposed his marriage which, in the event, was a complete failure. His wife later pursued him with verbal and literary attacks to the point of madness. After his mother's death in 1843 he succeeded to the family property, Knebworth House, Hertfordshire, and added his mother's maiden name, Lytton, to his own. He also rebuilt the house as a mansion in the Gothic style.

Despite the hostility of reviewers and critics, his novels on both contemporary and historical themes, e.g. *Pelham* (1828), *Paul Clifford* (1830), *Eugene Aram* (1832), *The Last Days of Pompeii* (1834), *Rienzi* (1843), *The Last of the Barons* (1843), and a prophetic work, *The Coming Race* (1871) among many others, proved most popular. He also wrote magazine articles of all kinds, edited a magazine, the *New Monthly*, for a time and, after his election to Parliament in 1831, spoke frequently on behalf of Liberal reforms. He was at this time a friend of J. S. Mill and an admirer of Bentham, but never became identified with utilitarianism. In fact his political views became more conservative in later years. He served as Secretary for the Colonies under Lord Derby for two years from 1858 and was elevated to the peerage in 1866.

His main connection with Dickens is literary and dramatic. Together they started the Guild of Literature and Art in 1850 to raise money for a scheme designed to help impoverished authors with pensions and with houses to be built at Knebworth. They toured with their company of amateur actors in a repertory of plays which included Bulwer's specially written comedy *Not So Bad as We Seem*. The scheme collapsed because it failed to elicit a single impoverished writer who would admit to being such. Bulwer Lytton, as he now was, chaired the farewell dinner before Dickens's second American tour in 1859. In his speech he praised Dickens as the happy man:

> Who makes clear his title deeds to the royalty of
> genius while he yet lives to enjoy the gratitude
> and reverence of those he has subjected to his sway ...
> seldom has that kind of royalty been quietly
> conceded to any man of genius until his tomb
> becomes his throne and yet there is not one of us
> now present who thinks it strange that it is granted
> without a murmur to the guest whom we receive
> tonight.

It was Bulwer who advised Dickens to change the ending of *Great Expectations* (see pp. 153–4).

MACLISE, DANIEL (1806–70), was considered the greatest genre painter of the age. His major work is the series of epic cartoons in the Royal Gallery of the House of Lords, depicting Wellington at Waterloo and the death of Nelson at Trafalgar. He was also a highly talented portraitist and first made his reputation with a drawing of Sir Walter Scott whom he sketched unseen as a boy in his native town of Cork, in Ireland. He exhibited at the Royal Academy from 1829 until his death a wide range of paintings on historical and literary subjects. It was Forster who introduced him to Dickens with whom he remained for many years on intimate terms until, probably over-taxed by the seven years he spent on his House of Lords project, he became solitary and valetudinarian. Dickens spoke an eloquent tribute to his old friend at the funeral which took place three months before his own death. Maclise painted several members of Dickens's family as well as the brilliant Nickleby portrait (page ii), of which Thackeray said 'we have here the real, identical man, Dickens, the inward as well as the outward of him'. Maclise was extremely handsome as a younger man, engaging and humorous; a central figure in many of Dickens's escapades and convivial projects.

MACREADY, WILLIAM CHARLES (1793–1873), the son of an actor, made his first appearance on the stage as Romeo in 1810 and was made famous by his performance in 1819 as Richard III which established him as a dangerous rival to Edmund Kean. At this time he met many leading literary figures including Charles Lamb and Thomas Talfourd. He played for many years at Covent Garden and took over the management of the theatre in 1837 for two years of great artistic success and financial disaster. He opened his last season with an address written by Talfourd, and produced plays by his contemporaries including Bulwer, as well as an impressive repertory of Shakespearian drama. Dickens, together with Bulwer, Forster, Maclise and Clarkson Stanfield who painted the sets, helped mount his *Henry V* with immense success. During these years he also toured Europe and America, where, in New York in 1849, his appearance as Macbeth ended in the calling out of troops of cavalry and infantry to quell the hostile rioters who were objecting to his appearance. Macready angered the Americans by his tactless quarrelsomeness, a quality he frequently displayed. His friendships, however, seemed to survive these outbursts and it was he who cared for the children during Dickens's first tour of America. Dickens also called his second daughter Kate after him.

Macready retired from the stage in 1851 to a great farewell dinner at which Dickens and Thackeray both spoke. Bulwer took the chair and Forster read a sonnet composed by Tennyson for the occasion.

The remarkable sketch by Thomas Sibson (reproduced on p. 52) of Dickens at the theatre with his wife and sister-in-law, turning round to look over his shoulder at Thackeray, portrays a stage scene which looks like *Macbeth*. The actor on stage may well be Macready. The sketch is from the Forster Collection. Macready wrote his *Reminiscences* and left a diary which is an important source of information about Dickens and other leading literary and dramatic figures who were his friends.

SMITH, DR THOMAS SOUTHWOOD (1788–1861) was a leading figure in the medical study of epidemics who was moved by his experiences as a hospital physician among the poor of East London to urge practical reform of sanitation and housing for the poor. Dickens made his acquaintance after reading his report for the Poor Law Commissioners on the housing of the poor in Bethnal Green, and often dined with him at home. This was always done in the presence of Jeremy Bentham whose remains were preserved seated in a mahogany case in one corner of the dining room. Smith had been a friend and disciple of Bentham to whom Bentham left his body for dissection with the instruction that Smith was to deliver an anatomy lecture on it.

Smith had not always been a Benthamite. He began his career as a Unitarian Minister in Edinburgh having been encouraged towards the ministry by William Blake, of whom Smith wrote a memoir. It was in Edinburgh that he qualified as a doctor. Southwood Smith's work led directly to the first Public Health Act of 1848 and the proceeds of one of the 1846 performances of Dickens's company of amateur players were given to the nursing home that Smith was setting up in Devonshire Terrace. The cholera outbreaks of 1850 and 1854 added an urgency to Smith's reports on behalf of which Dickens campaigned in *Household Words*. Smith continued his researches in epidemiology and his philanthropic labours until his death. Dickens loved and respected him but wrote to Stanfield on the occasion of the benefit performance for the sanitorium, 'Smith was born to confuse mankind' a hasty judgment he would never have stood by, as it was Southwood Smith who was the main influence behind the work on housing and welfare in Bethnal Green that Dickens directed on behalf of Angela Burdett-Coutts (see pp. 65–7). A portrait bust of him by J. Hart is in the National Portrait Gallery, London.

TALFOURD, SIR THOMAS NOON (1795–1854) studied law and, while reading for the Bar, supported himself by writing dramatic criticism, reviews and articles. He was an admirer of Charles Lamb, whose executor he became and of whom he wrote a memoir. Lamb introduced him to Wordsworth and Coleridge, and he frequented the leading writers of the day. In 1839 Edward Bulwer dedicated *Lady of Lyons* to him. Dickens and he first met in 1835 as reporters when Talfourd was law reporter for *The Times*. In 1837, as MP for his native town of Reading, he tried to introduce a new Copyright Bill. One of the writers he had consulted on the matter was Dickens, who dedicated *The Pickwick Papers* to him. The Parliamentary Bill was defeated but he and Dickens remained firm friends, and Talfourd wrote a sonnet in praise of *Oliver Twist*. Dickens and he kept in close touch on the issue of Copyright and International Copyright, and it was Talfourd who advised Dickens not to accept *ex gratia* payments from American publishers. In Part One we have seen the consequences of Dickens's raising of the issue during his first tour of America. (International Copyright was only settled by the Berne Convention of 1885, but without American participation. A Universal Copyright Convention was not achieved until 1952 under the auspices of UNESCO.)

Talfourd was not a great success as a Parliamentary speaker; 'his highly rhetorical style, effective as it may have been in legal cases, was unsympathetic to Parliamentary ears' as his obituary noted. He is best remembered as a man of letters and author of *Ion*, a tragic drama in which Macready appeared with great success in 1836. Talfourd was extremely vain about the success of this play and appeared without fail, as Dickens acidly noted, in the audience at each representation. Otherwise he was known as a most generous man and kind friend, as one may see from the terms of Dickens's dedication to him of *Pickwick*. He enjoyed helping young writers and he it was who introduced Dickens to both Lady Holland and Lady Blessington, the most fashionable hostesses to London's literary and political society. He also secured Dickens's early election to the Athenaeum Club. There is a portrait of him by Pickersgill in the National Portrait Gallery, London.

A Dickens geography

Dickens's life contains three kinds of geography belonging to the three periods of his life. In childhood he lived in Chatham on the north Kent coast and in London. As a reporter in London he travelled widely, but mainly in the south and south west of England. These two layers taken together form, in their large and small features, the landscape of the majority of his novels, stories, sketches and descriptive pieces. He knew extremely well and could describe with great fidelity and freedom the places he lived in or travelled to professionally in the years up to 1836. With the exception of the landscapes of *Dombey and Son*, his landscapes, towns and villages, houses and modes of transport suggest a world recalled rather than one observed and experienced. The difference is the one that absorbs much of his imaginative energy in *Dombey and Son*. In that novel the background to the leading events evokes a world in rapid change. Staggs's Garden and The Wooden Midshipman belong in the past and have been overwhelmed by railway palaces and the railway.

The third layer is that which belongs to his long years as an established, high-earning writer. It is a strikingly modern world of rapid easy transit, time-tables, family holidays by the sea in the summer months, whether at Broadstairs on the Kent coast, or Boulogne across the water in northern France. This Dickens is not a traveller in the sense that his friend Henry Layard was a traveller who deliberately sought and found the exotic and remotely distant. Modern schedules, such as regular Atlantic crossings by steamer, ante-date, if only by a few years, Dickens's first trip to America in 1841, by which time he was already an international celebrity — an early example of the modern superstar and, above all, a tourist and sightseer. The sight of Niagara Falls was a high point of the journey. The same may be said of his sabbatical years on the continent of Europe, whether in Italy (1844–5), Switzerland (1846) or Paris, which he loved all his life after his first visit in 1844. He learnt to speak French well and to write it very adequately. Modern communications made it easy to dash over to Paris for an occasional long weekend in a fashion that only half a generation earlier would have been unthinkable. The story of *A Tale of Two Cities* opens as the coach to Paris flounders up Shooter's Hill along a misty, muddy Dover Road. The passengers have to walk up that hill.

When he returned late in life to live among the scenes of his earliest memories at Gad's Hill Place on the main road between Chatham and Gravesend, the newly-built railway enabled him to commute daily with his London office, though he still chose

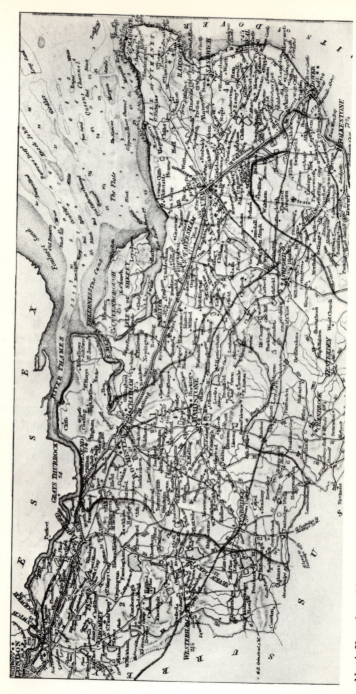

North Kent from Chatham to Dover

occasionally to walk the thirty odd miles between home and work.

His work as a journalist often led him to make quick sallies into the provinces; to Barnard Castle and the remote village of Bowes in North Yorkshire in 1838 to investigate the boarding school of William Shaw; to Preston, Lancashire, early in 1854 to cover a strike of mill-workers, which became the basis of *Hard Times*. Two days at the very end of 1848 in Yarmouth with friends gave him enough of the atmosphere of the place for what he needed for the Yarmouth chapters of *David Copperfield* which includes (chapter fifty-five) the magnificent description of the storm in which Steerforth and Ham are drowned. His later reading tours took him round the provinces, into Scotland and over to Ireland as well as to America in triumph for a second time.

But it is the geography of his childhood that stirs the eye, the memory and the imagination of Dickens in the majority of the novels. The London of that time is so intimately linked with Dickens's name, and is so important a feature of his artistic perception, that I have dealt with it separately (see Part One, pp. 70–90), but the Kent landscape is equally firmly depicted in the novels so that it requires special emphasis in this section.

The north coast of Kent lies along the southern shore of the Thames estuary until, at Margate, North Foreland, Broadstairs and Ramsgate it turns southwards to face the open North Sea and the sea route from Dover to France and the continent of Europe. The direct road dating from Roman times between London and Dover passes through Rochester and Canterbury which were both Roman settlements. The river and the sea are seldom out of sight from the gently rolling hills that characterise the landscape. Dickens knew it in intimate detail from his earliest years in Chatham, the Naval Dockyard town on the river Medway at the point where the river spills out into an estuary of small islands and muddy creeks, and flows into the Thames. He describes his attachment to the town and his youthful experiences there in a paper on 'Chatham Dockyard' in *The Uncommercial Traveller*. The Medway district is dominated by the cathedral town of Rochester with its eleventh-century castle. The Pickwick Club visit Rochester and it figures largely in two other novels. It is 'our town' in *Great Expectations* and features as Cloisterham in *Edwin Drood* which is set in and around the cathedral precinct. Now mainly a tourist centre, the heart of the old town has many associations with the life and work of Dickens, who remains its chief tourist attraction. There is a Dickens Museum and Study Centre, a festival which is to become an annual event and a number of locations which appear, sometimes lightly disguised and with details transposed, in a large number of his essays and fictions. The chalet from his garden in which he wrote has been restored and placed in the garden of the Eastgate museum. Nearby, in Bakers

Walk, is a large Elizabethan red-brick house, Restoration House, out of which Dickens made Satis House. The original of The Blue Boar is the Royal Victoria and Bull Hotel in the High Street, which stands almost facing the Guildhall.

Several of the surrounding villages are also closely associated with *Great Expectations*. Dickens and his bride spent their honeymoon at Chalk, near Gravesend; a cottage and adjoining forge there may well have been the original of the Gargery dwelling. The village itself where Pip was brought up seems most likely to be Cooling, just inland from the Halstow Marshes. As Forster reports in the *Life*, visitors were often taken there on long walks from Gad's Hill Place to look at the thirteen lozenge-shaped tombstones of the children of the Comport family buried by the church there.

At Gad's Hill Place one can still see Dickens's extensions to both sides of the original house. The extended front sitting room has a door from the conservatory ('positively my last improvement') through which he could enter as on to a stage to read to his assembled guests. On the opposite side of the entrance hall is the comfortable room that was his study. He had a tunnel built under the main road to connect the front garden and The Wilderness across the way where, in 1864, he installed the wooden Swiss chalet presented to him by Charles Fechter as a writing study. He wrote to an American friend:

> I have put five mirrors in the Chalet where I write and they reflect and refract, in all kinds of ways, the leaves that are quivering at the windows, and the great fields of waving corn, and the sail-dotted river. My room is up among the branches of the trees and the birds and the butterflies fly in and out, and the green branches shoot in at the open window, and the lights and shadows of the clouds come and go with the rest of the company.

Along the road a few score yards towards Chatham is the Sir John Falstaff inn which in its name commemorates that other notable association of the locality with literature.

One of Dickens's favourite walks from Gad's Hill was to Cobham Hall and Cobham Park, the owner of which, Lord Darnley, gave Dickens the freedom to come and go as he pleased. Cobham Park, Cobham village and its inn, the Leather Bottle, feature in *The Pickwick Papers*. Dickens and his friends often stayed there. It has suffered the inevitable ravages of modernisation, but still possesses an interesting collection of Dickens ephemera: illustrations, complete sets of cigarette cards of Dickensian characters and Pickwickiana of various sorts, which moulder slowly on the walls of the rear bar room and on the hotel staircase. The church on the opposite side of the street contains a splendid Renaissance tomb of the

Cobham family and a large number of medieval memorial brasses. The adjacent Almshouses, originally built as a priest's college, are described in the essay 'Titbull's Almshouses' from *The Uncommercial Traveller*.

Of the seaside holiday towns on the Kent coast, Dickens always preferred Broadstairs where one can still feel something of the atmosphere of 'Our English Watering Place' as Dickens described it in a piece for *Household Words* in 1851, when it was still a small fishing village. He and Catherine visited it in 1837 for the first of many family holidays and weekend respites from London and work. He often wrote while on holiday; he was engaged on *Pickwick* during the first visit, wrote parts of *Oliver Twist* and *Nicholas Nickleby* either in lodgings or, later, at the Albion Hotel which stands between the main street and the sea, overlooking a crescent-shaped sandy bay which lies below the cliff and the small harbour. In later years he rented Fort House, a somewhat forbidding crenellated structure on the northern end of the old town above the harbour, where he finished *David Copperfield*. In tune with the saturation of the whole district in Dickensian associations since his own time, the house, which bears a conspicuous plaque, has been renamed Bleak House with which novel it has no connection. Among all the claims that have been made on behalf of actual locations and persons that they inspired Dickens, of Broadstairs it is asserted that there, and not at Dover, lived the original of Miss Betsy Trotwood in just such a cottage. One house in the town sports a discreet notice asserting briefly 'Charles Dickens did not live here'.

While the whole enterprise to establish 'a local habitation and name' mistakes the very nature of imaginative, creative endeavour, it remains true that, in his novels, Dickens did not invent locations for his fictitious actions which he had not visited or known. Although I have asserted elsewhere in this book that the journalist and novelist are separate figures, they often come very close together in his descriptions of places, whether these are the towns and villages of North Kent or the snow-bound passes of the Great St Bernard in Switzerland, as in *Little Dorrit*. Dickens's imagination was Autolycus-like: it seemed able to snap up any unconsidered trifle of eye or memory to be delivered over later and transformed into art. What one does notice about a very large number of his fictional geographical descriptions is that they are laid in places close to running tidal water or to the sea:

> Running water is favourable to day-dreams, and a strong tidal river is the best of running water for mine.
>
> *The Uncommercial Traveller*, ('Chatham Dockyard')

Dickens's Reputation

It were, in our opinion, an offence against humanity
to place Mr Dickens among the greatest novelists . . .
he has created nothing but figures. He has added
nothing to our understanding of human character. He
is master of but two alternatives: he reconciles us
to what is commonplace, and he reconciles us to what
is odd . . . Mr Dickens is a great observer and a great
humourist, but he is nothing of a philosopher.
> (from a review of *Our Mutual Friend* by Henry James, 1865)

When I first began to write I suffered intensely from
reading reviews and I made a solemn compact with
myself that I would only know them for the future
from such general report as might reach me. For five
years I have never broken this rule once, I am
unquestionably the happier for it.
> (Charles Dickens to a young writer, 1843)

The changes of fortune that Dickens's reputation has undergone in
the last hundred years or so stem partly from changes in the nature
of criticism itself. From his earliest days, however, his reputation
has never lacked critical attention from admirers and detractors
alike. Contemporary novelists could scarcel avoid him. Elizabeth
Gaskell's *Cranford* began to appear in *Household Words* in 1851, but
it is not for this reason that *The Pickwick Papers* is praised in the
opening chapter for its humane spirit of modernity. Dickens is
mentioned in Charlotte M. Yonge's *The Heir of Redclyffe*, a popular
romance of 1853, and two years later, he is satirised in his role of
campaigning journalist as editor of 'The Jupiter' in Anthony Trollope's *The Warden*.

Critical attention and the establishment of a reputation in art
begins with Henri Taine's study of his talent and his works in 1856.
Henry James, quoted in the epigraph above, is an early exponent
of the general view that Dickens had neither philosophy nor intel-
lect. It is central to G. H. Lewes's summarising review of 1872,
'Dickens in Relation to Criticism', where it is sharply expressed in
the course of what claims to be a sympathetic account:

He set in motion the secret springs of sympathy by touching the
domestic affections. He painted nothing ideal, heroic; but all the
resources of the bourgeois epic were in his grasp. The world of
thought and pattern lay beyond his horizon. But the joys and
pains of childhood, the petty tyrannies of ignoble natures, the

genial pleasantries of happy natures, the life of the poor, the struggles of the street and back parlour, the insolence of office, the sharp social contrasts, east-wind and Christmas jollity, hunger, misery, and hot punch — these he could deal with, so that we laughed and cried, were startled at the revelation of familiar facts hitherto unnoticed, and felt our pulses quicken as we were hurried along with him in his fanciful flight.

Despite the conscious force of the attack, what Lewes writes subverts his position. Just as the very young Henry James who, sent to bed as too young to listen, sat transfixed on the stairs to overhear the instalment of *David Copperfield* read aloud by his father to the rest of the family, so Lewes is inevitably drawn towards admitting the power of his subject. His quotation from *Hamlet* which falls so easily into place should have told him with what sort of greatness he was dealing, without having to fall back on laughter and tears as a sufficient explanation for that power. The final answer to this stream of criticism is surely that of Coleridge in the *Biographia Literaria* in his assertion of the status of Shakespeare as a philosophical poet. A similar claim can be made for Dickens's novels.

Forster's riposte to Lewes in the *Life* (completed in 1874) is to assert Dickens's serious attention to the craft of letters, his powers of characterisation and the instructive purity of the morality of the novels. On the appearance of the third and final volume, Carlyle wrote to Forster, 'by those sparkling, clear and sunny utterances of Dickens's own . . . which were at your disposal and have been intercalated every now and then, you have given to every intelligent eye the power of looking down to the very bottom of Dickens's mode of existing in this world . . . . So long as Dickens is interesting to his fellow-men, here will be seen, face to face, what Dickens's manner of existing was; a steady practicality with all; the singularly solitary business talent he had; and deeper than all, if one had the eye to see deep enough, dark fateful silent elements, tragical to look upon, and hiding amid dazzling radiances as of the sun, the elements of death itself.' Carlyle, in characteristic manner, sees further than Forster that there are in Dickens and in his work depths of seriousness and tragedy which do not readily occur to later critics. George Gissing's fragmentary sympathetic study *The Immortal Dickens* (1898) emphasises Dickens's powerful social appeal on behalf of the ordinary, everyday life of the poor and the dispossessed, although he notes, 'Morally he would change the world; socially, he is a thorough conservative.' As a novelist, Gissing acknowledged the enormous importance of Dickens to him and his admission is characteristic. Later English novelists could scarcely avoid his presence in the very language and techniques available to them as part of their inheritance. H. G. Wells's *Kipps* (1905) is a sadly diluted imitation of *Great Expectations*, and the atmosphere of Joseph

Conrad's London novel, *The Secret Agent*, displays a powerful consciousness of the atmosphere of Dickens's evocation of the City. (See especially the description of Verloc's seedy shop in Soho and, in chapter eight, The Verloc family's cab-ride across alien parts of London.) Even Henry James's first important novel *Roderick Hudson* (1875–6) is a comedy owing much to Dickens in style and tone. There is a perceptible debt in the social satires of Evelyn Waugh and in the work of his contemporary George Orwell.

Of foreign writers who acknowledge the importance of the debt they owe to Dickens, foremost is Leo Tolstoy, the Russian novelist. After reading *David Copperfield* in translation, he learned English in order to be able to read it properly. In her essay 'Dickens and Tolstoy: The Case for a Serious View of *David Copperfield*' (in *Dickens The Novelist*) Q. D. Leavis distinguishes very consciously those episodes of *War and Peace* that seem to her to owe much to its author's reading of *David Copperfield* twenty years earlier, and to Dickens's use, in that novel, of symbolic action and dialogue to carry the theme. Dostoevsky and Turgenev equally shared the enthusiasm for Dickens that swept over literary Russia in the 1840s and later. Franz Kafka should also be mentioned in this connection as well as the similarities critics have noted between the Dickens of *Dombey and Son* (especially in the passage from chapter fourteen quoted in Part Two on pp. 120–1 in which the scene is dramatised from the point of view of the ailing consciousness of Paul) and *David Copperfield* and the whole method of recollection employed by Marcel Proust in *A la Recherche du Temps Perdu*.

George Orwell wrote a long sensitive study of Dickens, published in 1940 in *Inside the Whale*, in which, having chastised him for limitations some of which Orwell invents, and for a near total lack of political consciousness, he takes the centre of Dickens's achievement to be not unlike that which Gissing chose, a 'native generosity of mind' and 'a good-tempered antinomianism — one of the marks of Western popular culture'. Also like Gissing, Orwell praises Dickens's characteristic Englishness, a quality which is nevertheless totally free from nationalistic prejudice. Confronted by Dickens, Orwell suffers that characteristic left-wing inability to reconcile totally his admiration for the author with his own political stance which his subject does not share, but the essay is otherwise full of sharp insights that grow out of a sense of the problems involved in the making of fiction.

Orwell is the last critic from the age of innocence of Dickens criticism. The balance of his appreciation is still that of the tradition of reviewing from the middle of the nineteenth century in that it lies rather towards the earlier broadly comic novels than towards the later masterpieces. He can be read with Forster, Gissing and G. K.

Chesterton's *Charles Dickens* (1906), which is a full-length study that makes an intelligent, witty revision of Gissing's judgements.

The tradition was broken in 1941 by the appearance in America of Edmund Wilson's essay 'Dickens: The Two Scrooges' which uses the novels to evoke a driven, neurotic, guilt-ridden creator behind them. It is almost as if Wilson had undertaken to explore the implications of the insight Carlyle expressed in his letter to Forster. Since that date Dickens has been an absorbing subject of a largely academic critical interest. This new age of critical experience has produced a number of important studies which emphasise, as I am also conscious of having done, the later novels from *Dombey and Son* onwards at the expense of the sparkling comedy of the earlier period. Perhaps it is only that comedy is recalcitrant to critical contemplation and needs it not at all for enjoyment. I signal what I take to be the most rewarding and interesting of these studies in the accompanying bibliography.

It was the German poet Rainer Maria Rilke who said that fame, finally, is the sum of all the misunderstandings that surround a new name. Instead of misunderstandings I would prefer to think of continuous re-interpretations and recreations which, as I stressed in my opening argument, are marks of the complexity and transcendent vitality of a creator of genius.

Further reading and reference

Bibliographical research has grown into a considerable and special-
ised branch of Dickens scholarship. The constant flow of scholarly
critical and historical studies bears witness to the continued vitality
of its object. I indicate below some useful bibliographical sources,
but have restricted the scope of this section to those titles which I
have found informative, helpful and occasionally provoking in
forming my view of the novelist and his work. Many of the titles
signalled contain their own select bibliographies, and the following
sub-headings follow the general order of the first two parts of the
present volume.

Editions

New Oxford Illustrated Dickens, 21 vols., Oxford University Press,
1947–59. It is being superseded by the Clarendon Dickens, Clarendon Press, 1966–, in which series *Oliver Twist* (ed. K. Tillotson),
The Mystery of Edwin Drood (ed. M. Cardwell), *Dombey and Son* (ed. A.
Horsman) *David Copperfield* (ed. N. Burgis), *Martin Chuzzlewit* (ed.
M. Gardwell) and *Little Dorrit* (ed. H. P. Sucksmith) have so far
appeared.

The definitive edition of Dickens's letters is the Pilgrim Edition
edited by M. House and G. Storey and published by the Clarendon
Press, 1965–. To date, five volumes covering the years to 1849 have
appeared.

Bibliographies

A. NISBET, 'Dickens' in *Victorian Fiction: A Guide to Research*, ed. L.
　Stevenson, Harvard University Press, 1963.
R. C. CHURCHILL, *A Bibliography of Dickensian Criticism: 1836–1974*,
　Garland Publishing, 1978.
The Dickensian. Cumulative analytical index 1905–74, compiled by
　F. T. Dunn, 1976.

Life and times

J. FORSTER, *The Life of Charles Dickens*, 3 vols., 1872–4, ed. J. W. T.
　Ley, Everyman (Dent), 1927; revised by A. J. Hoppé, 2 vols.,
　1966. Forster's *Life* is still the one indispensable biography of
　Dickens and the sole source of much information and material.

UNA POPE-HENNESSY, *Charles Dickens*, Chatto and Windus, 1945; Penguin, 1970.

E. JOHNSON, *Charles Dickens, His Tragedy and Triumph*, 2 vols., Little Brown, 1952; revised in one volume, Allen Lane, 1977.

H. HOUSE, *The Dickens World*, Oxford University Press, 1942.

A. WILSON, *The World of Charles Dickens*, Secker and Warburg, 1970; Penguin, 1972. This is a splendid introduction to the life and work and is very well illustrated.

P. COLLINS, *Charles Dickens: The Public Readings*, Clarendon Press, 1975.

K. J. FIELDING, *The Speeches of Charles Dickens*, Clarendon Press, 1960.

P. COLLINS, *Dickens and Crime*, Macmillan, 1962.

N. POPE, *Dickens and Charity*, Macmillan, 1978.

M. SLATER, *Dickens and Women*, Deutsch, 1983.

M. and M. HARDWICK, *The Charles Dickens Encyclopedia*, Osprey, 1973.

A. L. HAYWARD, *The Dickens Encyclopaedia*, 1924; reprinted Routledge and Kegan Paul, 1969.

E. HEALEY, *Lady Unknown: the Life of Angela Burdett-Coutts*, Sidgwick, 1978.

E. JOHNSON, *Letters from Charles Dickens to Angela Burdett-Coutts, 1841–65*, 1953.

J. BUTT and K. TILLOTSON, *Dickens at Work*, Methuen, 1958.

J. H. BUCKLEY, *The Victorian Tempers: A Study in Literary Culture*, Harvard University Press, 1951.

W. E. HOUGHTON, *The Victorian Frame of Mind, 1830–1870*, Yale University Press, 1957.

K. CHESNEY, *The Victorian Underworld*, Temple Smith, 1970.

S. MARGESTON, *Leisure and Pleasure in the Nineteenth Century*, Cassell, 1969.

D. THOMSON, *England in the Nineteenth Century*, Penguin 1950.

G. M. YOUNG, *Victorian England*, Oxford University Press, 1936.

A. BRIGGS, *Victorian People*, Odhams Press, 1954; Pelican 1965.

General critical surveys

P. COLLINS (ed.), *Dickens, The Critical Heritage*, Routledge and Kegan Paul, 1971.

G. FORD and L. LANE JNR. (eds.), *The Dickens Critics*, Cornell University Press, 1961. Contains an extensive bibliography.

J. GROSS and G. PEARSON (eds.), *Dickens and the Twentieth Century*, Routledge and Kegan Paul, 1962.

F. R. and Q. D. LEAVIS, *Dickens the Novelist*, Chatto and Windus, 1970.

s. MARCUS, *Dickens, From Pickwick to Dombey*, Chatto and Windus, 1965.

J. H. MILLER, *Charles Dickens: The World of his Novels*, Harvard University Press, 1958.

G. ORWELL, 'Charles Dickens', in *Inside the Whale*, Gollancz, 1940; Penguin, 1957.

M. SLATER (ed.), *Dickens 1970*, Chapman and Hall, 1970. See especially 'Dickens and the Symbol' by J. Holloway.

E. WILSON, 'Dickens, the Two Scrooges', in *The Wound and the Bow*, Secker and Warburg, 1947.

See also:

s. WALL (ed.), *Charles Dickens, A Critical Anthology*, Penguin Critical Anthologies, 1970.

B. FORD (ed.), *From Dickens to Hardy*, The Pelican Guide to English Literature, Vol. 6, Penguin, 1958.

J. LUCAS, *The Melancholy Man*, Methuen, 1970 Harvester, 1980.

London

P. COLLINS, 'Dickens and London', in *The Victorian City: Images and Reality*, edited by H. Dyos and M. Wolff, 2 vols., Routledge and Kegan Paul, 1973.

F. S. SCHWARZBACH, *Dickens and the City*, Athlone Press, 1979.

A. WELSH, *The City of Dickens*, Clarendon Press, 1971.

C. HIBBERT, *London, the Biography of a City*, Longman, 1969; revised edition, Allen Lane, 1971.

D. J. OLSEN, *The Growth of Victorian London*, Batsford, 1976; Peregrine, 1979.

A. BRIGGS, *Victorian Cities*, Odhams, 1963; second edition, Penguin, 1968.

M. and M. HARDWICK, *Dickens's England*, Dent, 1970.

Childhood

P. COLLINS, *Dickens and Education*, Macmillan, 1963.

P. COVENEY, *The Image of Childhood*, Peregrine, 1967. It would be difficult to overstress the importance and influence of this work on the literary handling of the theme of childhood in nineteenth-century English poetry and fiction.

F. R. DONOVAN, *The Children of Dickens*, Frewin, 1969.

H. STONE, *Dickens and the Invisible World*, Macmillan, 1980.

A. WILSON, 'Dickens on Children and Childhood', in (Dickens 1970).

Great Expectations

N. PAGE (ed.), 'Dickens, *Hard Times, Great Expectations* and *Our Mutual Friend*', Macmillan Casebook, 1979. Contains a number of useful essays. See especially those by Barbara Hardy and Julian Moynihan.

Q. D. LEAVIS, 'How We Must Read *Great Expectations*', in *Dickens The Novelist*.

D. VAN GHENT, 'On *Great Expectations*', in *The English Novel: Form and Function*, Rinehart and Co., 1953, Harper Torchbook, 1961.

H. STONE, *Dickens and the Invisible World*, chapters 8 and 9.

Appendix A: Dickens's personal statement

Such a statement, in which anger is hotly directed against calumnies that may not be specified, was bound to do Dickens more harm than good with his readers. He appealed to them in the role of his private self and at the same time demanded that the unspecified event, whatever it was, claimed respect 'as being of a sacredly private nature'. They were no doubt ignorant of the occasion that had provoked the appeal and bewildered by their author's attempt to have it both ways.

One can allow that he made such a fuss of his wife's family's inferences from the fact that Georgina took her brother-in-law's part rather than that of her own sister, merely in order to divert attention from the truth that he wanted to be free to take up, if only in secret, with Ellen Ternan. Rumours of this relationship were at least as current in Dickens's own circles as were the Hogarths' innuendoes, but it is almost as though, having once had the role offered to him of the injured innocent, he played it as he played other roles, to the very end and without regard for himself or for others.

In writing to Forster he asserted that a whole history of incompatibility supported his present view of his wife, that 'nothing on earth could make her understand me, or suit us to each other. Her temperament will not go with mine.' Forster's very reticent account in the *Life* reveals his attempt to distance himself from the pain and the disapproval he clearly felt at these events.

From about this time Forster was less intimate with Dickens than hitherto, and so relates the separation from Catherine to a general restlessness, to growing difficulties with invention and writing since *David Copperfield*, and to Dickens's preoccupation with the idea of paying for Gad's Hill by giving public readings for profit. He gave the first of such readings in London to a paying audience in the same week as the personal statement appeared in *Household Words*.

"Familiar in their Mouths as HOUSEHOLD WORDS."—Shakespeare.

HOUSEHOLD WORDS.

A WEEKLY JOURNAL.

CONDUCTED BY CHARLES DICKENS.

N⁰· 429.]　　　　SATURDAY, JUNE 12, 1858.　　　　{ Price 2d.
{ Stamped 3d.

PERSONAL.

THREE-AND-TWENTY years have passed since I entered on my present relations with the Public. They began when I was so young, that I find them to have existed for nearly a quarter of a century.

Through all that time I have tried to be as faithful to the Public, as they have been to me. It was my duty never to trifle with them, or deceive them, or presume upon their favor, or do any thing with it but work hard to justify it. I have always endeavoured to discharge that duty.

My conspicuous position has often made me the subject of fabulous stories and unaccountable statements. Occasionally, such things have chafed me, or even wounded me ; but, I have always accepted them as the shadows inseparable from the light of my notoriety and success. I have never obtruded any such personal uneasiness of mine, upon the generous aggregate of my audience.

For the first time in my life, and I believe for the last, I now deviate from the principle I have so long observed, by presenting myself in my own Journal in my own private character, and entreating all my brethren (as they deem that they have reason to think well of me, and to know that I am a man who has ever been unaffectedly true to our common calling), to lend their aid to the dissemination of my present words.

Some domestic trouble of mine, of longstanding, on which I will make no further remark than that it claims to be respected, as being of a sacredly private nature, has lately been brought to an arrangement, which involves no anger or ill-will of any kind, and the whole origin, progress, and surrounding circumstances of which have been, throughout, within the knowledge of my children. It is amicably composed, and its details have now but to be forgotten by those concerned in it.

By some means, arising out of wickedness, or out of folly, or out of inconceivable wild chance, or out of all three, this trouble has been made the occasion of misrepresentations, most grossly false, most monstrous, and most cruel—involving, not only me, but innocent persons dear to my heart, and innocent persons of whom I have no knowledge, if, indeed, they have any existence—and so widely spread, that I doubt if one reader in a thousand will peruse these lines, by whom some touch of the breath of these slanders will not have passed, like an unwholesome air.

Those who know me and my nature, need no assurance under my hand that such calumnies are as irreconcileable with me, as they are, in their frantic incoherence, with one another. But, there is a great multitude who know me through my writings, and who do not know me otherwise ; and I cannot bear that one of them should be left in doubt, or hazard of doubt, through my poorly shrinking from taking the unusual means to which I now resort, of circulating the Truth.

I most solemnly declare, then—and this I do, both in my own name and in my wife's name—that all the lately whispered rumours touching the trouble at which I have glanced, are abominably false. And that whosoever repeats one of them after this denial, will lie as wilfully and as foully as it is possible for any false witness to lie, before Heaven and earth.

CHARLES DICKENS.

Appendix B: The ending of *Great Expectations*

Forster appends the following note to his discussion of the novel in the *Life*.

There was no Chapter 59 as now; but the sentence which opens it ('For eleven years' in the original, altered to 'eight years') followed the paragraph about his business partnership with Herbert, and led to Biddy's question whether he is sure he does not fret for Estella ('I am sure and certain, Biddly' as originally written, altered to 'O no — I think not, Biddly): from which point here was the close. 'It was two years more before I saw herself. I had heard of her as leading a most unhappy life, and as being separated from her husband who had used her with great cruelty, and who had become quite renowned as a compound of pride, brutality and meanness. I had heard of the death of her husband (from an accident consequent of ill-treating a horse), and of her being married again to a Shropshire doctor, who, against his interest, had once very manfully interposed, on an occasion when he was in professional attendence on Mr Drummle, and had witnessed some outrageous treatment of her. I had heard that the Shropshire doctor was not rich, and that they lived on her own personal fortune. I was in England again — in London, and walking along Piccadilly with little Pip — when a servant came running after me to ask would I step back to a lady in a carriage who wished to speak to me. It was a little pony carriage, which the lady was driving; and the lady and I looked sadly enough on one another. 'I am greatly changed, I know; but I thought you would like to shake hands with Estella too, Pip. Lift up that pretty child and let me kiss it!' (She supposed the child, I think, to be my child.) I was very glad afterwards to have had the interview; for in her face and in her voice, and in her touch, she gave me the assurance, that suffering had been stronger than Miss Havisham's teaching, and had given her a heart to understand what my heart used to be.'

I agree, finally, with George Bernard Shaw's judgment of the change that 'though psychologically wrong, [it] is artistically much more congruous than the original. The scene, the hour, the atmosphere, are beautifully touching and exactly right.' One might add only that the changed ending emphasises without obtrusiveness the parallels that are to be drawn from the story between the apparently very different lives of Estella and Pip.

Acknowledgements

We are grateful to the following for permission to reproduce photographs:

BBC Hulton Picture Library, page 73; British Library, pages 76 (from Bourne, *Drawings of London and Birmingham Railway*) and 187; Cambridge University Library, page 174 (from Dugdale, *Curiosities in Great Britain*, plate 21); Dickens House Museum, pages 21, 27, 31, 32, 48, 131, 132, 160, 162 and 163; Fitzwilliam Museum, Cambridge, page 45; Mary Evans Picture Library, page 135; National Portrait Gallery, page 65; Tate Gallery, page ii; Victoria and Albert Museum, pages 29, 37, 42, 52 and 58; Wisbech and Fenland Museum, page 129.

The painting *London Street Scene* by John Parry, 1835, is reproduced on the cover by permission of Alfred Dunhill Ltd.

General Index

Index to Dickens's Works